ISBN 0-8373-5405-6

5 REGENTS COLLEGE PROFICIENCY EXAMINATION SERIES

Regents College Proficiency Examination Program
Subject Examination In...

Biology

Test Preparation Study Guide

Questions and Answers

All rights reserved, including the right of reproduction in whole or in part, in any form or by any means, electronic or mechanical, including photocopying, recording, or by any information storage and retrieval system, without permission in writing from the Publisher.

Copyright © 1999 by

National Learning Corporation

212 Michael Drive, Syosset, New York 11791
(516) 921-8888

PRINTED IN THE UNITED STATES OF AMERICA

PASSBOOK®

NOTICE

This book is *SOLELY* intended for, is sold *ONLY* to, and its use is *RESTRICTED* to *individual*, bona fide applicants or candidates who qualify by virtue of having seriously filed applications for appropriate license, certificate, professional and/or promotional advancement, higher school matriculation, scholarship, or other legitimate requirements of educational and/or governmental authorities.

This book is *NOT* intended for use, class instruction, tutoring, training, duplication, copying, reprinting, excerption, or adaptation, etc., by:

(1) Other Publishers
(2) Proprietors and/or Instructors of "Coaching" and/or Preparatory Courses
(3) Personnel and/or Training Divisions of commercial, industrial, and governmental organizations
(4) Schools, colleges, or universities and/or their departments and staffs, including teachers and other personnel
(5) Testing Agencies or Bureaus
(6) Study groups which seek by the purchase of a single volume to copy and/or duplicate and/or adapt this material for use by the group as a whole without having purchased individual volumes for each of the members of the group
(7) Et al.

Such persons would be in violation of appropriate Federal and State statutes.

PROVISION OF LICENSING AGREEMENTS. — Recognized educational commercial, industrial, and governmental institutions and organizations, and others legitimately engaged in educational pursuits, including training, testing, and measurement activities, may address a request for a licensing agreement to the copyright owners, who will determine whether, and under what conditions, including fees and charges, the materials in this book may be used by them. In other words, a licensing facility *exists* for the legitimate use of the material in this book on other than an individual basis. However, it is asseverated and affirmed here that the materials in this book *CANNOT* be used without the receipt of the express permission of such a licensing agreement from the Publishers.

NATIONAL LEARNING CORPORATION
212 Michael Drive
Syosset, New York 11791

Inquiries re licensing agreements should be addressed to:
The President
National Learning Corporation
212 Michael Drive
Syosset, New York 11791

PASSBOOK SERIES®

THE *PASSBOOK SERIES®* has been created to prepare applicants and candidates for the ultimate academic battlefield—the examination room.

At some time in our lives, each and every one of us may be required to take an examination—for validation, matriculation, admission, qualification, registration, certification, or licensure.

Based on the assumption that every applicant or candidate has met the basic formal educational standards, has taken the required number of courses, and read the necessary texts, the *PASSBOOK SERIES®* furnishes the one special preparation which may assure passing with confidence, instead of failing with insecurity. Examination questions—together with answers—are furnished as the basic vehicle for study so that the mysteries of the examination and its compounding difficulties may be eliminated or diminished by a sure method.

This book is meant to help you pass your examination provided that you qualify and are serious in your objective.

The entire field is reviewed through the huge store of content information which is succinctly presented through a provocative and challenging approach—the question-and-answer method.

A climate of success is established by furnishing the correct answers at the end of each test.

You soon learn to recognize types of questions, forms of questions, and patterns of questioning. You may even begin to anticipate expected outcomes.

You perceive that many questions are repeated or adapted so that you gain acute insights, which may enable you to score many sure points.

You learn how to confront new questions, or types of questions, and to attack them confidently and work out the correct answers.

You note objectives and emphases, and recognize pitfalls and dangers, so that you may make positive educational adjustments.

Moreover, you are kept fully informed in relation to new concepts, methods, practices, and directions in the field.

You discover that you are actually taking the examination all the time: you are preparing for the examination by "taking" an examination, not by reading extraneous and/or supererogatory textbooks.

In short, this PASSBOOK®, used directedly, should be an important factor in helping you to pass your test.

ACT PEP: REGENTS COLLEGE EXAMINATIONS

General Information

The ACT PEP: Regents College Examinations, hereafter referred to as PEP Examinations, give you an opportunity to obtain recognition for college-level learning, no matter how or where the learning took place. You may have acquired such learning in a number of ways: advanced courses in high school; evening, extension, or correspondence courses; on-the-job training; the armed forces; television courses; or reading on your own. Now you would like some official recognition of that learning—whether to apply it toward a college degree, to satisfy a professional licensing or certification requirement, to show you have skills for a better position, or perhaps simply to find out for yourself whether you are capable of college-level achievement before you apply to a college degree program.

The ACT Proficiency Examination Program can help you obtain recognition for college-level learning. PEP consists of examinations designed to let you demonstrate your proficiency in various college-level subjects. On the basis of your results on one or more examinations, colleges and universities, academic departments, and various other certifying agencies may grant you actual course or area credit, waive prerequisite course or area requirements, allow you to begin college coursework at an appropriate advanced or intermediate level in your field of knowledge, or verify skills and knowledge required for certification, licensing, or promotion.

American College Testing does **not** grant credit. **Before you register for any PEP examination, be sure to check directly with the appropriate institution, agency or company to determine whether it will grant the credit you seek on the basis of PEP examination results.** A list of institutions that grant credit for one or more PEP examinations is **a separate four-page document** in the registration packet.

The ACT Proficiency Examination Program makes available nationwide the examinations used by the University of the State of New York's Regents College Degrees. Since 1963, colleges and universities in New York and other states have granted more than one million course credits on the basis of results of these examinations, which are recommended by the American Council on Education, Office on Education Credit and Credentials for college credit. The Regents College Degrees, which awards course credit on the basis of these examinations, has been fully accredited by the New York State Education Department and the Middle States Association of Colleges and Schools, Commission on Higher Education.

The PEP examinations have been carefully designed to test your college-level proficiency. They cover undergraduate coursework in a broad range of areas, including arts and sciences, business, education, and nursing. The examinations generally cover material studied in comparable one- or two-semester courses; a few advanced examinations in business subjects deal with broader areas. All the examinations test not only how well you know facts and terminology, but also how well you can apply essential concepts and skills.

All of the ACT Proficiency Examinations are 3 hours long. Most of the examinations are objective; some are entirely essay. The list on the inside front cover indicates the kinds of questions each examination contains.

PEP examinations have been prepared by college and university faculty members who have taught comparable courses in their own schools. Each examination has been developed by a committee of teachers and scholars in the subject. This committee writes and reviews all examination items and the outlines on which they are based. Test specialists have worked with each committee to ensure that the examinations actually measure the proficiency required of students taking comparable courses. The examinations are continually reviewed and revised to ensure that they are kept up to date with current developments in each subject area.

Each examination is based on an outline that defines its scope and content. Each outline is like a syllabus for a typical course, though it may not be identical with the syllabus for the equivalent course given by the college from which you may wish to receive credit. The outline for a PEP examination is contained in the PEP Study Guide for that examination, which you can obtain by writing to ACT. The outline for an examination can be used in several ways. It will help you determine whether the test is appropriate for you and how much of the material you already know. You can identify areas with which you are not sufficiently familiar and devote more study time to them. And since each outline indicates the weight given to each area covered by the examination, you can apportion your preparation time appropriately.

American College Testing, a nonprofit educational service organization, has no affiliation with nor does it endorse or recommend any profit-making educational counseling center. Initial counseling/advising for college degrees is usually provided free by degree-granting institutions.

Study Guides/Textbooks

ACT strongly recommends that all candidates use the study guides before taking PEP examinations.

An ACT Proficiency Examination Program Study Guide is available free of charge for **each** PEP examination. Each study guide contains a course outline and a reading list. The study guide is comparable to a syllabus for a course you might take at a college or other institution. The outline indicates the scope and content of the examination, and the approximate weight given to each area covered on the examination. The reading lists suggest resources to which you may refer as you prepare for an examination. The sample questions give you an idea of the kinds of questions in each exam.

Study guides are routinely updated; therefore you should request a copy of the most recent guide within two months of the anticipated test date or call ACT PEP to check if you already have the most recent study guide copy.

To request a PEP study guide, use the order form on the back cover of this guide. Indicate the examination title and code number for each exam you plan to take. Send your order to ACT PEP Study Guides, P.O. Box 4014, Iowa City, Iowa 52243-4014, or you may call (319) 337-1363.

Selected textbooks listed in the study guides may now be ordered direct from SUNY Empire State College, External Programs Bookstore. To receive information, call or write:

SUNY Empire State College, External Programs Bookstore
5 Grande Blvd.
Saratoga Springs, NY 12866-9060
1-800-338-9179 (during business hours, EST)

from the official announcement for instructional purposes

©1994 by The American College Testing Program. All rights reserved.

ACT Proficiency Examination Content Descriptions

ACT PEP examinations measure college-level knowledge and understanding. Most are comparable to end-of-course tests for one- or two-semester courses.

The following descriptions summarize the content of each test offered in 1994-95. Following each description is a list of the number of semester hours of credit recommended by ACE and awarded by Regents College for passing scores on PEP exams as well as the level of the examination: Upper Level=U, or Lower Level=L. Where appropriate, the specific course(s) covered by the examination is indicated. **If you requested your score report be sent to an institution other than Regents College, you should check with that institution for information about their policies and criteria for granting credit for ACT PEP exams.**

Arts and Sciences

Abnormal Psychology (459)
Corresponds to a one-semester course in abnormal psychology. Includes the historical background of abnormal psychology, the major conceptualizations, and the nature and description of abnormal disorders, as well as their definitions, classifications, etiology, and major treatments. Assumes knowledge of concepts typically learned in an introductory psychology course. 3 credits, U

The American Dream (Part I) (460)
Reflects an interdisciplinary course of study which reveals both the conflict and the consensus that resulted as groups and individuals struggled to define and shape the American dream in a variety of ways prior to the Civil War. Draws from the literature, history, and political science of the United States. 6 credits, U

Anatomy and Physiology (506)
Corresponds to an introductory, two-semester sequence of courses in anatomy and physiology. Includes an understanding of anatomical and physiological factors involved in the functioning of major body systems, with emphasis on systems that maintain, integrate, and control body functions. Assumes familiarity with basic biological terminology and with concepts such as basic cell structure and function. 6 credits, L

Foundations of Gerontology (407)
Corresponds to an introductory, one-semester course in gerontology. Includes biological, psychological, and social aspects of aging, and an understanding of issues, needs, and realities involved in the aging process. Multidisciplinary in nature and covers theories, concepts, empirical patterns and their implications for policy and practice. 3 credits, U

The History of Nazi Germany (432)
Reflects a study of the history of National Socialism. Includes the Nazis' rise to power, politics and the economy, everyday life in the Third Reich, the role of the SS in the Nazi state, the Holocaust, and the legacy of National Socialism. 3 credits, U

International Conflicts in the Twentieth Century (510)
Reflects an interdisciplinary course of study of the origins of the great international conflicts in the 20th century and their relevance to ongoing efforts to maintain international security in the post–Cold War era. 3 credits, U

Microbiology (558)
Corresponds to an introductory, one-semester course in microbiology. Tests for a knowledge and understanding of bacteria, algae, fungi, protozoa, viruses, and their relationships with humans. Includes introduction to microbiology, biology of microorganisms, control of microorganisms, disease and resistance, biology of infectious diseases, and industrial and environmental microbiology. Assumes general knowledge of chemistry, biology, and anatomy and physiology. 3 credits, L

The New Rule of Reason: Philosophy and Society in the Seventeenth Century (560)
Reflects an interdisciplinary course of study of seventeenth-century Western European philosophy viewed in the context of four major social changes: capitalism, modern science, the nation-state, and challenges to religious dogma. Based on the writings of individual philosophical thinkers of the period, as well as on selected modern critical interpretations. 3 credits, U

Religions of the World (509)
Reflects an interdisciplinary course of study of the major religions as viewed in their social and historical context. Draws content from sociology, psychology, and philosophy. Questions require student to apply an understanding of the content to an analysis and comparison of religious beliefs and practices. 3 credits, U

Statistics (408)
Corresponds to an introductory, one-semester course in statistics. Includes the fundamental concepts of descriptive and inferential statistics in a service course applicable to many majors. Assumes a basic knowledge of algebra. 3 credits, L

The War in Vietnam (1945–1975): A Global Perspective (511)
Reflects a study of the various stages of war in Vietnam from the conflict's beginnings in traditional Vietnamese culture to the aftermath of Communist victory in 1975. Throughout the chronological history of the war, the examination focuses on three major themes: the role of culture, the temporal and international context of the war, and the conflicting interpretations of the war. 3 credits, U

Business

Business Policy and Strategy (579)
Corresponds to a one-semester, upper division course in business policy and strategy. Tests for achievement typically expected of a student who has completed a capstone course at the end of an undergraduate program in business. Requires the integration of facts and concepts from core business subjects, the application of these concepts to address business problems encountered in case studies, as well as demonstrated understanding of the influence of business environments on solving business problems. 3 credits, U

Corporation Finance (581)
Corresponds to a one-semester course in corporation finance. Includes goals of financial management and introduction to strategic decisions of financial management; tools of financial analysis; management of current assets and current liabilities; intermediate and long-term financial instruments; the investment decision; the financing decision; the dividend decision; and international finance. 3 credits, L

Note: These examinations are administered in New York State by Regents College. You may register by calling (518) 464-8500.

Human Resource Management (482)
Corresponds to a one-semester, upper-division course in human resource management. Resembles an end-of-course test required of management majors in the junior or senior year. Includes the role and context of human resource management, human resource planning and staffing, performance and the individual, compensation, labor-management relations, and performance and the organization. Tests for knowledge of facts and terminology, and understanding of personnel management concepts and principles, and particularly for the ability to apply these concepts to typical personnel management situations. Assumes knowledge of the principles of management. 3 credits, U

Introductory Accounting (431)
Corresponds to a two-semester, six-credit sequence of courses in introductory accounting designed for all majors in business. Includes basic accounting concepts and principles; the accounting recording process; financial statements and analysis; accounting for assets, liabilities, owner's equity, revenues and expenses; manufacturing accounting; and analysis for managerial decision making. 6 credits, L

Labor Relations (535)
Corresponds to a one-semester, upper-division course in labor relations; comparable to an end-of-course test required of business administration majors in the junior or senior year. Includes labor relations in the United States, American labor law, collective bargaining, contract administration, and miscellaneous related topics. Tests for knowledge of facts and terminology, an understanding of basic concepts, and particularly for the ability to apply this knowledge and understanding of typical business situations. 3 credits, U

Organizational Behavior (429)
Corresponds to a one-semester, upper-division course in organizational behavior; comparable to an end-of-course test required of business administration majors in the junior or senior year. Includes individual behavior, group and interpersonal behavior, and organizational and intergroup behavior. Tests for knowledge of facts and terminology, understanding of basic concepts, and particularly for the ability to apply this knowledge and understanding to typical business situations. Assumes knowledge of the principles of management. 3 credits, U

Principles of Management (430)
Corresponds to an introductory, one-semester course in principles of management designed for all majors in business. Includes the evolution of management thought; planning and decision making; organizing, leading, influencing, and controlling functions; and special issues in management. 3 credits, L

Principles of Marketing (483)
Corresponds to an introductory, one-semester, three-credit course in principles of marketing designed for all majors in business. Includes the role of marketing in the organization and society, analysis for markets, the functional areas of marketing, and special topics. 3 credits, L

Production/Operations Management (582)
Corresponds to a one-semester course in production/operations management. Includes definition and description of production/operations management, design of the productive system, planning the use of the productive system, and the control of the productive system. Assumes a knowledge of generally accepted production/operations management principles, principles of economics, statistics, and basic computer science concepts. 3 credits, L

Education

Reading Instruction in the Elementary School (555)
Corresponds to a two-semester sequence of courses in elementary school reading instruction. Includes theoretical framework, early stages of reading, word identification strategies, comprehension, instructional strategies, and classroom assessment and evaluation. 6 credits, L

Nursing

Fundamentals of Nursing (403)
Corresponds to a course in fundamentals of nursing. Includes concepts basic to nursing practice; communication and interpersonal relations; protection and promotion of safety; comfort, rest, and activity; nutrition; elimination; oxygenation; and fluid and electrolyte. 8 credits, L

Maternal and Child Nursing: Associate Degree Level (453)
Corresponds to one or more courses in maternal and child nursing at the associate degree level. Includes maternity nursing and care of the well and ill child from birth through adolescence. Assumes a basic knowledge of anatomy and physiology, and growth and development. 6 credits, L

Maternal and Child Nursing: Baccalaureate Degree Level (457)
Measures knowledge and understanding of material typically taught in a sequence of courses in maternal and child nursing at the baccalaureate degree level. The exam tests for the ability to utilize the nursing process in the nursing management of family health and reproduction, low-risk pregnancy, the normal neonate and family, the family with a high-risk mother or high-risk neonate, the well child and family, and the ill child and family. 8 credits, U

Maternity Nursing (559)
Corresponds to a course in maternity nursing. Assumes a basic knowledge and understanding of anatomy, physiology, and developmental tasks. 3 credits, L

Adult Nursing (554)
Measures knowledge and understanding of material typically taught in a sequence of courses in medical-surgical or adult nursing at the baccalaureate degree level. The exam measures knowledge and understanding of the health and nursing care of young, middle-aged, and older adults, including the ability to use the nursing process in the nursing management of adults with cardiovascular, respiratory, urinary, reproductive, endocrine, gastrointestinal, sensorimotor, musculoskeletal, immune, or integumentary system dysfunction. 8 credits, U

Psychiatric/Mental Health Nursing (503)
Measures knowledge and understanding of material typically taught in a sequence of courses in psychiatric/mental health nursing at the baccalaureate degree level. The exam measures knowledge and understanding of the theoretical/therapeutic foundations for psychiatric mental health nursing practice, and tests the application of this knowledge and understanding to the nursing care of functional and dysfunctional clients using the nursing process as an organizing framework. Within this framework, the client system is defined as the individual, the family, the small group, or the community, with major emphasis on the individual. 8 credits, U

Commonalities in Nursing Care: Area A (427)
Includes concepts of nursing care and nursing actions common to all patients throughout the life cycle. Assumes the technical vocabulary and knowledge of anatomy and physiology, microbiology, emotional and physical development, and nutrition generally expected of the associate degree nurse. Focuses on the nursing care of patients related to the health continuum, comfort, rest, and sleep, activity/mobility, environmental safety, biological safety, and psychological safety. 5 credits, L

Commonalities in Nursing Care: Area B (478)
Includes concepts of nursing care and nursing actions common to all patients throughout the life cycle. Assumes the technical vocabulary and knowledge of anatomy and physiology, microbiology, and emotional and physical development generally expected of the associate degree nurse. Focuses on the nursing care of patients related to nutrition, elimination, oxygenation, and fluid and electrolyte balance. 5 credits, L

Differences in Nursing Care: Area A (479)
Includes nursing care of patients experiencing problems of oxygenation or abnormal cell growth, as well as the development of the fetus and the physiological changes associated with normal pregnancy. Focuses on acute and long-term problems of medical, surgical, obstetric, and pediatric patients. Assumes knowledge of anatomy and physiology, emotional and physical development, pharmacology, and nutrition. 5 credits, L

Differences in Nursing Care: Area B (531)
Includes nursing care of patients experiencing problems with behavioral responses, metabolic mechanisms, regulatory mechanisms, and congenital anomalies, genetic disorders, and developmental problems. Focuses on both acute and long-term problems of medical, surgical, psychiatric, and pediatric patients. Assumes knowledge of anatomy and physiology, emotional and physical development, pharmacology, and nutrition. 5 credits, L

Differences in Nursing Care: Area C (578)
Includes nursing care of patients experiencing infections and communicable disease problems; tissue trauma; and neurological, sensory, and musculoskeletal dysfunctions. Focuses on both acute and long-term problems of medical, surgical, and pediatric patients. Assumes knowledge of anatomy and physiology, emotional and physical development, and nutrition. 5 credits, L

Occupational Strategies in Nursing (532)
Focuses on the roles and functions of the associate degree nurse within the occupation of nursing. Includes the health care delivery system; the health team; legal, educational, and ethical aspects of current nursing practice; and influences of nursing history, nursing organizations, and licensure on the nurse's function in the delivery of care. 3 credits, L

Professional Strategies in Nursing (426)
Measures knowledge and understanding of the professional role within the occupation of nursing. The exam focuses on trends and events that have influenced the development of the profession of nursing, accountability for professional practice, design and management of professional practice, and the health care delivery system. 4 credits, U

Health Support: Area I (530)
Measures knowledge and understanding of health promotion and prevention of illness in the nursing care of the client. While the client may be the individual, family, or community, emphasis is placed on the family and community. The exam tests the ability to apply the nursing process to support the health of the client. Emphasis is placed on health promotion and the primary and secondary aspects of health protection. The concepts of wellness tested are theoretical and philosophical; ecological and epidemiological; individual, family, and community assessment; and nursing strategies to promote and support health. The patterns of risk tested are environmental safety, nutrition, and childbearing and childrearing. 4 credits, U

Health Support: Area II (577)
Measures knowledge and understanding of nursing action related to factors which affect a client's wellness and place the client at risk for major health problems. While the client may be the individual, family, or community, emphasis is placed on the family and community. The exam tests the ability to apply the nursing process to support the health of the client. Emphasis is placed on the primary and secondary prevention aspects of health protection. The patterns of risk tested are mental health; cardiovascular and respiratory; neoplasms; infections, communicable diseases, and immune responses; neuromuscular and endocrine/regulatory; and birth defects and genetic problems. 4 credits, U

Health Restoration: Area I (425)
Measures the ability to apply the nursing process to assist clients in dealing with major health problems. While the client may be the individual, family, or community, emphasis is placed on the individual at all stages of the life cycle. The major health problems tested are cardiovascular, respiratory, neoplasms, accidents and traumatic injuries, endocrine, and autoimmune. 4 credits, U

Health Restoration: Area II (477)
Measures the ability to apply the nursing process to assist clients in dealing with major health problems. While the client may be the individual, family, or community, emphasis is placed on the individual at all stages of the life cycle. The major health problems tested are emotional and behavioral; neurological and sensory; gastrointestinal and genitourinary; infections and communicable diseases; complications of pregnancy, problems of the high-risk mother and problems of the high-risk infant; and birth defects and genetic problems. 4 credits, U

Registration Instructions

Registration materials are included in the packet with this *Registration Guide.* To register for one or more PEP exams, you must complete the ACT PEP Registration Form according to the instructions below, and mail the properly completed form along with the correct total fee in the preaddressed return envelope provided.

Once your registration form has been mailed, all PEP policies apply. No changes can be made to the test date choice or examination choices; however, you may request a test center change (see page 6 for information).

Registration materials must be postmarked no later than the registration deadline for the desired test date (see front cover). If there is a discrepancy between the metered postmark and an official U.S. Postal Service postmark, the latter will be considered official. It is advisable not to mail registration materials too close to the postmark deadline, because mail is sometimes postmarked a day or two after mailing. ACT PEP will not be responsible for registration materials lost in the mail.

Due to limited seating capacity at some PEP test centers, the sooner you send in your registration form, the more likely it will be that you can test at your first-choice test center.

Restrictions on Retesting

Candidates may retake an examination if 60 days have passed since they last took it.

For example, if you take an exam in October 1994, you could not retake it in November 1994 because 60 days would not have passed. You would have to wait for the next test date (February 1995) to retake the exam. **Scores for exams retaken before 60 days have passed will not be reported and fees will not be returned.**

Your ACT PEP Registration Form

Be sure you follow all the instructions in this guide and on the Registration Form carefully. Errors may delay or prevent your registration. Your ACT PEP registration will **not** be processed unless the registration form is completed fully and properly and is accompanied by a cashier's check or money order payable to ACT PEP for the correct total fee. Cash will not be accepted.

We reserve the right to return unprocessed any improperly completed forms, incomplete forms, unsigned forms, simulated forms, and forms not accompanied by correct and complete payment of the total test fee. This delay may cause you to miss the registration deadline for your test date.

Because the registration form will be processed by machine, be sure to:

- use a soft-lead (No. 2) pencil and print legibly
- blacken ONE oval under each letter or number you enter
- blacken the blank ovals below each empty box
- erase any errors completely

Do **NOT** staple your payment to the form.

Begin on Side 1 of your Registration Form.

A: Name and Mailing Address. Print your name and current mailing address on the lines provided.

B: Name. Enter your name in the sections labeled Last Name, First Name, MI (middle initial). Begin in the first box for each part of your name. If there is not enough space for your name, enter as much as possible using one box for each letter, but do not extend any part of your name beyond its designated area. Blacken the corresponding ovals.

C, D, E, and F: Mailing Address, City, State Code, and ZIP Code. The address you enter will be used for mailing your Registration Acknowledgment Form. Enter each part of the address where you are certain to receive mail from ACT PEP. If you live in an apartment, enter the apartment number after the name of the street. For example:

1420 FLDCRST #315

Leave a space between the parts of your street address. If you need to abbreviate in block C, use the abbreviations below. (Letter ovals are in the upper part and number ovals in the lower part of block C.)

Abbreviations for Street Addresses

Apartment	#	Expressway	EXPY	Route	RT
Avenue	AVE	Fort	FT	South	S
Beach	BCH	Garden	GDN	Springs	SPGS
Boulevard	BLVD	Heights	HTS	Square	SQ
Canyon	CYN	Highway	HWY	State, Street	ST
Center	CTR	Lake	LK	Terrace	TER
Circle	CIR	Mount	MT	Trail	TRL
City	CY	Mountain	MTN	Trailer	TRLR
Court	CT	North	N	Turnpike	TPKE
Crescent	CRES	Parkway	PKY	University	UNIV
Drive	DR	Place	PL	Village	VLG
East	E	Point	PT	West	W
Estates	EST	Road	RD		

For block E, State Code, see the list of state codes located adjacent to block E.

Blacken the corresponding ovals for blocks C, D, E, and F.

G: Telephone. Enter the telephone area code and numbers for both your home and work. We may need to reach you to verify information. If you do not have a telephone, indicate the number of a friend or relative with whom we can leave a message.

Turn to Side 2 of the Registration Form.

H: Social Security Number. Enter your Social Security number. If you do not have a Social Security number or do not wish to provide it, enter zeros. Canadian students should also enter zeros. ACT PEP will use your Social Security number only for positive identification of your record and will routinely include it in the score reports sent to you and reports sent at your request to agencies or institutions. Blacken the corresponding ovals.

I: Sex. Blacken the appropriate oval.

J: Date of Birth. Enter the month, day, and last two digits of the year in which you were born. Enter a zero for any blank. Blacken the corresponding ovals.

K: Test Date. **Blacken the correct oval for the test date on which you wish to take the ACT PEP examinations you mark on Side 2 of the form.** The schedule of test dates and registration deadlines is on the front cover of this guide. **Your registration will be processed for the date you indicate and must be postmarked by the deadline. An error in test date selection may cause you to miss your test date.**

L: Test Center Codes. The test center list begins on page 11 in this guide. **Note that many test centers are open only on selected test dates. It is your responsibility to check carefully that the test centers you list are open on the dates for which you are registering.** Find and print the code number for your first choice of test center; then print the code number for your second choice of test center. Blacken the corresponding ovals. If your first choice is closed or filled to capacity, you will automatically be assigned to your second choice center. If you cannot be assigned to either center because of capacity limitations, your registration form will be returned to you and your fee refunded in full. If neither of the centers you list is scheduled to be open on the test date you indicated in block K, your registration form and fee will be returned to you unprocessed.

M: Additional Registration Packet. If you plan to take additional PEP exams on a later test date and need another registration packet, blacken the appropriate oval. Packets are also available at test centers on the test dates, and you may request one at that time.

Selecting Your ACT PEP Examinations. You may register for a maximum of four PEP examinations. For test security reasons, exams may be taken **only** during the test session for which they are listed on the registration form. The **only** exception to this policy is if you wish to take two exams that are offered during the **same** session. If you wish to take two exams scheduled for the same session, blacken the oval for both exams; the ACT PEP office will reschedule one of the conflicting exams to a session during which you are not testing. **For each exam** registered, blacken the corresponding oval and write the exam fee next to the title in the space marked "Fee Enclosed."

N: Total Fee Enclosed. After you have marked the exams you wish to take, complete block N. Write the total fee for each session, then add all sessions to arrive at the total fee you must submit with the registration form. Enclose a cashier's check or money order, payable to ACT PEP, for the correct total amount. **Do *not* staple your payment to the registration form and do *not* send cash.** Your registration cannot be processed without the correct payment.

Retain your copy of your money order or cashier's check for receipt of payment. If your employer requires additional proof for reimbursement of exam fees, your copy of your ACT PEP score report is an official document and may serve as proof of payment.

O: Student's Certification. Read the statement in block O, then sign (do not print) and date the form. Your registration cannot be processed without your signature.

Mailing Your Registration Form. Carefully fold your registration form the way it was folded when you received it. Mail the completed form with the appropriate fee in the preaddressed envelope provided.

Keep this registration guide for reference. Completed registration materials, as well as all other correspondence, inquiries, requests for study guides, and requests concerning registration materials, administration, and processing, should be directed to:

ACT PEP
P.O. Box 4014
Iowa City, Iowa 52243-4014
Telephone: (319) 337-1363
TDD for hearing impaired (must call from a TDD)
(319) 337-1701

Additional Information

Registration Acknowledgment

Normally, within 3 weeks after your PEP Registration Form and fee have been received at ACT, a Registration Acknowledgment will be sent to you. If you do not receive an acknowledgment within 3 weeks, contact ACT PEP. Note, however, that if you submit your registration form far in advance of the test date you wish, it will take longer than 3 weeks. Registration Acknowledgments for such future registrations will be sent when processing for that date begins.

When you receive your Registration Acknowledgment, review it carefully to be sure that it lists the exams you registered for (check both code number and title) as well as the correct test center and test date. If there are any discrepancies or if you have any questions, call (319) 337-1363 immediately. TDD for hearing impaired (must call from a TDD) (319) 337-1701.

Note: Your Registration Acknowledgment Form may be used to request a reregistration or refund (see page 8); therefore **it is important for you to retain this form.** The reverse side of the Registration Acknowledgment Form gives instructions for requesting either a reregistration or refund.

Changing Your Test Center

All test center changes are subject to the availability of test materials for the exam(s) you desire and seating space.

If you cannot take a PEP examination at the test center to which you have been assigned, you may request a test center change. To initiate this change, call (319) 337-1363. Collect calls will not be accepted. Be sure that the new center you request is scheduled to be open on that test date.

There is no charge for a test center change for the same test date; however, you must pay for any last-minute communications. All changes will be made after the registration deadline but not later than 10 calendar days before the test.

Guidelines for Taking the ACT PEP Tests

Please read these guidelines carefully. They can help you do your best on the ACT PEP tests.

1. Get sufficient rest the night before taking the tests so that you are in good physical and mental shape for taking them.
2. Due to variations in room temperature at the test centers, we suggest you take a sweater or jacket to ensure your comfort.
3. Listen closely to all directions. Ask questions if you do not understand what you are to do.
4. You must complete identifying information and mark your answers on the machine-scored answer sheet. Be very precise in doing so. Be sure that you blacken the correct ovals and rectangles (see sample on page 13).
5. When taking the tests, position your answer sheet next to your test booklet so you can mark answers quickly without moving either the booklet or the answer sheet.
6. Select only one answer to each question.
7. When you are marking your answers, be sure that the number of the line of ovals on the answer sheet is the same as the number of the question you are answering. Then mark your answer in the oval that has the same number as your answer choice.
8. If you wish to change an answer, erase the unintended mark completely.
9. Read each question and the possible answers fully so that you are sure you understand them before answering.
10. **IMPORTANT: ANSWER EVERY QUESTION. THERE IS NO PENALTY FOR GUESSING.**

11. When you are unsure of the correct answer to a question, first eliminate every wrong answer you can. Then pick the best answer from those left.
12. Pace yourself throughout each test. Do not spend too much time on any one question. If a question is too hard for you, choose the answer you think is best and go on to the next question.
13. You may want to take a watch for your personal use. Each test is timed, and time remaining will not be announced. Note: Alarms may not be used during testing.
14. If you complete the test before time is called, look for any careless mistakes by rereading the questions and your answers.

Test Day Information

Important Instructions!

On the test day, you may indicate **one** institution or agency to which you wish your ACT PEP results reported for no additional fee. When completing your answer sheet, the Test Supervisor will ask you to mark the code number of the institution you wish to receive your scores. Therefore, **before the test day,** you should refer to the "List of ACT PEP Participating Institutions" (a separate 4-page list included in the registration packet) to determine the proper code number. Circle this code number for easy reference on the test day; **take this list with you to the test center. You will also receive a copy of your score report.** Because ACT maintains confidentiality of your ACT record, no other copies of your scores will be released without your permission.

Time of Examination

Morning test sessions normally begin at 8:30 a.m.; afternoon sessions normally begin at 1:30 p.m. **You are advised to report at least 15 minutes before these starting times.** No one will be admitted to the examination room after testing has begun.

NOTE: Occasionally, when a test center reporting address changes at the last minute, there is insufficient time to notify you. Be prepared to report to an address other than the one listed on your registration acknowledgment (signs should be posted). Reporting to the center 15 minutes early should allow enough time if this occurs.

Special Testing Requirements

American College Testing recognizes its obligation to make the PEP examinations equally accessible to candidates with physical or mental handicaps or disabilities. Reasonable accommodation to specific handicaps will be made whenever necessary and possible. However, it is the candidate's responsibility to advise ACT of the need for special accommodation or procedures **at the time he or she registers to take an examination.** ACT PEP reserves the right to require medical documentation of any handicap or disability and to refuse special accommodation when the applicant fails to provide adequate notice or medical justification.

Admission and Identification

The test center supervisor must positively identify each candidate before permitting admission to the testing room. The candidate's photograph, attached to the PEP Identification Card, will be used to facilitate this identification process. Candidates must provide a photograph and completed PEP ID Card **each test date,** even if they have tested on previous test dates. Attach permanently (with transparent tape or glue) a current, representative 2" x 2" photograph of yourself to the space indicated on the ID card. The photograph becomes the property of ACT PEP and will NOT be returned to you. Please note that formal portraits are not necessary; recent, representative snapshots are sufficient.

Each candidate must have signed the PEP ID Card. The supervisor may request additional identification and may, if necessary, inspect such documents to ascertain that they have not been altered and that they belong to the person displaying them. Each candidate's right thumbprint will be taken at the test center.

If you are taking more than one test on a test date, you need only to present one ID card at the first test session. Example: If you are scheduled to test Thursday morning and Friday afternoon, you need only to present the ID card on Thursday morning. The Test Supervisor will pull your card Friday afternoon to reverify your identification.

To avoid potential embarrassment or inconvenience in the identification process, candidates are advised to provide a recent, representative photograph of sufficient quality to make positive identification a routine procedure.

Test Center Regulations

The following regulations will be observed at all test centers in order to ensure uniform testing procedures:

1. Each candidate must bring his or her PEP Identification Card, properly completed and signed. Each candidate's right thumbprint will be taken at the test center. **No candidate will be admitted without being thumbprinted, and no candidate will receive scores without a properly completed and signed PEP ID Card for that test date.**
2. Candidates must bring at least three soft lead (No. 2) pencils and a good eraser for the objective multiple-choice examinations.
3. For examinations that are essay, candidates must bring a **black**-ink ballpoint pen.
4. Candidates are not permitted to take books, notes, slide rules, calculators, dictionaries, tables, electronic devices (pagers or similar communication devices), or aids of any kind into the examination room. Candidates also are not permitted to duplicate or record, by copying, photographing, or any other means, any part of the PEP examinations. All test materials must be returned to the test administrator; no portion of such materials may be retained by the candidate.
5. Candidates are not permitted to smoke, eat, or drink while actually testing.
6. No candidate will be admitted to the examination room after testing has started.
7. For security reasons, examinees are not allowed to receive or place telephone calls during testing.

8. Access to the examination room will be restricted to test center personnel and candidates.
9. Once the seal of the test booklet has been broken, the candidate is considered to have tested (i.e., ineligible for refund or reregistration). An exception may be made if a candidate becomes ill or ceases to test because of an emergency situation during the first 15 minutes of the examination. That candidate should return the test booklet and answer document(s) to the test supervisor, who will mark the answer document(s) VOID and indicate on the Irregularity Report that the document(s) should not be scored. No special testing arrangements can be made for a candidate in this situation. The candidate may request reregistration for a later test date or refund according to the established procedures explained below.
10. Answer documents may be voided at the request of the candidate. If a candidate discontinues testing during the first 15 minutes because of an emergency situation or illness, that candidate must request that the answer sheet not be scored in order to be eligible for refund or reregistration. In addition, a candidate who continues testing after the first 15 minutes and/or completes an examination but does not wish his or her answer documents scored must personally ask the test center supervisor to void the answer documents at the test center. The supervisor will mark the answer documents VOID and will note on the Irregularity Report the reason for voiding and that the answer document(s) are not to be scored. Such candidates are not eligible for refund or reregistration.
11. An examinee receiving or giving assistance of any kind may be required to surrender his or her test booklet(s) and answer document(s) to the supervisor and may be dismissed from the examination room. Such answer documents will be marked VOID and will not be scored; the test supervisor will attach an explanation to the Irregularity Report. Irregularities in the administration of the PEP exams can result in the cancellation of scores by ACT PEP.
12. If any question of authenticity or other irregularity in the testing process is discovered by or reported to ACT PEP, and a review confirms its significance, the candidate will be notified and given the opportunity to provide an explanation. If a significant question of authenticity or other irregularity remains, the candidate's PEP scores in question may be cancelled.
13. If you feel your performance on an examination may have been affected by an unusual situation at the test center, you may request a special review by writing to ACT PEP within ONE WEEK of the test date.

Reregistration and Refunds

Attention!

If you **cannot** test on the date assigned, reregistration for a later test date is possible; however, certain restrictions apply (see **Reregistration for a Later Test Date**).

If you originally register for one or more examinations and then do not take all of those examinations, you may request one of the following options:

1. Reregistration for **all** of the examinations that you did not take on the original test date form **to one** of the remaining valid 1994-95 test dates for an additional total fee of $10.
2. Refund of test fees for **all** of the examinations that you did not take on the original test date form minus a total fee of $15.

Note: The deadline for refund requests for the 1994-95 testing year is August 31, 1995.

You MUST make your request for a refund or reregistration for **all** exams you did not take by completing Side 2 of the Registration Acknowledgment Form which lists those exams.

The instructions outlined on Side 2 of your Registration Acknowledgment Form must be followed carefully to assure proper handling of your request. If you do not follow these procedures exactly, your request will be delayed and you may miss the registration deadline for the test date you requested.

Reregistration for a Later Test Date

Important!

All reregistration requests must be postmarked on or before the published registration deadline date for the new test date desired.

You may **not** request both reregistration and a refund for the same examination.

If you *cannot* test on the date assigned, reregistration for a later test date is possible; however, you may **not** register for the next month's test date. For example, if you originally registered for the October test date, you may **not** reregister for the November test date; likewise, you may **not** change your test date from February to March or from May to June.

The last test date for 1994-95 is June 1-2, 1995. If you miss that test date, you may apply for a refund but **not** for reregistration. If you wish to register for a test date during the next testing year, you must follow the steps for regular registration and submit a completed Registration Form and full fee.

If you cannot or choose not to take any particular PEP examination(s) on the requested test date, you may reregister for the **same** examination(s) for one of the remaining valid test dates in the current testing year (September 1–August 31). To reregister, you must send the following to ACT PEP:

1. Your PEP Registration Acknowledgment Form with Side 2 properly completed.
2. A cashier's check or money order for $10, payable to ACT PEP. Cash will not be accepted.

If you no longer have your Registration Acknowledgment Form, you must make your request for reregistration in writing. The request also must account for ALL OF THE EXAMINATIONS FOR WHICH YOU ORIGINALLY REGISTERED. That is, for each examination originally requested on your PEP Registration Form, you must state that you took the exam or that you wish to reregister to take that exam on one of the remaining test dates in the current testing year.

If you wish to register for any **different** examination(s), you must fully complete a new Registration Form and submit it along with full test fee payment. You may apply for a refund if appropriate.

The reregistration policy applies as soon as you have mailed your Registration Form to ACT PEP.

Refund of Examination Fee

> The deadline for refund requests for the 1994-95 testing year is August 31, 1995.

If you cannot or choose not to take any particular PEP examination(s) on the test date for which you were originally registered, **and** you cannot or do not wish to reregister, you may apply for a refund. To receive a refund, you MUST complete Side 2 of the Registration Acknowledgment Form that lists those examinations for which you are requesting a refund. The request should be made within two weeks after the original test date.

If you no longer have your Registration Acknowledgment Form, you must make your request in writing and state the original test date, test center, and the titles of the examinations.

The test fee(s) will be refunded minus a $15 service charge for processing, administrative, materials, and handling costs incurred. The maximum refund is the total test fee minus $15 even if the request is made before the test date for which you initially registered. **Refunds are not issued until after the test date** and may take 4-6 weeks to process.

Score Reports

In order to keep your scores confidential, they will not be given to anyone by telephone.

PEP results for examinations that include any essay questions are generally mailed 60 to 90 days after a test date. PEP results for entirely objective examinations are generally mailed 3 to 6 weeks after a test date.

On the test day, you may indicate one institution or agency to which you wish your ACT PEP results reported. Take the white 4-page "List of ACT PEP Participating Institutions" (included in the registration packet) with you to the test center to enter on your answer sheet the correct code for the institution of your choice. **You will also receive a copy of your score report.** These two reports are provided at no additional charge.

If you lose your score report, you will have to request and pay for an Additional Score Report (see next section).

Examinations that include essay questions will normally be graded by the appropriate faculty committee from the University of the State of New York, which develops the exams. However, the faculty at other institutions may review the essays themselves. If you indicate one of these institutions on your answer sheet, a copy of your answer documents will be sent to them also for evaluation.

ACT will retain your original PEP answer sheet for one year after the test date; score report data will be retained indefinitely. Your score report data, which include individually identifiable student information, may be used by the test developer (Regents College) to conduct research related to the test. In order to preserve the confidentiality of your PEP records, no report of your scores will be released to any institution or agency without your written authorization.

Stringent quality control procedures ensure the validity of scoring keys for objective PEP examinations each test date. However, if you question your scores because they are inconsistent with your previous performance on standardized tests or your level of prior learning, you may request that your scores be reverified. Your request must be in writing and must list by test code and title the PEP exams that you wish hand-scored, the test date(s) on which you took each exam, the test center where the tests were administered, and your full name, address, and date of birth. You must request this service **within six months** of the test date(s) in question. Requests after that time will **not** be honored. Results of hand-scoring are normally issued within 10 working days of receipt of the request. If you are dissatisfied with the hand score results, you may travel to Iowa City (at your expense) and witness the hand score of your answer sheet (objective tests only). However, neither your answer sheet nor test booklet will be released to you for review.

Additional Score Reports

If you wish, you may wait until you receive your copy of your score report before having your results reported to an institution or agency. All reports requested after the test date will require an additional fee.

The fee for regular Additional Score Reports (ASRs) is $4.00 per exam. A separate request form must be filed for each different institutional address. Regular ASRs are normally issued within 10 working days of receipt of the request and are mailed first-class. An ACT PEP Additional Score Request Form will be mailed to you with your score report.

In unusual situations, rush mailgram ASRs may be issued for $10.00 per exam; however do NOT request this service until you have received your score report copy. Before you request this service, we suggest that you check with the appropriate individual in the Admissions and Records department at your institution to ensure that they will accept scores listed on a mailgram from ACT PEP. Mailgram ASRs are normally issued within 48 hours after receipt of the request. If your situation requires mailgram ASR service, mark the Additional Score Request Form "RUSH" and include the fee payment of $10.00 per exam.

Diagnostic Reports

Diagnostic reports will be sent to those examinees who take objective examinations and receive a score of 44 or less. These reports are designed to assist you in evaluating your performance on the examination(s) and to provide information that may be useful in preparing to retake the exam(s).

Cancellation of Test Scores by ACT

ACT reserves the right to cancel test scores when there is reason to believe the scores are invalid. Cases of irregularities in the test administration process—for example, falsifying one's identity, impersonating another examinee (surrogate testing), unusual similarities in the answers of examinees at the same test center, or other indicators, including but not limited to student misconduct—may result in ACT's canceling the test scores. When ACT plans to cancel an examinee's test scores, the examinee is always notified prior to ACT taking that action. This notification includes information about the options available regarding the planned score cancellation, including procedures for appealing that decision. In all instances, the final and exclusive remedy available to examinees who want to appeal or otherwise challenge a decision by ACT to cancel their test scores shall be binding arbitration through written submissions to the American Arbitration Association.

Sample ACT PEP Answer Sheet

STUDY THE SAMPLES ON THIS PAGE TO BECOME FAMILIAR WITH THE FRONT SIDE OF THE ANSWER SHEET YOU WILL BE COMPLETING AT THE TEST CENTER.

BLOCK B: *NAME:* Print your Last Name, First Name, and MI (Middle Initial) in the boxes for each. Begin in the first box in each case and print only one letter per box. If your last or first name has more than one part, **leave one empty box between the parts.** If there are more letters in your last or first name than the number of boxes, print as many letters as possible, one letter per box. If you use the initial from your first name along with your middle name, print the initial in the first box for first name, leave one empty box, and print as many letters as possible of your middle name. Leave the box for middle initial blank. In the column directly below each box, blacken either the oval (only one) containing the same letter as the box or the blank rectangle below each empty box.

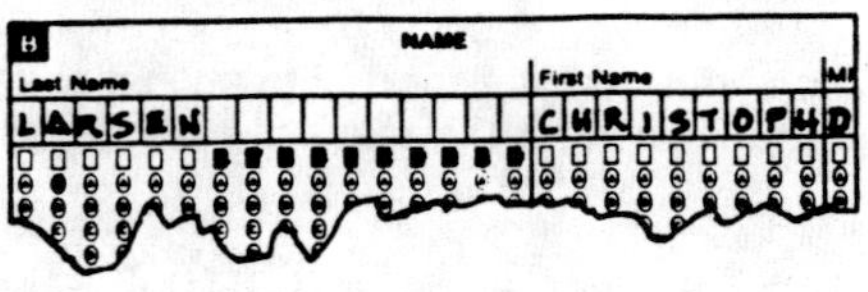

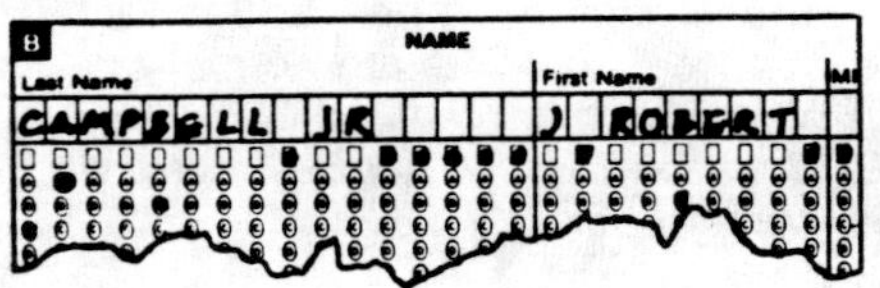

BLOCK C: *MAILING ADDRESS.* Print your street mailing address, one letter or number per box. Begin in the first box and **leave one empty box between the parts.** Use numbers instead of words in street names that include numbers. Abbreviate when possible. In the column directly below each box, blacken the corresponding oval (only one) or the blank rectangle.

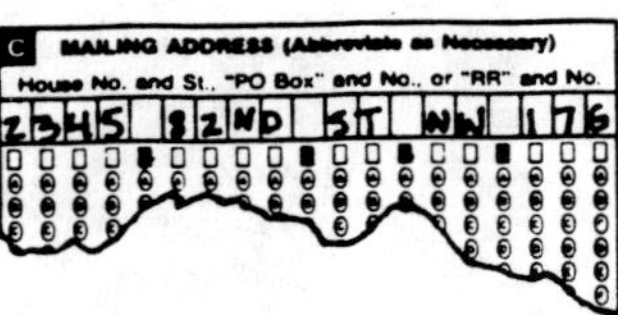

SUGGESTED ABBREVIATIONS

Beach	BCH	Highway	HWY
Boulevard	BLVD	Mile	MLE
Canyon	CYN	Parkway	PKY
Center	CTR	Place	PL
Circle	CIR	Santa, Santo	SN
City	CY	Springs	SPGS
Court	CT	Square	SQ
Crescent	CRES	State, Street	ST
Estates	EST	Terrace	TER
Expressway	EXPY	Turnpike	TPKE
Freeway	FWY	University	UNIV
Heights	HTS	Village	VLG

BLOCK D: *CITY.* Begin in the first box and print your city mailing address, one letter per box. If the city name has more than one part, **leave one empty box between the parts.** If the name requires more than the 14 boxes, abbreviate when possible and print as many letters as possible, one letter per box. Blacken either the appropriate oval (only one) or the blank rectangle in every column.

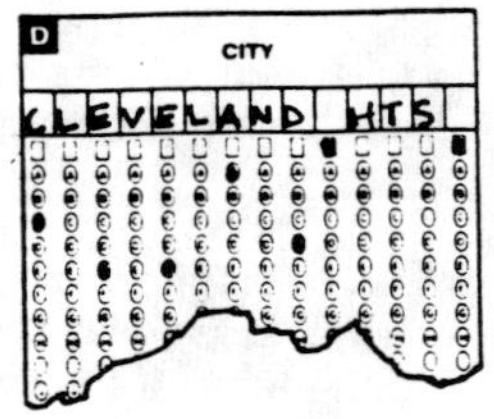

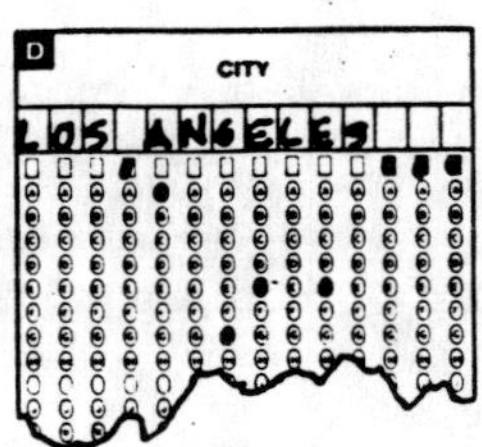

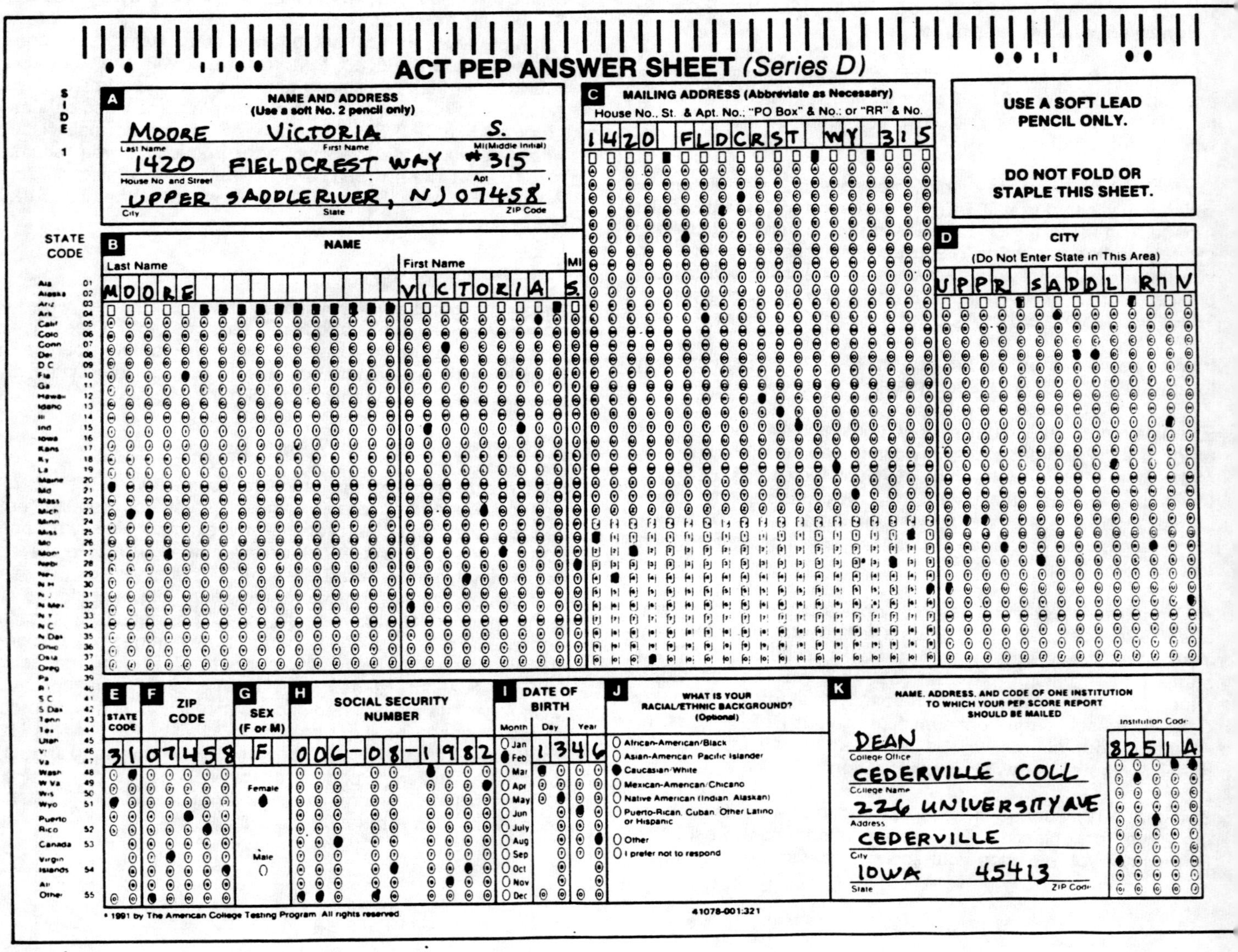

ACT PEP ANSWER SHEET *(Series D)*

SIDE 1

A — NAME AND ADDRESS (Use a soft No. 2 pencil only)

MOORE VICTORIA S.
Last Name — First Name — MI(Middle Initial)

1420 FIELDCREST WAY #315
House No. and Street — Apt.

UPPER SADDLERIVER, NJ 07458
City — State — ZIP Code

C — MAILING ADDRESS (Abbreviate as Necessary)
House No., St. & Apt. No.; "PO Box" & No.; or "RR" & No.

1420 FLDCRST WY 315

USE A SOFT LEAD PENCIL ONLY.

DO NOT FOLD OR STAPLE THIS SHEET.

STATE CODE

Ala	01
Alaska	02
Ariz	03
Ark	04
Calif	05
Colo	06
Conn	07
Del	08
D C	09
Fla	10
Ga	11
Hawaii	12
Idaho	13
Ill	14
Ind	15
Iowa	16
Kans	17
Ky	18
La	19
Maine	20
Md	21
Mass	22
Mich	23
Minn	24
Miss	25
Mo	26
Mont	27
Nebr	28
Nev	29
N H	30
N J	31
N Mex	32
N Y	33
N C	34
N Dak	35
Ohio	36
Okla	37
Oreg	38
Pa	39
R I	40
S C	41
S Dak	42
Tenn	43
Tex	44
Utah	45
Vt	46
Va	47
Wash	48
W Va	49
Wis	50
Wyo	51
Puerto Rico	52
Canada	53
Virgin Islands	54
All Other	55

B — NAME
Last Name: MOORE — First Name: VICTORIA — MI: S

D — CITY (Do Not Enter State in This Area)
UPPR SADDL RIV

E — STATE CODE: 31

F — ZIP CODE: 07458

G — SEX (F or M): F
Female / Male

H — SOCIAL SECURITY NUMBER: 006-08-1982

I — DATE OF BIRTH
Month: Jan, Feb, Mar, Apr, May, Jun, July, Aug, Sep, Oct, Nov, Dec — Day — Year
Feb 13 46

J — WHAT IS YOUR RACIAL/ETHNIC BACKGROUND? (Optional)
- African-American/Black
- Asian-American, Pacific Islander
- Caucasian/White
- Mexican-American/Chicano
- Native American (Indian, Alaskan)
- Puerto-Rican, Cuban, Other Latino or Hispanic
- Other
- I prefer not to respond

K — NAME, ADDRESS, AND CODE OF ONE INSTITUTION TO WHICH YOUR PEP SCORE REPORT SHOULD BE MAILED

DEAN
College Office
CEDERVILLE COLL
College Name
226 UNIVERSITY AVE
Address
CEDERVILLE
City
IOWA 45413
State — ZIP Code

Institution Code: 8251A

© 1991 by The American College Testing Program. All rights reserved.

41078-001:321

ACT PEP Test Centers

Enter the correct four digit test center code for your **first and second choice** test centers in block L of your PEP Registration Form. It is your responsibility to **be sure that the test centers you indicate are open on the test date for which you are registering.** If the test center you wish is not open on a particular date, you must choose an alternate center that is open, or wait to register for the next date your desired center is open. If neither of the test centers you list is open on the test date you check in block K of your registration form, your registration form and fee will be returned to you unprocessed with an explanation that you did not indicate an open test center for the test date you selected.

X = Test center is OPEN for that test date.

City	Code	Test Center	Oct. 6-7, 1994	Nov. 3-4, 1994	Feb. 2-3, 1995	Mar. 2-3, 1995	May 4-5, 1995	June 1-2, 1995
ALABAMA								
Birmingham	0078	Lawson State Comm. Coll.	X	X	X	X	X	
Mobile	0009	Bishop State Comm. Coll.	X	X	X	X	X	X
Montgomery	0008	Alabama State Univ.	X	X	X		X	X
ARIZONA								
Flagstaff	0086	Northern Arizona Univ.	X	X		X	X	
Phoenix	0103	Rio Salado Comm. Coll.		X	X		X	X
Tempe	0088	Arizona State Univ.	X	X	X	X	X	X
ARKANSAS								
Blytheville	0129	Mississippi County Comm. Coll.	X	X	X	X		
Fort Smith	0122	Westark Comm. Coll.		X	X			X
Little Rock	0132	Univ. Conference Center	X	X	X	X	X	X
State Univ.	0116	Arkansas State Univ.		X		X	X	X
CALIFORNIA								
Berkeley	0162	Armstrong Univ.	X	X	X	X	X	X
Carmichael	9343	San Juan Unified School District	X		X	X		
Chico	0212	California State Univ., Chico						X
El Cajon	0279	Grossmont Coll. (testing at LaMesa)	X	X	X	X	X	X
Fresno	0489	California State Univ.–Fresno	X	X	X	X	X	X
Imperial	0292	Imperial Valley Coll.	X	X	X	X		X
Long Beach	0300	Long Beach City Coll.	X	X	X	X	X	X
Los Angeles	0448	Moseley Salvatori Conference Ctr.	X	X	X	X	X	X
Monterey	0336	Monterey Peninsula Coll.	X	X		X	X	X
Montrose	0274	Montrose Campus–Glendale Comm. Coll.	X	X	X	X	X	X
Oakland	9341	HEC–Samuel Merritt College	X	X	X	X	X	X
Orange	0210	Chapman Univ.	X		X	X	X	X
Sacramento	0158	American River College	X	X	X	X	X	
San Diego	0394	Univ. of San Diego	X	X	X	X	X	X
Whittier	0379	Rio Hondo Coll.			X	X		X
COLORADO								
Colorado Springs	0509	Pikes Peak Comm. Coll.		X	X			X
Ft. Morgan	0544	Morgan Comm. Coll.	X			X		
Grand Junction	0518	Mesa State Coll.	X	X	X	X	X	X
Greeley	0502	Univ. of Northern Colorado	X		X		X	
Littleton	0497	Arapahoe Comm. Coll.	X			X		
Westminster	0507	Front Range Comm. Coll.	X	X	X	X	X	X
CONNECTICUT								
Danbury	0558	Western Connecticut State Univ.	X	X	X	X	X	X
Fairfield	0560	Fairfield Univ.	X			X	X	
Newington	0627	Charter Oak State Coll.		X			X	
West Hartford	0606	Univ. of Hartford		X	X		X	X
FLORIDA								
Boca Raton	0729	Florida Atlantic Univ.	X	X	X	X	X	X
Daytona Beach	0720	Bethune-Cookman Coll.	X	X	X	X	X	X
Ft. Myers	9271	St. Cecilia's Church	X	X	X	X	X	X
Jacksonville	0717	Florida Comm. Coll. at Jacksonville		X	X	X		X
Lakeland	0732	Florida Southern Coll.	X	X	X	X	X	X
Miami	0770	Miami-Dade Comm. Coll.	X	X	X	X	X	X
Miami Shores	0718	Barry Univ.	X	X	X	X	X	X
N. Miami	9233	Florida Int'l. Univ.		X	X	X	X	
Panama City	0738	Gulf Coast Comm. Coll.		X			X	
Tallahassee	0734	Florida State Univ.		X	X		X	
Tampa	6394	Hillsborough Comm. Coll.	X	X	X	X	X	X
Tampa	0762	Univ. of Tampa	X	X	X	X	X	X
GEORGIA								
Atlanta	5571	Atlanta Area Technical Inst.		X	X		X	X
Atlanta	0810	Emory Univ.	X	X	X	X	X	X
Atlanta	0826	Georgia State Univ.	X	X	X	X	X	X
Augusta	0796	Augusta Coll.	X			X		X
Dahlonega	0848	North Georgia Coll.		X	X		X	
Savannah	0786	Armstrong State Coll.		X		X		X

City	Code	Test Center	Oct. 6-7, 1994	Nov. 3-4, 1994	Feb. 2-3, 1995	Mar. 2-3, 1995	May 4-5, 1995	June 1-2, 1995
HAWAII								
Hilo	0904	Univ. of Hawaii–Hilo	X		X			X
Honolulu	0902	Univ. of Hawaii–Manoa		X	X		X	
IDAHO								
Boise	0914	Boise State Univ.		X	X		X	
Pocatello	0918	Idaho State Univ.	X		X		X	
ILLINOIS								
Champaign	1015	Parkland Coll.		X			X	
Chicago	0934	City Colleges of Chicago–Harold Washington Coll.		X	X		X	X
De Kalb	1102	Northern Illinois Univ.		X	X		X	X
Dixon	1127	Sauk Valley Comm. Coll.		X	X		X	
East Peoria	1035	Illinois Central Coll.			X			X
Lisle	1132	Illinois Benedictine Coll.	X	X	X	X		X
Quincy	0956	Blessing Rieman Coll. of Nrsg.	X		X			X
Rockford	1122	Rockford Coll.	X		X	X	X	
University Park	1028	Governors State Univ.	X	X	X	X	X	X
INDIANA								
Evansville	1188	Univ. of Evansville				X		X
Fort Wayne	1238	Saint Francis Coll.	X			X		X
Indianapolis	1214	Indiana Univ.–Purdue Univ.	X	X	X	X	X	X
Mishawaka	1178	College Park Missionary Church	X			X	X	
IOWA								
Cedar Falls	1322	Univ. of Northern Iowa	X		X			X
Cedar Rapids	1275	Kirkwood Comm. Coll.		X	X	X	X	
Des Moines	1302	Drake Univ.	X			X		X
Mason City	1336	No. Iowa Area Comm. Coll.		X	X		X	
Ottumwa	1269	Indian Hills Comm. Coll.	X					X
Sioux City	1276	Briar Cliff Coll.	X		X		X	X
West Burlington	1280	Southeastern Comm. Coll.	X	X	X	X	X	X
KANSAS								
Wichita	1472	Wichita State Univ.		X			X	
KENTUCKY								
Hopkinsville	1569	Hopkinsville Comm. Coll.	X					X
Lexington	1554	Univ. of Kentucky	X	X	X	X	X	X
Louisville	1556	Univ. of Louisville	X	X	X	X	X	X
LOUISIANA								
Hammond	1608	Southeastern Louisiana Univ.	X	X	X	X	X	X
Lake Charles	1594	McNeese State Univ.		X		X		X
New Orleans	1611	Southern Univ. at New Orleans	X	X	X	X	X	X
Shreveport	1613	Southern Univ.	X	X	X	X	X	X
MAINE								
South Portland	9342	Southern Maine Tech. Coll.	X			X	X	
Wiscasset	1667	Lincoln County Court House		X	X		X	X
MARYLAND								
Baltimore	1727	College of Notre Dame	X	X	X	X	X	X
Catonsville	1684	Catonsville Comm. Coll.	X	X		X	X	X
College Park	1746	Univ. of Maryland	X	X	X	X	X	X
Cumberland	1679	Allegany Comm. Coll.		X				X
Largo	1731	Prince George's Comm. Coll.	X	X	X	X	X	X
MASSACHUSETTS								
Chestnut Hill	1788	Boston Coll.	X	X	X	X	X	X
Holyoke	1844	Holyoke Comm. Coll.		X		X		X
Lynn	1875	North Shore Comm. Coll.	X	X	X	X	X	X
Newton	1911	Aquinas College at Newton	X	X	X	X	X	X
No. Dartmouth	1906	Univ. of Massachusetts–Dartmouth						X
Wellesley Hills	1861	Massachusetts Bay Comm. Coll.	X	X	X	X	X	X

City	Code	Test Center	Oct. 6-7, 1994	Nov. 3-4, 1994	Feb. 2-3, 1995	Mar. 2-3, 1995	May 4-5, 1995	June 1-2, 1995
MICHIGAN								
Ann Arbor	1977	Concordia Coll.	X	X	X	X	X	X
Detroit	2024	Marygrove Coll.	X	X	X	X	X	X
Detroit	2060	Univ. of Detroit Mercy	X	X	X		X	X
Grand Rapids	2004	Grand Rapids Comm. Coll.		X	X	X	X	X
Kalamazoo	2066	Western Michigan Univ.	X			X		X
Traverse City	2040	Northwestern Michigan Coll.	X		X			X
University Center	2057	Saginaw Valley State Univ.	X	X	X	X	X	X
MINNESOTA								
Duluth	2157	Univ. of Minnesota–Duluth		X		X	X	
Inver Grove Hts.	2103	Inver Hills Comm. Coll.				X		
Minneapolis	2156	Univ. of Minnesota	X	X	X		X	X
White Bear Lake	2125	Lakewood Comm. Coll.						X
MISSISSIPPI								
Cleveland	2190	Delta State University	X			X	X	X
Jackson	2204	Jackson State Univ.		X	X		X	
Mississippi St.	2220	Mississippi State Univ.	X	X	X	X	X	X
MISSOURI								
Kansas City	2380	Univ. of Missouri–Kansas City	X	X	X	X	X	X
Springfield	2370	Southwest Missouri State Univ.		X	X		X	
St. Louis	2352	St. Louis Univ.–Frost Campus		X	X		X	X
St. Louis	2383	Univ. of Missouri–St. Louis	X	X	X	X	X	X
MONTANA								
Bozeman	2420	Montana State Univ.		X			X	
NEBRASKA								
Kearney	2468	Univ. of Nebraska–Kearney		X			X	
Lincoln	2482	Univ. of Nebraska–Lincoln		X			X	X
McCook	2460	McCook Comm. Coll.	X		X	X		X
Omaha	2464	Univ. of Nebraska at Omaha		X	X			X
NEVADA								
N. Las Vegas	2498	Comm. Coll. of Southern Nevada		X	X		X	
Reno	2499	Truckee Meadows Comm. Coll.	X	X	X	X	X	X
Reno	2494	Univ. of Nevada–Reno	X	X	X	X	X	X
NEW HAMPSHIRE								
Keene	2510	Keene State Coll.	X	X	X	X	X	X
Manchester	2522	St. Anselm Coll.	X	X	X	X	X	X
NEW JERSEY								
Camden	2598	Rutgers Univ.	X	X	X	X	X	X
Lodi	2559	Felician Coll.	X	X	X	X	X	X
Morristown	2546	College of St. Elizabeth	X	X	X	X	X	X
Pemberton	2543	Burlington County Coll.	X		X		X	X
Trenton	2568	Mercer County Comm. Coll.	X	X	X	X	X	X
Trenton	2612	Thomas Edison State Coll.	X			X		
NEW MEXICO								
Albuquerque	2650	Univ. of New Mexico	X	X	X	X	X	X
Clovis	2631	Clovis Comm. Coll.	X	X	X	X	X	
Silver City	2646	Western New Mexico Univ.		X		X		
NEW YORK These examinations are administered in New York State by Regents College. You may register with Regents College by calling (518) 464-8500.								
NORTH CAROLINA								
Belmont	3070	Belmont Abbey Coll.	X	X	X	X	X	X
Chapel Hill	3162	Univ. of North Carolina	X		X		X	
High Point	3108	High Point Univ.	X	X	X	X		X
Raleigh	3177	Wake Technical Coll.	X		X	X		X
OHIO								
Cincinnati	3340	Univ. of Cincinnati	X	X	X	X	X	X
Columbus	3275	Franklin Univ.	X	X	X	X	X	X
Dayton	3295	Wright State Univ.	X	X	X	X	X	X
Elyria	3287	Lorain County Comm. Coll.		X	X		X	X
St. Clairsville	3317	Ohio Univ.–Eastern Campus	X			X		
Steubenville	3258	Franciscan Univ. of Steubenville		X		X	X	
Westerville	3318	Otterbein Coll.		X		X	X	X
Youngstown	3368	Youngstown State Univ.	X	X	X	X	X	X
OKLAHOMA								
Midwest City	3403	Rose State Coll.		X		X		
Norman	3442	Univ. of Oklahoma			X		X	
Oklahoma City	3423	Oklahoma State Univ.	X		X			X
Stillwater	3424	Oklahoma State Univ.	X		X			X
Tulsa	5340	Langston Univ./UCT		X		X	X	
OREGON								
Eugene	3498	Univ. of Oregon	X			X		X
Klamath Falls	3484	Oregon Institute of Technology		X			X	
Portland	3491	Oregon Polytechnic Institute	X	X	X	X	X	X
PENNSYLVANIA								
Bethlehem	3645	Northampton Comm. Coll.	X			X	X	
Blue Bell	3641	Montgomery County Comm. Coll.	X	X	X	X	X	X
Harrisburg	3589	Harrisburg Area Comm. Coll.	X	X	X	X	X	X
Indiana	3704	Indiana Univ. of Pennsylvania		X				X
Johnstown	3735	Univ. of Pittsburgh–Johnstown		X	X		X	X
Kutztown	3706	Kutztown Univ. of Pennsylvania		X		X		X
Philadelphia	3608	La Salle Univ.	X	X	X	X	X	X
Philadelphia	3724	Temple Univ.		X	X		X	
Philadelphia	9237	Thomas Jefferson Univ.	X	X	X	X	X	X
Pittsburgh	3560	Duquesne Univ.	X			X		X
Pittsburgh	3734	Univ. of Pittsburgh	X	X	X	X	X	X
Radnor	3532	Cabrini Coll.	X	X	X	X	X	X
Reading	3718	Reading Area Comm. Coll.			X		X	
Wilkes-Barre	3604	King's Coll.		X	X		X	X
RHODE ISLAND								
Providence	3810	Rhode Island Coll.	X	X	X	X	X	X
SOUTH CAROLINA								
Charleston	6465	Medical Univ. of South Carolina	X	X	X		X	X
Florence	3856	Francis Marion Univ.	X	X	X	X	X	X
Orangeburg	3876	South Carolina State Coll.	X	X	X	X	X	X
Spartanburg	3889	Univ. of South Carolina–Spartanburg	X	X	X	X	X	X
TENNESSEE								
Chattanooga	4022	Univ. of Tennessee–Chattanooga		X			X	X
Clarksville	3944	Austin Peay State Univ.	X	X	X	X	X	X
Jackson	4020	Union Univ.		X	X		X	X
Johnson City	3958	East Tennessee State Univ.	X	X	X	X	X	X
Knoxville	4026	Univ. of Tennessee	X	X	X	X	X	X
Murfreesboro	3994	Middle Tennessee State Univ.	X	X	X	X	X	X
Nashville	3946	Belmont Univ.			X	X	X	X
TEXAS								
College Station	4198	Texas A&M Univ.	X	X	X	X	X	X
Dallas	9344	The Bill J. Priest Inst. for Economic Dev.	X	X	X	X	X	X
El Paso	4090	El Paso Comm. Coll.	X	X	X		X	X
Fort Worth	4222	Texas Wesleyan Univ.	X	X	X	X	X	X
Houston	4236	Univ. of Houston	X	X	X	X	X	X
Houston	4170	Univ. of Houston–Downtown	X	X	X	X	X	X
Killeen	4081	Central Texas Coll.	X	X	X	X	X	X
Midland	4127	Midland Coll.	X			X	X	
Odessa	4138	Odessa Coll.		X	X		X	X
Plano	4046	Collin Co. Comm. Coll.	X	X	X	X	X	X
Prairie View	4202	Prairie View A&M Univ.	X	X	X	X	X	X
Richardson	4243	Univ. of Texas–Dallas					X	
San Antonio	4158	St. Marys Univ.	X	X	X	X	X	X
Wharton	4252	Wharton County Jr. Coll.	X	X	X	X	X	X
UTAH								
Orem	4278	Utah Valley Comm. Coll.	X	X	X	X	X	X
Salt Lake City	4274	Univ. of Utah	X	X	X	X	X	X
VERMONT								
Johnson	4316	Johnson State Coll.		X		X	X	
VIRGINIA								
Hampton	4358	Hampton Univ.	X		X	X	X	
Norfolk	4425	Norfolk State Univ.	X	X	X	X	X	X
Petersburg	4424	Virginia State Univ.		X	X		X	X
Roanoke	4351	Virginia Western Comm. Coll.	X	X	X	X	X	X
WASHINGTON								
Bellingham	4490	Western Washington Univ.	X	X	X		X	X
Bothell	4497	Univ. of Washington Bothell		X	X		X	
Seattle	4484	Univ. of Washington	X	X	X	X	X	X
Spokane	4458	Gonzaga Univ.		X	X		X	
WEST VIRGINIA								
Beckley	4510	The Coll. of West Virginia	X	X	X	X	X	X
Parkersburg	4542	West Virginia Univ. at Parkersburg		X	X		X	
WISCONSIN								
Madison	4582	Edgewood Coll.		X	X		X	
Menomonie	4652	Univ. of Wisconsin–Stout	X	X	X		X	
Milwaukee	4558	Alverno Coll.		X	X		X	
Oshkosh	4674	Univ. of Wisconsin–Oshkosh	X	X	X	X	X	X
Stevens Point	4680	Univ. of Wisconsin–Stevens Point	X		X			X

ACT PEP Test Center Addendum

STATE, City	CODE	TEST CENTER	OCT	NOV	FEB	MAR	MAY	JUN
IOWA, Clinton	1292	Clinton Community Coll (at Best Western Frontier Motor Inn)	X	X		X		X

List of ACT PEP Participating Institutions

Note: This is **NOT** a list of PEP test centers. The test center list can be found on pages 11-12 of the PEP *Candidate Registration Guide.*

IMPORTANT INSTRUCTIONS!
Take this list with you to the test center on the test day. You will need it to complete your answer sheet.

The institutions listed below grant credit for successful completion of one or more ACT PEP examinations or use them to facilitate transfer to other institutions. If you have questions about which examinations are used, amount of credit awarded, minimum scores required, or deadlines, contact the institution directly. Because the number of institutions participating in ACT PEP continues to grow, the list may not be complete. If the institution of your choice is not listed, check directly with the appropriate department office or the registrar at that institution to determine whether it will grant the credit you seek on the basis of PEP examination results.

On the test date you will be asked to indicate on each of your answer sheets the name, address, and code number (four numbers and one letter) for one institution to which your PEP scores should be reported. To be sure that you list the correct code number. **It is crucial that you take this list with your to the test center on the test day to use in completing your answer sheet. The institution code number is essential for proper reporting of your PEP results. Note:** This is **NOT** a list of PEP test centers. The test center list can be found on pages 11-12 of the PEP *Candidate Registration Guide.*

ALABAMA
0009A Bishop State Comm. Coll. (Mobile)
4256A Comm. Coll. of the Air Force (Maxwell AFB)
0003A Faulkner Univ. (Montgomery)
0039A Jefferson Davis State Jr. Coll. (Brewton)
0047A Jefferson State Jr. Coll. (Birmingham)
0078A Lawson State Comm. Coll. (Birmingham)
0029A Mobile Coll. (Mobile)
0030A Oakwood Coll. (Huntsville)
0038A Southeastern Bible Coll. (Birmingham)
0133A Troy State Univ. in Montgomery (Montgomery)
0052A Univ. of Alabama–The New Coll. (University)
0059A Univ. of South Alabama Sch. of Nrsg. (Mobile)
0054A Walker Coll. (Jasper)

ALASKA
0137A Univ. of Alaska (Anchorage)
4828A Wayland Baptist Univ. (Anchorage)

ARIZONA
0088A Arizona State Univ. (Tempe)
0092A Grand Canyon Univ. (Phoenix)
0104A Navajo Comm. Coll. (Tsaile)
0086A Northern Arizona Univ. (Flagstaff)
9222A Ottawa Univ.–Phoenix Ctr.
0103A Rio Salado Comm. Coll. (Phoenix)
9255A Univ. of Phoenix (Mesa)
9203A Univ. of Phoenix (Phoenix)
9254A Univ. of Phoenix (Tucson)
0179A Western International Univ. (Phoenix)

ARKANSAS
0116A Arkansas State Univ. (State University)
0114A Arkansas Tech. Univ. (Russellville)
0131A Baptist System Sch. of Nrsg. (Little Rock)
0109A East Arkansas Comm. Coll. (Forrest City)
0115A Garland County Comm. Coll. (Hot Springs Nat. Pk.)
0126A Henderson State Univ. (Arkadelphia)
0161A Jefferson Sch. of Nrsg. (Pine Bluff)
0129A Mississippi County Comm. Coll. (Blytheville)
0134A Ouchita Baptist Univ. (Arkadelphia)
0142A Southern Arkansas Univ. (Magnolia)
0132A Univ. of Arkansas (Little Rock)
0110A Univ. of Arkansas at Monticello (Monticello)
0108A Univ. of Arkansas at Pine Bluff (Pine Bluff)
6869A Univ. of Arkansas Med. Sci. Campus (Little Rock)
0118A Univ. of Central Arkansas (Conway)
0122A Westark Comm. Coll. (Fort Smith)

CALIFORNIA
9271A American Coll. of Nrsg. (San Francisco)
0158A American River Coll. (Sacramento)
0166A Azusa Pacific Coll. (Azusa)
0165A Butte Coll. (Oroville)
9213A CA Dept. of Consumer Afrs., Bd. of Accountancy (Sacramento)
0173A Cabrillo Coll. (Aptos)
0175A Calif. Baptist Coll. (Riverside)
0489A Calif. Statewide Nrsg. Program (Carson)
0228A Cogswell Coll. (San Francisco)
0232A Coll. of Marin, Reg. Nrsg. Pro. (Kentfield)
0473A Columbia Pacific Univ. (San Rafael)
0256A Dominican Coll. of San Rafael (San Rafael)
9221A Empire Coll. (Santa Rosa)
0274A Glendale Comm. Coll. (Glendale)
0278A Golden Gate Univ. (San Francisco)
0288A Humphreys Coll. (Stockton)
0292A Imperial Valley Coll. (Imperial)
9245A Kensington Univ. (Glendale)
0294A La Sierra Univ. (Riverside)
0333A Merced Coll. (Merced)
0348A Merritt Coll. (Oakland)
0336A Monterey Peninsula Coll. (Monterey)
0439A National Univ. (San Diego)
0353A New Coll. of California (San Francisco)
0346A Northrop Univ. (Los Angeles)
0265A Ohlone Coll. (Fremont)
0356A Pacific Christian Coll. (Fullerton)
0360A Pacific Western Univ. (Encino)
0370A Point Loma Coll., Div. of Nrsg. (San Diego)
0380A Sacramento City Coll. (Sacramento)
0386A St. Mary's Coll. (Moraga)
0412A Samuel Merritt Coll. (Oakland)
0186A San Francisco Art Inst. (San Francisco)
0436A San Joaquin Delta Coll. (Stockton)
0410A San Jose State Univ. (San Jose)
0450A Univ. of Calif.–San Francisco, Sch. of Nrsg. (San Francisco)
0295A Univ. of La Verne (La Verne)
9253A Univ. of Phoenix (Fountain Valley)
9248A Univ. of Phoenix (San Diego)
9252A Univ. of Phoenix (San Jose)
0371A Univ. of San Diego–Philip Y. Hahn Sch. of Nrsg. (San Diego)
0470A Univ. of So. California, Dept. of Nrsg. (Los Angeles)
0481A Woodbury Univ. (Burbank)

COLORADO
0497A Arapahoe Comm. Coll. (Littleton)
9258A Columbia Coll. (Aurora)
0511A Comm. Coll. of Denver (Denver)
0539A Front Range Comm. Coll. (Ft. Collins)
0507A Front Range Comm. Coll. (Westminster)
0518A Mesa Coll. (Grand Junction)
0519A Metropolitan State Coll. (Denver)
0544A Morgan Comm. Coll. (Ft. Morgan)
0509A Pikes Peak Comm. Coll. (Colorado Springs)
0526A Regis Univ. (Denver)
6057A Univ. of CO Health Sci. Cen. (Denver)
0502A Univ. of Northern Colorado (Greeley)
9251A Univ. of Phoenix (Aurora)
0524A Univ. of Southern Colorado (Pueblo)

CONNECTICUT
0551A Asnuntuck Comm. Coll. (Enfield)
9228A Bridgeport Hosp. Sch. of Nrsg. (Bridgeport)
0627A Charter Oak Coll./Bd. St. Acd. Awds. (Farmington)
0616A Eastern Connecticut State Univ. (Willimantic)
0560A Fairfield Univ. (Fairfield)
0564A Holy Apostles Coll. (Cromwell)
0569A Manchester Comm. Coll. (Manchester)
0573A Mohegan Comm. Coll. (Norwich)
0577A Norwalk Comm. Coll. (Norwalk)
0589A Sacred Heart Univ. (Bridgeport)
9217D St. Francis Hospital Sch. of Nrsg. (Hartford)
9214A St. Mary's Hospital Sch. of Nrsg. (Waterbury)
0592A St. Vincent's Coll. of Nrsg. (Bridgeport)
0593A Southern Connecticut State Univ. (New Haven)
0602A Univ. of Bridgeport (Bridgeport)
0604A Univ. of Connecticut (Storrs)
0606A Univ. of Hartford (West Hartford)
0558A Western Connecticut State Univ. (Danbury)

DELAWARE
0635A Wilmington Coll. (New Castle)

WASHINGTON, D.C.
0654A Catholic Univ. of America
9220A District of Columbia Bd. of Accountancy
0674A Howard Univ. (Washngton, D.C.)
0695A Univ. of District of Columbia (Washington, D.C.)

FLORIDA
0718A Barry Univ. Sch. of Nrsg. (Miami Shores)
0720A Bethune Cookman Coll. (Daytona Beach)
0769A Brevard Comm. Coll. (Cocoa)
0722A Chipola Jr. Coll. (Marianna)
0723A Daytona Beach Comm. Coll. (Daytona Beach)
0727A Edison Comm. Coll. (Ft. Myers)
0725A Embry-Riddle Aeronautical Univ. (Bunnell)
0726A Florida A&M Univ. (Tallahassee)
0729A Florida Atlantic Univ. (Boca Raton)
0717A Florida Comm. Coll. (Jacksonville)
0776A Florida Int'l. Univ. (Miami)
9233A Florida Int'l. Univ.–Sch. of Nrsg. (No. Miami Beach)
0747A Florida Keys Comm. Coll. (Key West)
0734A Florida State Univ. (Tallahassee)
0738A Gulf Coast Comm. Coll. (Panama City)
6394A Hillsborough Comm. Coll. (Tampa)
0774A Indian River Comm. Coll. (Fort Pierce)
0766A Lake City Comm. Coll. (Lake City)
0737A Lake-Sumter Comm. Coll. (Leesburg)
9216D Martin Memorial Hospital (Stuart)
0770A Miami-Dade Comm. Coll. (Miami)
0714A Nova Univ. (Fort Lauderdale)
0744A Palm Beach Jr. Coll. (Lake Worth)
0757A Polk Comm. Coll. (Winter Haven)
0755A Saint Leo Coll. (Saint Leo)
0778A Santa Fe Comm. Coll. (Gainesville)
0779A Seminole Comm. Coll. (Sanford)
0711A Univ. of North Florida (Jacksonville)
5472A Univ. of Sarasota (Sarasota)
5828A Univ. of South Florida (Ft. Myers)
0761A Univ. of South Florida (Tampa)
0762A Univ. of Tampa (Tampa)
0771A Univ. of West Florida (Pensacola)

GEORGIA
0786A Armstrong State Coll. (Savannah)
1110A Atlanta Bible Coll. (Morrow)
0796A Augusta Coll. (Augusta)
0800A Brenau Coll. (Gainesville)
0810A Emory Univ.–Nell Hodgson Woodruff Sch. of Nrsg. (Atlanta)
9217A Floyd Jr. Coll. (Rome)
0819A Georgia Baptist Coll. of Nrsg. (Atlanta)
0836A Medical Coll. of Georgia Sch. of Nrsg. (Augusta)
0848A North Georgia Coll. (Dahlonega)

HAWAII
0903A Hawaii Loa Coll. (Kaneohe)
0900A Hawaii Pacific Univ. (Honolulu)
0904A Univ. of Hawaii–Hilo (Hilo)

IDAHO
0914A Boise State Univ. (Boise)
0924A Northwest Nazarene Coll. (Nampa)

ILLINOIS
0941A Aero-Space Inst. (Chicago)
0950A Aurora Univ. (Aurora)
0952A Barat Coll. (Lake Forest)
0954A Belleville Area Coll. (Belleville)
0956A Blessing Rieman Coll. of Nrsg. (Quincy)
4965A Board of Governors Bach. of Arts Deg. Prog. (Springfield)
1170A Carl Sandburg Coll. (Galesburg)
0992A Chicago State Univ.–BOG (Chicago)
City Colleges of Chicago:
0934A City Wide Coll.
9267A European Office (APO New York)
0978A Kennedy-King Coll.
0975A Harold Washington Coll. (Loop)
0972A Malcolm X Coll.
0974A Olive-Harvey Coll.
0971A Richard J. Daley Coll.
0970A Truman Coll.
0980A Wright Coll.
1004A Concordia Univ. (River Forest)
5032A Concordia Coll.–WSCN (Oak Park)
1012A De Paul Univ. (Chicago)
1016A Eastern Illinois Univ.–BOG (Charleston)
1020A Elmhurst Coll. (Elmhurst)
1028A Governors State Univ.–BOG (Univ. Park)
1029A Highland Comm. Coll. (Freeport)
0995A IECC-Frontier Comm. Coll. (Fairfield)
1067A IECC-Lincoln Trail Coll. (Robinson)
1113A IECC-Olney Central Coll. (Olney)
1162A IECC-Wabash Valley Coll. (Mt. Carmel)
1132A Illinois Benedictine Coll. (Lisle)
1035A Illinois Central Coll. (East Peoria)
1044A Illinois Wesleyan Univ. Sch. of Nrsg. (Bloomington)
1017A John A. Logan Coll.–Carterville (Carterville)
1019A John Wood Comm. Coll. (Quincy)
1048A Joliet Jr. Coll. (Joliet)
0964A Kaskaskia Coll. (Centralia)
1050A Kendall Coll. (Evanston)
1051A Kishwaukee Coll. (Malta)
1057A Lakeview Med. Ctr. Sch. of Nrsg. (Danville)
1058A Lewis Univ. (Romeoville)
1038A Lewis and Clark Comm. Coll. (Godfrey)
1068A MacMurry Coll. (Jacksonville)
1076A McKendree Coll. (Lebanon)

1081A Mennonite Coll. of Nrsg. (Bloomington)
1087A Moraine Valley Comm. Coll. (Palos Hills)
1090A Morton Coll. (Cicero)
1094A National–Louis Univ. (Lombard)
0993A Northeastern Illinois Univ.–BOG (Chicago)
1102A Northern Ilinos Univ. (De Kalb)
1098A North Park Coll. (Chicago)
1112A Olivet Nazarene Coll. (Kankakee)
1120A Quincy Coll. (Quincy)
1091A Rend Lake Coll. (Ina)
1121A Robert Morris Coll. (Carthage)
1122A Rockford Coll. (Rockford)
1124A Roosevelt Univ. (Chicago)
1117A Rush Univ. (Chicago)
6432A St. Anthony Coll. of Nrsg. (Rockford)
1138A St. Francis Medical Center (Peoria)
1135A St. Joseph Coll. of Nrsg. (Joliet)
1134A Saint Xavier Coll. (Chicago)
1127A Sauk Valley Coll. (Dixon)
1173A Shawnee Coll. (Ullin)
1148A South Suburban Coll. (S. Holland)
1161A Southeastern Illinois Coll. (Harrisburg)
1165A Trinity Christian Coll. (Palos Heights)
1159A Waubonsee Comm. Coll. (Sugar Grove)
1158A Western Illinois Univ.–BOG (Macomb)

INDIANA

1176A Ball State Univ. (Muncie)
1178A Bethel Coll. (Mishawaka)
1180A Butler Univ. (Indianapolis)
1203A Holy Cross Jr. Coll. (Notre Dame)
1204A [illegible]v. of Indianapolis (Indianapolis)
1216A [illegible]ana Univ. East (Richmond)
1218A [illegible]ana Univ. Northwest (Gary)
1225A [illegible]diana Univ.–South Bend (South Bend)
1235A Indiana Voc. Tech. Coll. (Madison)
1257A Ivy Tech. Coll. (Bloomington)
9247A Lutheran Coll. of Health Professions (Fort Wayne)
1233A Purdue Univ.–Calumet (Hammond)
1238A St. Francis Coll. of Fort Wayne (Fort Wayne)
1188A Univ. of Evansville (Evansville)
1258A Vincennes Univ. (Vincennes)

IOWA

1273A Allen Memorial Hosp. Sch. of Nrsg. (Waterloo)
1276A Briar Cliff Coll. (Sioux City)
1290A Clarke Coll. (Dubuque)
1294A Coe Coll. (Cedar Rapids)
1302A Drake Univ. (Des Moines)
1314A Graceland Coll. (Lamoni)
1316A Grand View Coll. (Des Moines)
1312A Iowa Central Comm. Coll. (Ft. Dodge)
1310A Iowa Lakes Comm. Coll. (Estherville)
1334A Marycrest Coll. (Davenport)
1340A Mt. Mercy Coll. (Cedar Rapids)
1280A Southeastern Comm. Coll. (West Burlington)
6260A Spencer Sch. of Business (Spencer)
1377A St. Luke's Sch. of Nrsg. (Sioux City)
1370A Teikyo Westmar Univ. (LeMars)
1356A Univ. of Iowa Coll. of Nrsg. (Iowa City)
1358A Univ. of Dubuque (Dubuque)
1360A Upper Iowa Univ. (Fayette)

KANSAS

1467A Baker Univ.–Stormont/Vail Campus (Topeka)
1399A Colby Comm. Coll. (Colby)
1408A Fort Hays State Univ. (Hays)
1412A Friends Univ. (Wichita)
1418A Highland Comm. Jr. Coll. (Highland)
1420A Hutchinson Comm. Coll. (Hutchinson)
1425A Johnson County Comm. Coll. (Overland Park)
1428A Kansas State Univ. (Manhattan)
1434A Kansas Wesleyan Univ. (Salina)
1440A McPherson Coll. (McPherson)
1445A Mid-America Nazarene Coll. (Olathe)
1446A Ottawa Univ. (Overland Park)
1464A Southwestern Coll. (Winfield)
1472A Wichita State Univ. (Wichita)

KENTUCKY

1486A Asbury Coll. (Wilmore)
1564A Ashland Comm. Coll. (Ashland)
1490A Bellarmine Coll. (Louisville)
1512A Eastern Kentucky Univ. (Richmond)
1513A Elizabethtown Comm. Coll. (Elizabethtown)
1572A Hazard Comm. Coll. (Hazard)
1557A Henderson Comm. Coll. (Henderson)
1569A Hopkinsville Comm. Coll. (Hopkinsville)
1571A Jefferson Comm. Coll. (Louisville)
1518A Kentucky Wesleyan Coll. (Owensboro)
1531A Lexington Comm. Coll. (Lexington)
1533A Madisonville Comm. Coll. (Madisonville)
1527A Maysville Comm. Coll. (Maysville)
1530A Morehead State Univ. (Morehead)
1538A Paducah Comm. Coll. (Paducah)
1541A Prestonsburg Comm. Coll. (Prestonsburg)
1570A Somerset Comm. Coll. (Somerset)
1555A Southeast Comm. Coll. (Cumberland)
1534A Spaulding Coll. (Louisville)
5535A Sullivan Jr. Coll. (Louisville)
1560A Thomas More Coll. (Crestview Hills)
1554A Univ. of Kentucky, Coll. of Nrsg. (Lexington)
1568A Univ. of Kentucky–Elizabethtown Campus (Elizabethtown)

LOUISIANA

1578A Dillard Univ. (New Orleans)
1582A Grambling State Univ. (Grambling)
1658A La Salle Univ. (Slidell)
1592A Loyola Univ.–City Coll. (New Orleans)
1594A McNeese State Univ. (Lake Charles)
1580A Nicholls State Univ. (Thibodaux)
1574A Our Lady of Holy Cross Coll. (New Orleans)
1621A Our Lady of the Lake Coll. of Nrsg. & Allied Health (Baton Rouge)
1608A Southeastern Louisiana Univ. (Hammond)
1611A Southern Univ. of New Orleans (New Orleans)
1613A Southern Univ.–Shreveport (Shreveport)

MAINE

1639A Central Maine Medical Center Sch. of Nrsg. (Lewiston)
9218A Kennebec Valley Tech. Coll. (Fairfield)
1659A Saint Joseph's Coll. (No. Windham)
9342A S. Maine Voc. Tech. Inst. (So. Portland)
1642A Univ. of Maine at Fort Kent (Fort Kent)

MARYLAND

1679A Allegany Comm. Coll. (Cumberland)
1693A Antietam Bible Coll. (Hagerstown)
1712A Bowie State Coll. (Bowie)
1681A Cecil Comm. Coll. (North East)
1727A Coll. of Notre Dame (Baltimore)
1688A Coppin State Coll. (Baltimore)
1700A Harford Comm. Coll. (Bel Air)
1704A Johns Hopkins Univ. Sch. of Nrsg. (Baltimore)
1722A Morgan State Univ. (Baltimore)
1716A Salisbury State Coll. (Salisbury)
1718A Towson State Univ. (Towson)
9264A Traditional Acupuncture Inst. (Columbia)
1749A Union Memorial Hosp. Sch. of Nrsg. (Baltimore)
1746A Univ. of Maryland (College Park)
1758A Univ. of Maryland–Sch. of Nrsg. (Baltimore)
9202J Univ. of Maryland–Asian Div. (APO San Francisco)
9201J Univ. of Maryland–European Div. (APO New York)
1753A Villa Julie Coll. (Stevenson)

MASSACHUSETTS

1772A American International Coll. (Springfield)
1784A Atlantic Union Coll. (South Lancaster)
1849A Becker Coll. (Worcester)
1788A Boston Coll. Sch. of Nrsg. (Chestnut Hill)
1803A Bristol Comm. Coll. (Fall River)
1799A Bunker Hill Comm. Coll. (Charlestown)
1807A Cape Code Comm. Coll. (W. Barnstable)
1814A Curry Coll. (Milton)
1822A Emmanuel Coll. (Boston)
9221D Framingham Union Hosp. Sch. of Nrsg. (Framingham)
1839A Greenfield Comm. Coll. (Greenfield)
1844A Holyoke Comm. Coll. (Holyoke)
1848A Lasell Jr. Coll. (Newton)
9240A Lawrence Memorial Hosp. Sch. of Nrsg. (Medford)
1861A Massachusetts Bay Comm. Coll. (Wellesley Hills)
1862A Massasoit Comm. Coll. (Brockton)
1865A Middlesex Comm. Coll. (Bedford)
9214D New England Baptist Hosp. Sch. of Nrsg. (Boston)
9256A New England Deaconess Hosp. Sch. of Nrsg. (Boston)
1878A Nichols Coll. (Dudley)
1875A North Shore Comm. Coll. (Lynn)
1880A Northeastern Univ. (Boston)
1877A Northern Essex Comm. Coll. (Haverhill)
1888A Quincy Jr. Coll. (Quincy)
1885A Quinsigamond Comm Coll. (Worcester)
1886A Regis Coll. (Weston)
9206D St. Elizabeth Hosp. Sch. of Nrsg. (Brighton)
1910A Salem State Coll. (Salem)
1892A Simmons Coll. (Boston)
1918A Stonehill Coll. (North Easton)
1925A Univ. of Massachusetts, Boston (Boston)
1906A Univ. of Massachusetts, Dartmough (N. Dartmouth)

MICHIGAN

1954A Adrian Coll. (Adrian)
1992A Andrews Univ. (Berrien Springs)
1972A Central Michigan Univ. (Mt. Pleasant)
1977A Concordia Coll. (Ann Arbor)
1990A Eastern Michigan Univ. (Ypsilanti)
2004A Grand Rapids Comm. Coll. (Grand Rapids)
2005A Grand Valley State Colleges (Allendale)
2013A Hurley Medical Center Sch. of Nrsg. (Flint)
2014A Jackson Comm. Coll. (Jackson)
2011A Jordon Coll. (Cedar Springs)
1964A Kellogg Comm. Coll. (Battle Creek)
2020A Lawrence Inst. of Technology (Southfield)
2022A Madonna Coll. (Livonia)
2030A Michigan Technological Univ. (Houghton)
2045A Northeastern Sch. of Commerce (Bay City)
2041A Northwood Inst. (Midland)
2033A Oakland Univ. (Rochester)
2057A Saginaw Valley State Coll. (University Center)
2055A Southwestern Michigan Coll. (Dowagiac)
2060A Univ. of Detroit–Mercy (Detroit)
9231A Univ. of Michigan Dept. of Geol. Sci. (Ann Arbor)

MINNESOTA

2090A Brainerd Comm. Coll. (Brainerd)
2088A Bethel Coll. (St. Paul)
2094A Coll. of St. Benedict (St. Joseph)
2149A Coll. of St. Catherine–St. Mary's Campus (Minneapolis)
2098A Coll. of St. Scholastica (Duluth)
2116A Hibbing Comm. Coll.–Arrowhead (Hibbing)
2103A Inver Hills Comm. Coll. (Inver Grove Heights)
2125A Lakewood Comm. Coll. (White Bear Lake)
2126A Mankato State Univ. (Mankato)
9260A Metropolitan State Univ. (St. Paul)
2148A St. Mary's Coll. (Winona)
2102A Univ. of St. Thomas (St. Paul)

MISSISSIPPI

2190A Delta State Univ. (Cleveland)
2202A Itawamba Jr. Coll. (Fulton)
2212A Millsaps Coll. (Jackson)
2251A Univ. of Mississippi Med. Ctr. Sch. of Nrsg. (Jackson)
2253A Wesley Coll. (Florence)

MISSOURI

2287A Berean Coll. of the Assemblies of God (Springfield)
2276A Columbia Coll. (Columbia)
2280A Conception Seminary Coll. (Conception)
2293A Deaconess Coll. of Nrsg. (St. Louis)
1314A Graceland Coll. (Independence)
2320A Hannibal–LaGrange Coll. (Hannibal)
2313A Jefferson Coll. (Hillsboro)
2305A Jewish Hosp. Sch. of Nrsg. (St. Louis)
2316A Kemper Military Sch. and Coll. (Bonneville)
2330A Missouri Valley Coll. (Marshall)
2340A Park Coll. (Parkville)
2347A Research Coll. of Nrsg. (Kansas City)
2281A St. Charles County Comm. Coll. (O'Fallon)
2297A St. Louis Comm. Coll. at Florissant Valley (St. Louis)
2352A St. Louis Univ. Sch. of Nrsg. (St. Louis)
2357A St. Luke's Coll. (Kansas City)
2368A Southwest Baptist Univ. (Bolivar)
2380A Univ. of Missouri–Kansas City (Kansas City)
2383A Univ. of Missouri–St. Louis (St. Louis)
2388A Webster Univ. (Kansas City)
2388A Webster Univ. (St. Louis)
2394A William Jewell Coll. (Liberty)

MONTANA

2417A Flathead Valley Comm. Coll. (Kalispell)
2418A Montana Coll. of Mineral Sci. & Tech. (Butte)
2426A Rocky Mountain Coll. (Billings)
2428A Western Montana Coll. (Dillon)

NEBRASKA

2437A Bellevue Coll. (Bellevue)
2436A Bishop Clarkson Coll. (Omaha)
2440A Coll. of St. Mary (Omaha)
2444A Creighton Univ. Sch. of Nrsg. (Omaha)
2454A Grace Coll. of the Bible (Omaha)
2468A Kearney State Coll. (Kearney)
2460A McCook Comm. Coll. (McCook)
9227A Methodist Sch. of Nrsg. (Omaha)
2491A Mid Plains Comm. Coll. (North Platte)
2462A Midland Lutheran Coll. (Fremont)
5572A Nebraska Coll. of Business (Omaha)
2474A Nebraska Wesleyan Univ. (Lincoln)

NEVADA

2498A Comm. Coll. of Southern Nevada (N. Las Vegas)
2500A Morrison Coll.–Reno (Reno)
2496A Univ. of Nevada–Las Vegas (LasVegas)
2494A Univ. of Nevada (Reno)

NEW HAMPSHIRE

2506A Colby-Sawyer Coll. (New London)
2503A Hesser Coll. (Manchester)
2510A Keene State Coll. (Keene)
2514A New Hampshire Coll. (Manchester)
2517A New Hampshire Tech. Coll. (Berlin)
2507A New Hampshire Tech. Coll. (Manchester)
2530A New Hampshire Tech. Coll.–Stratham (Stratham)
2520A Rivier Coll.–St. Joseph Hosp. Sch. of Nrsg. (Nashua)
2522A St. Anselm Coll. (Manchester)
2524A Univ. of New Hampshire (Durham)
2519A Univ. of New Hampshire (Manchester)

NEW JERSEY

2541A Bergen Comm.Coll. (Paramus)
2540A Bloomfield Coll. (Bloomfield)
2553A Brookdale Comm. Coll. (Lincroft)
2543A Burlington County Coll. (Pemberton)
2544A Centenary Coll. (Hackettsotwn)
2546A Coll. of Saint Elizabeth (Morristown)
9236A Cumberland County Coll. (Vineland)
9223A Elizabeth Gen. Med. Ctr. Sch. of Nrsg. (Elizabeth)
9216A Englewood Hosp. Sch. of Nrsg. (Englewood)
2552A Fairleigh Dickinson Univ. (Rutherford)
2559A Felician Coll. (Lodi)
2562A Georgian Court Coll. (Lakewood)
2575A Helene Fuld Sch. of Nrsg. in Camden Co. (Camden)
9270A Helene Fuld Sch. of Nrsg. (Trenton)
2570A Jersey City State Coll. (Jersey City)
2582A Kean Coll. of New Jersey (Union)
2568A Mercer County Comm. Coll. (Trenton)
2571A Monmouth Coll. (West Long Branch)
9249A Mountainside Hosp. Sch. of Nrsg. (Montclair)
2585A Ocean County Coll. (Toms River)
2586A Our Lady of Lourdes Sch. of Nrsg. (Camden)
2583A Passaic County Comm. Coll. (Paterson)
2591A Ramapo Coll. of New Jersey (Mahwah)
2609A Raritan Valley Comm. Coll. (Somerville)
2598A Rutgers, The State Univ. of NJ (Camden)
9265A St. Francis Med. Ctr. (Trenton)
9242A St. Peter's Coll. (Englewood Cliffs)
2604A St. Peter's Coll. (Jersey City)
2606A Seton Hall Univ. (South Orange)
2589A Stockton State Coll. (Pomona)
2612A Thomas Edison Coll. of New Jersey (Trenton)
9223D Winifred B. Baldwin Sch. of Nrsg. (Orange)

NEW MEXICO

2631A Eastern New Mexico Univ. (Clovis)
9241A Navajo Comm. Coll. (Shiprock)
2650A Univ. of New Mexico Coll. of Nrsg. (Albuquerque)
2646A Western New Mexico Univ. (Silver City)

NEW YORK
2662A Academy of Aeronautics (Flushing)
2664A Adelphi Univ. (Garden City)
2667A Adirondack Comm. Coll. (Glens Falls)
2661A Albany Business Coll. (Albany)
2666A Alfred Univ. (Alfred)
2669A American Acad. McAllister Inst. (New York City)
2674A Bard Coll. (Annandale on Hudson)
2686A Berkeley Claremont Sch., Hicksville (Hicksville)
2688A Berkeley Claremont Sch., New York City (New York City)
2950J Bernard M. Baruch Coll. (New York City)
9208A Borough of Manhattan Comm. Coll. (New York City)
2950J Bronx Comm. Coll. (Bronx)
2950J Brooklyn Coll. (Brooklyn)
2684A Broome Comm. Coll. (Binghamton)
2676A Bryant and Stratton Bus. Inst., Buffalo (Buffalo)
2690A Canisius Coll. (Buffalo)
2668A Cayahuga County Comm. Coll. (Auburn)
2696A Cazenovia Coll. (Cazenovia)
4801A Central City Bus. Inst. (Syracuse)
2950J City Coll. (New York City)
2694A Clinton Comm. Coll. (Plattsburgh)
2072A Colgate Univ. (Hamilton)
4976A Coll. of Insurance, The (New York City)
2823A Coll. of Mt. St. Vincent (Riverdale)
2712A Coll. of New Rochelle (New Rochelle)
2714A Coll. of St. Rose (Albany)
2715A Columbia Greene Comm. Coll. (Hudson)
2704A Comm. Coll. of the Finger Lakes (Canandaigua)
2722A Concordia Coll. (Bronxville)
2724A Cooper Union for the Advanc. of Sci. and Art (New York City)
2727A Corning Comm. Coll. (Corning)
2874A Daemen Coll. (Amherst)
2730A Dominican Coll. of Blauvelt (Blauvelt)
2665A Dowling Coll. (Oakdale)
2732A D'Youville Coll. (Buffalo)
2729A Edna McConnell Clark Sch. of Nrsg. (New York City)
2736A Elmira Coll. (Elmira)
2737A Empire State Coll. (Saratoga Springs)
2742A Erie Comm. Coll. (Buffalo)
2747A Friends World Coll. (Lloyd Harbor)
2749A Fulton-Montgomery Comm. Coll. (Johnstown)
2751A Genesse Comm. Coll. (Batavia)
2756A Hartwick Coll. (Oneonta)
9209A Herbet H. Lehman Coll. (Bronx)
2765A Herkimer County Comm. Coll. (Herkimer)
2759A Hilbert Coll. (Hamburg)
2758A Hobart and William Smith Coll. (Geneva)
2760A Hofstra Univ. (Hempstead)
2766A Houghton Coll. (Houghton)
2950J Hunter Coll. (New York City)
2772A Ithaca Coll. (Ithaca)
2774A Jamestown Comm. Coll. (Jamestown)
2775A Jefferson Comm. Coll. (Watertown)
9210A John Jay Coll. of Crim. Just.-CUNY (New York City)
2778A Juilliard Sch. (New York City)
2787A Katharine Gibbs Sch., Melville (Melville)
2700A Katharine Gibbs Sch., New York City (New York City)
2782A Keuka Coll. (Keuka Park)
2784A Kings Coll. (Briarcliff Manor)
9211A Kingsborough Comm. Coll. (Brooklyn)
2950J Laguardia Comm. Coll. (Long Island City)
2790A LeMoyne Coll. (Syracuse)
2792A Long Island Univ. Brooklyn Ctr. (Long Island)
2687A Long Island Univ. C. W. Post Ctr. (Greenvale)
2907A Long Island Univ., Southampton Coll. (Southampton)
2796A Manhattan Coll. (Riverdale)
2809A Manhattan Sch. of Music (New York City)
2800A Manhattanville Coll. (Purchase)
2803A Maria Coll. of Albany (Albany)
2804A Marist Coll. (Poughkeepsie)
2810A Marymount Coll. (Tarrytown)
2811A Marymount Manhattan Coll. (New York City)
2799A Mater Dei Coll. (Ogdensburg)
2822A Medaille Coll. (Buffalo)
2814A Mercy Coll. (Dobbs Ferry)
2818A Mohawk Valley Comm. Coll. (Utica)
2820A Molloy Coll. (Rockville Centre)
2821A Monroe Comm. Coll. (Rochester)
2819A Mount St. Mary Coll. (Newburgh)
2825A Nassau Comm. Coll. (Garden City)
2826A Nazareth Coll. (Rochester)
2828A New Sch. for Soc. Res. (New York City)
2950J New York City Tech. Coll. (New York City)
2832A New York Inst. of Tech. (Old Westbury)
2829A New York Sch. of Int. Design (New York City)
2838A New York Univ. (New York City)
2843A Niagra County Comm. Coll. (Sanborn)
2842A Niagra Univ. (Niagra University)
2864A North Country Comm. Coll. (Saranac Lake)
2846A Nyack Coll. (Nyack)
2847A Onondaga Comm. Coll. (Syracuse)
2848A Orange County Comm. Coll. (Middletown)
2852A Pace Univ. (Pleasantville)
2862A Pratt Inst. (Brooklyn)
2950J Queens Coll. (Flushing)
2950J Queensborough Comm. Coll. (Bayside)
2868A Roberts Wesleyan Coll. (Rochester)
2870A Rochester Inst. of Tech. (Rochester)
2873A Rockland Comm. Coll. (Suffern)
2882A St. Bonaventure Univ. (St. Bonaventure)
2886A St. John Fisher Coll. (Rochester)
2888A St. John's Univ. (Jamaica)
2890A St. Joseph's Coll. (Brooklyn)
2896A St. Lawrence Univ. (Canton)
2897A St. Thomas Aquinas Coll. (Sparkill)
2892A Schenectady County Comm. Coll. (Schenectady)
2895A Sch. of Vis. Arts (New York City)
2878A Siena Coll. (Loudonville)
2906A Skidmore Coll. (Saratoga Springs)
2910A SUNY-Ag. and Tech. Coll. at Alfred (Alfred)
2912A SUNY-Ag. and Tech. Coll. at Canton (Canton)
2914A SUNY-Ag. and Tech. Coll. at Cobleskill (Cobleskill)
2916A SUNY-Coll. of Technology at Delhi (Delhi)
2918A SUNY-Ag. and Tech. Coll. at Farmingdale (Farmingdale)
2920A SUNY-Ag. and Tech. Coll. at Morrisville (Morrisville)
2978A SUNY at Buffalo (Buffalo)
2952A SUNY at Stony Brook (Stony Brook)
2981A SUNY Upstate Med. Str. (Syracuse)
2930A SUNY-Coll. at Buffalo (Buffalo)
2932A SUNY-Coll. at Cortland (Cortland)
2934A SUNY-Coll. at Fredonia (Fredonia)
2938A SUNY-Coll. at New Paltz (New Paltz)
2940A SUNY-Coll. at Oneonta (Oneonta)
2942A SUNY-Coll. at Oswego (Oswego)
2944A SUNY-Coll. at Plattsburgh (Plattsburgh)
2946A SUNY-Coll. at Potsdam (Potsdam)
2931A SUNY-Coll. at Purchase (Purchase)
2936A SUNY-Coll. of Arts and Sci. at Geneseo (Geneseo)
2948A SUNY-Coll. of Envir. Sci. and Forest. at Syracuse (Syracuse)
2953A SUNY-Coll. of Tech. at Utica-Rome (Utica)
2954A SUNY-Maritime Coll. at Fort Schuyler (Bronx)
2965A Suffolk County Comm. Coll. (Selden)
2967A Sullivan County Comm. Coll. (Loch Sheldrake)
2968A Syracuse Univ. (Syracuse)
2963A Tompkins Cortland Comm. Coll. (Dryden)
2961A Touro Coll. (New York City)
2964A Trocaire Coll. (Buffalo)
2971A Ulster County Comm. Coll. (Stone Ridge)
2980A Univ. of Rochester, Sch. of Nrsg. (Rochester)
2834A Univ. of State of New York/ Regents College Degrees (Albany)
2973A Utica Coll. of Syracuse Univ. (Utica)
6361A Utica Sch. of Commerce, The (Utica)
2984A Wagner Coll. (Staten Island)
2988A Wells Coll. (Aurora)
4972A Westchester Bus. Inst., The (White Plains)
2990A Westchester Comm. Coll. (Valhalla)
2992A Yeshiva Univ. (New York City)

NORTH CAROLINA
3070A Belmont Abbey (Belmont)
3076A Campbell Coll. (Buies Creek)
3096A Elon Coll. (Elon College)
3102A Gardner-Webb Coll. (Statesville)
3031A Montreat-Anderson Coll. (Montreat)
3060A North Carolina A & T St. Univ. (Greensboro)
3135A North Carolina Wesleyan Coll. (Rocky Mount)
3064A Univ. of North Carolina (Asheville)

NORTH DAKOTA
3210A Dickinson State Coll. (Dickinson)
3200A Jamestown Coll. (Jamestown)
3214A Minot State Coll. (Minot)
3206A North Dakota State Sch. of Science (Wahpeton)
3202A North Dakota State Univ. (Fargo)
3201A Univ. of Mary (Bismarck)
3196A UND Graduate Center–Bismarck State Coll. (Bismarck)

OHIO
3238A Bluffton Coll. (Bluffton)
3245A Cedarville Coll. (Cedarville)
9257A Christian Union Sch. of the Bible (Greenfield)
3247A Clark Tech. Coll. (Springfield)
3268A Dyke Coll. (Cleveland)
3377A Edison St. Comm. Coll. (Piqua)
3271A Fairview General Hosp. Sch. of Nrsg. (Cleveland)
3258A Franciscan Univ. of Steubenville (Steubenville)
3275A Franklin Univ. (Columbus)
3278A Heidelberg Coll. (Tiffin)
3279A Kettering Coll. of Medical Arts (Kettering)
3287A Lorain County Comm. Coll. (Elyria)
3598A Lourdes Coll. (Sylvania)
3351A Marion Tech. Coll. (Marion)
3296A Miami-Jacobs Jr. Coll. (Dayton)
3294A Miami Univ. (Hamilton)
3299A Miami Univ.–Middletown (Middletown)
3305A Muskingum Area Tech. Coll. (Zanesville)
3300A Muskigum Coll. (New Concord)
3312A Ohio State Univ. Coll. of Nrsg. (Columbus)
3314A Ohio Univ. (Athens)
3322A Ohio Univ. (Zanesville)
3318A Otterbein Coll. (Westerville)
3308A Raymond Walters Coll. of the Univ. of Cincinnati (Cincinnati)
3324A Rio Grande Coll. & Comm. Coll. (Rio Grande)
3336A Shawnee State Univ. (Portsmouth)
3276A Southern State Comm. Coll. (Hillsboro)
3349A Walsh Coll. (Canton)
3295A Wright State Univ. (Dayton)
3320A Xavier Coll. (Cincinnati)
3368A Youngstown State Univ. (Youngstown)

OKLAHOMA
3380A Bacone Coll. (Muskogee)
3386A Cameron Univ. (Lawton)
3430A Carl Albert Jr. Coll. (Poteau)
3390A Central State Univ. (Edmond)
3400A Langston Univ. (Langston)
3408A Northeastern Oklahoma State Univ. (Tahlequah)
3410A Northern Oklahoma Coll. (Tonkawa)
3406A Northeastern Oklahoma A & M (Miami)
3414A Oklahoma Baptist Univ. (Shawnee)
3435A OCU/St. Anthony Sch. of Nrsg. (Oklahoma City)
3416A Oklahoma City Univ. CBDP (Oklahoma City)
3423A Oklahoma State Univ.–Oklahoma City (Oklahoma City)
3424A Oklahoma State Univ. (Stillwater)
3398A Redlands Comm. Coll. (El Reno)
3420A Rogers State Coll. (Claremore)
3403A Rose State Coll. (Midwest City)
3436A Deminole Jr. Coll. (Seminole)
3441A Tulsa Jr. Coll. (Tulsa)
3442A Univ. of Oklahoma, The (Norman)
3418A Univ. of Science & Arts of Oklahoma (Chickasha)
3378A Western Oklahoma State Coll. (Altus)

OREGON
3461A Clatsop Comm. Coll. (Astoria)
3468A Marylhurst Coll. (Marylhurst)
3484A Oregon Inst. of Tech. (Klamath Falls)
3500A Univ. of Portland (Portland)

PENNSYLVANIA
9219D Abington Memorial Hosp. Sch. of Nrsg. (Abington)
3521A Alvernia Coll. (Reading)
3524A Beaver Coll. (Glenside)
3532A Cabrini Coll. (Radnor)
3694A Calif. Univ. of Pennsylvania (California)
9220D Chester County Hosp. Sch. of Nrsg. (West Chester)
3698A Clarion Univ. (Clarion)
3543A Comm. Coll. of Philadelphia (Philadelphia)
9250A Comm. Med. Ctr. Sch. of Nrsg. (Scranton)
3560A Duquesne Univ. Sch. of Nrsg. (Pittsburgh)
3562A Eastern Coll. (St. David's)
3702A Edinboro Univ. of Pennsylvania (Edinboro)
9208D Frankford Hosp. Sch. of Nrsg. (Philadelphia)
9266A Geisinger Med. Ctr. (Danville)
3578A Geneva Coll. (Beaver Falls)
3583A Gwynedd Mercy Coll. (Gwynedd)
3586A Hahnemann Medical Coll. & Hosp. (Philadelphia)
3589A Harrisburg Area Comm. Coll (Harrisburg)
3596A Immaculata Coll. (Immaculata)
3704A Indiana Univ. of Pennsylvania (Indiana)
3604A Kings Coll. (Wilkes-Barre)
3706A Kutztown Univ. (Kutztown)
3605A Lackawana Jr. Coll. (Scranton)
9207D Lancaster Gen. Hosp. Sch. of Nrsg. (Lancaster)
3607A LaRoche Coll. (Pittsburgh)
3608A LaSalle Coll. (Philadelphia)
3611A Lehigh County Comm. Coll. (Schnecksville)
9324A Memorial Hosp. Sch. of Nrsg.–Roxborough (Philadelphia)
3630A Messiah Coll. (Grantham)
3712A Millersville Univ. (Millersville)
3641A Montgomery County Comm. Coll. (Blue Bell)
3635A Mount Aloysius Coll. (Cresson)
3645A Northampton Comm. Coll. (Bethlehem)
3659A Peirce Jr. Coll. (Philadelphia)
3658A Philadelphia Coll. of the Bible (Langhorne)
3530A Point Park Coll. (Pittsburgh)
3718A Reading Area Comm. Coll. (Reading)
3674A Robert Morris Coll.–Moon Campus (Coraopolis)
3675A Robert Morris Coll. (Pittsburgh)
3682A St. Francis Coll. (Loretto)
3684A St. Joseph's Univ.–Univ. Coll. (Philadelphia)
9218D Sharon Regional Health System Sch. of Nrsg. (Sharon)
3716A Slippery Rock State Coll. (Slippery Rock)
9237A Thomas Jefferson Univ. (Philadelphia)
3724A Temple Univ. (Philadelphia)
3735A Univ. of Pittsburgh at Johnstown (Johnstown)
3734A Univ. of Pittsburgh Sch. of Nrsg. (Pittsburgh)
3736A Univ. of Scranton (Scranton)
3740A Valley Forge Military Jr. Coll. (Wayne)
3742A Villa Maria Coll. (Erie)
3744A Villanova Univ. (Coll. of Nrsg.) (Villanova)
3752A Westminster Coll. (New Wilmington)
3762A York Coll. of Pennsylvania (York)

RHODE ISLAND
3811A Comm. Coll. of Rhode Island (Warwick)
3804A Johnson and Wales Univ. (Providence)
3810A Rhode Island Coll. (Providence)
3818A Univ. of Rhode Island Coll. of Nrsg. (Kingston)

SOUTH CAROLINA
3832A Anderson Coll. (Anderson)
3848A Columbia Bible Coll. (Columbia)
3856A Francis Marion Univ. (Florence)
3860A Lander Coll. (Greenwood)
3862A Limestone Coll. (Gaffney)
6465A Medical Univ. of South Carolina (Charleston)
3829A Piedmont Tech. Coll. (Greenwood)
3876A South Carolina St. Coll. (Orangeburg)
3889A Univ. of South Carolina–Spartanburg (Spartanburg)

SOUTH DAKOTA
3902A Augustana Coll. (Sioux Falls)
3906A Dakota Wesleyan Univ. (Mitchell)
3912A Huron Coll. Regional Med. Ctr. Sch. of Nrsg. (Huron)
3914A Mount Marty Coll. (Yankton)
3924A South Dakota State Univ. (Brookings)

TENNESSEE
3944A Austin Peay State Univ. (Clarksville)
3946A Belmont Coll. (Nashville)
4009A Bristol Coll. (Bristol)
3950A Carson-Newman Coll. (Jefferson City)
3957A Cooper Institute, Inc. (Knoxville)
3956A David Lipscomb Univ. (Nashville)
3958A East Tennessee State Univ. (Johnson City)

3963A Ft. Sanders Presby. Hosp. Sch. of Nrsg. (Knoxville)
3974A Lambuth Coll. (Jackson)
3988A Maryville Coll. (Maryville)
3994A Middle Tennessee State Univ. (Murfreesboro)
4006A Southern Coll. of Seventh-Day Adventist (Collegedale)
4014A Tennessee Wesleyan Coll. (Athens)
4017A Tomlinson Coll. (Cleveland)
4022A Univ. of Tennessee at Chattanooga (Chattanooga)

TEXAS
4073A Amber Univ. (Garland)
1499A Calvary Coll. (Lewisville)
4081A Central Texas Coll. (Killeen)
9212A Central Texas Coll.–Overseas Europe (APO New York)
9261A Corpus Christi State Univ. (Corpus Christi)
4090A El Paso Comm. Coll. (El Paso)
4103A Galveston Coll. (Galveston)
4100A Howard Coll. at Big Spring (Big Spring)
4260A Kingwood Coll. (Kingwood)
4123A Lubbock Christian Univ. (Lubbock)
4139A North Harris Coll. (Houston)
4202A Prairie View A&M Unv. (Prairie View)
4158A St. Mary's Univ. (San Antonio)
4160A St. Philip's Coll. (San Antonio)
4178A Southwest Texas State Univ. (San Marcos)
4198A Texas A & M (College Station)
4222A Texas Wesleyan Coll. (Fort Worth)
4261A Tomball Coll. (Tomball)
4055A Univ. of Central Texas (Killeen)
4241A Univ. of Texas Medical Branch at Galveston (Galveston)
4239A Univ. of Texas at San Antonio (San Antonio)
4246A Wayland Baptist Coll. (Plainview)
4254A Wiley Coll. (Marshall)

UTAH
9259A Hawthorne Univ. (Salt Lake City)
9269A Univ. of Phoenix (Salt Lake City)

VERMONT
4329A Burlington Coll. (Burlington)
4314A Castleton State Coll. (Castleton)
4298A Champlain Coll. (Burlington)
4316A Johnson State Coll. (Johnson)
4308A Norwich Univ. (Northfield)
4322A Univ. of Vermont (Burlington)
4328A Vermont Coll. (Montpelier)

VIRGINIA
4338A Averett Coll. (Danville)
4354A Central Virginia Comm. Coll. (Lynchburg)
4336A Embry-Riddle Aero Univ. (NAS Norfolk)
4357A George Mason Univ. (Fairfax)
4358A Hampton Univ. (Hampton)
4364A Liberty Baptist Coll. (Lynchburg)
4374A Mary Baldwin Coll. (Staunton)
4378A Marymount Univ. (Arlington)
4376A Mountain Empire Comm. Coll. (Big Stone Gap)
4425A Norfolk State Univ. (Norfolk)
4384A Piedmont Virginia Comm. Coll. (Charlottsville)
4422A Radford Univ. (Radford)
4396A Shenandoah Coll. & Conservatory of Music (Winchester)
4401A Southwest Virginia Comm. Coll. (Richlands)
4407A Thomas Nelson Comm. Coll. (Hampton)
4353A Tidewater Comm. Coll. (Portsmouth)
4435A Upper Iowa Univ. Extension Division (Roanoke)
4379A Virginia Commonwealth Univ. (Richmond)
4351A Virginia Western Comm. Coll. (Roanoke)

WASHINGTON
4442A Big Bend Comm. Coll. (Moses Lake)
4505A City Univ. (Bellevue)
4457A Evergreen State Coll., The (Olympia)
4458A Gonzaga Univ. (Spokane)
4470A Pacific Lutheran Univ. (Tacoma)
4476A Seattle Pacific Univ. (Seattle)
9226A State Bd. of Accountancy (Olympia)
4497A Univ. of Washington–Bothell (Bothell)
9244A Univ. of Washington Grd. Sch. Nrsg. (Seattle)
4484A Univ. of Washington, Sch. of Nrsg. (Seattle)
4493A Univ. of Washington–Tacoma (Tacoma)
4491A Whatcom Comm. Coll. (Bellingham)

WEST VIRGINIA
4508A Alderson-Broaddus Coll. (Philippi)
4512A Bethany Coll. (Bethany)
4525A Southern W. V. Comm. Coll. (Logan)
4528A Univ. of Charleston (Charleston)
4534A West Liberty State Coll. (West Liberty)

WISCONSIN
4558A Alverno Coll. (Milwaukee)
4563A Bellin Coll. of Nrsg. (Green Bay)
4568A Cardinal Stritch Coll. (Milwaukee)
4574A Concordia Coll. (Milwaukee)
4582A Edgewood Coll. (Madison)
4556A Fox Valley Tech. Inst. (Appleton)
4615A Madison Area Tech.Coll. (Madison)
4620A Mt. Mary Coll. (Milwaukee)
4585A Northeast Wisconsin Tech. Inst. (Green Bay)
4644A St. Norbert Coll. (Depere)
4586A Silver Lake Coll. (Manitowoc)
4688A Univ. of Wisconsin–Green Bay (Green Bay)
4656A Univ. of Wisconsin–Madison (Madison)
4658A Univ. of Wisconsin–Milwaukee, Sch. of Nrsg. (Milwaukee)
4674A Univ. of Wisconsin–Oshkosh (Oshkosh)
4692A Univ. of Wisconsin Center–Manitowoc (Manitowoc)
4652A Univ. of Wisconsin–Stout (Menomonie)
4671A Waukesha County Tech. Inst. (Pewaukee)

WYOMING
5004A Northwest Comm. Coll. (Powell)
5006A Univ. of Wyoming (Laramie)
5005A Western Wyoming Comm. Coll. (Rock Springs)

FOREIGN

ANTILLES
5296A Universidat Di Aruba (Netherlands)

CANADA
9201A Canadian Sch. of Management (Toronto)

ENGLAND
9215A Centre for Business Studies (London)

FRANCE
5295A American Univ. of Paris (Paris)

GERMANY
5248A Schiller International Univ. (Heidelberg)

HAITI
9202A Haitian-American Institute (Port-Au-Prince)

SWITZERLAND
9268A Business School Lausanne (Lausanne)

THAILAND
5238A American Coll. of Thailand (Bangkok)

VIRGIN ISLANDS
5288A Coll. of the Virgin Islands (St. Thomas)

Note: If the institution you wish to receive a copy of your score report is not included in this list, print the institution's name and address in the space provided on your answer sheet. Your scores will be reported to that address.

BIOLOGY

OFFICIAL STATEMENT

The College Proficiency Examination in Biology is based upon the introductory college course in biology.

OBJECTIVES

The examination presupposes that in his study the candidate has emphasized the fact that fundamental principles apply to both plants and animals. The overall approach assumed is dynamic, including constant attention to functional morphology. Since evolution is a fundamental theme in biology, understanding will be expected of the interdependence of organism and environment, with stress on animal adaptations and behavior. Since a thorough understanding of concepts in biology involves chemistry, the candidate will be expected to have a background in that subject.

CONTENT

I. UNITY AMONG LIVING THINGS: PROTOPLASM, CELLS, AND CELLULAR METABOLISM

A. General structure of cells as revealed by electron microscopy

1. Cell wall, cell membrane, plasma membrane, endoplasmic reticulum, ribosomes, mitochondria, plastids, vacuoles, lysomes, centrioles, Golgi apparatus, nuclear membrane, nucleus, and chromosomes

B. Biochemistry

1. Fundamentals

(a) Properties and distribution of elements with emphasis on carbon, hydrogen, oxygen, nitrogen, phosphorus, and sulfur ions, valence, pH, concepts of free energy and entropy

(b) Compounds, particularly carbon compounds

2. Carbohydrates: pentoses, hexoses, monosaccharides, disaccharides, polysaccharides

3. Lipids: fats, saturated and unsaturated fatty acids, glycerol, steroids

4. Proteins: amino acids, peptide linkage, depeptides and polypeptides, simple and conjugated proteins, denaturation of proteins

5. Nucleic acids: DNA, RNA, nucleotides

C. Origin of energy sources and their transformation in cells

1. Photosynthesis

(a) Structure of chloroplasts, structure of grana, chemistry of chlorophyll, factors affecting synthesis of chlorophyll, chromatographic techniques for separating pigments, role of pigments in photosynthesis

(b) Dark and light phases of photosynthesis: important chemical reactions in CO_2 fixation, role of light, phosphorylation

(c) History of major experiments such as those of Van Helmont, Priestley, Ingenhousz, Blackman, Ruben and Kamen, Calvin and Benson

2. Respiration of carbohydrates

(a) ATP: composition, functions, phosphagens, *high energy* bond formation and transfer

(b) Anaerobic phase: important chemical reactions of glycolysis and alcoholic fermentation

(c) Aerobic phase: important chemical reactions, Krebs cycle

(d) Relative efficiency of aerobic and anaerobic phases

(e) Hydrogen and electron transfer systems: pyridine and flavin nucleotides, cytochrome system

(f) Enzymes:

(1) dehydrogenases, carboxylases, oxidases, phosphorylases

(2) major coenzymes and their functions

(3) vitamins in relation to enzymes and coenzymes

3. Respiration of fats and proteins

(a) Fats: beta oxidation, relation to the Krebs cycle and acetyl-CoA, glycol in relation to carbohydrates

(b) Proteins: deamination and transmination, formation of urea (arginine-ornithine cycle), relation of *carbohydrate fraction* of amino acids to metabolites of Krebs cycle

D. Basic synthesis of carbohydrates, proteins, fats

1. Carbohydrates: polymerization, dehydration synthesis, general structure of starch, cellulose, glycogen

2. Proteins: relation to ribosomes, endoplasmic reticulum, DNA, RNA, and genes

3. Fats: relation to the Krebs cycle and acetyl-CoA

E. Passage of materials into and out of cells

1. Chemical composition and structure of the cell wall and cell membrane

(a) Plasmodesmata in plant cells, effects of structure on selective permeability

(b) Relation of cell membrane to endoplasmic reticulum

2. Penetrating particles: concentration, charge, size, solubility

3. Effects of hypertonic, hypotonic, and isotonic solutions on cells

4. Active transport

5. Pinocytosis

F. Mitosis and cytokinesis

1. Structure and function of the nucleus

2. Mitotic apparatus

3. Phases of mitosis

4. Method of DNA replication

5. Cytokinesis in animal and plant cells

II. DIVERSITY AMONG LIVING THINGS: STRUCTURE, FUNCTION, REPRODUCTION, DEVELOPMENT, EVOLUTION, DISTRIBUTION, AND CLASSIFICATION

A. Viruses (including phages)

1. Questions as to their nature

2. Replication

B. Bacteria

1. Morphology and physiology: types, spore formation, respiration (aerobic facultative, and obligate anaerobic), fermentation

2. Modes of nutrition including photosynthesis and chemosynthesis

3. Relation to the carbon and nitrogen cycles

C. Fungi

1. Major characteristics of slime molds and true fungi

2. Reproduction in rhizopus, neurospora, puccinia

3. Economic importance

D. Green algae

1. Major characteristics

2. Reproduction to illustrate meiosis, zoospore formation, isogamy, heterogamy

3. Relationship to the evolution of higher plants: biochemical similarities, alteration of generations

E. Bryophyta: emphasis should be placed upon the adaptations to a terrestrial environment both in the vegative structures and in the methods of reproduction

1. Characteristics of mosses and liverworts

2. Life cycle of a representative form

F. Tracheophyta

1. Ferns: life cycle with the emphasis on alteration of generations

2. Pine: structure of the seed with the emphasis on its evolutionary significance

3. Angiosperms

(a) Reproduction and life cycle

(1) Flower - structure, details of the male and female gametophyte generations, relationships to insects in geologic time and in adaptations for pollination, initiation of flowering-photoperiodism

(2) Seed - development of embryo sporophyte in the seed, differences between monocots and dicots, dormancy, germination, economic importance

(3) Fruit - relationship to seed dispersal, auxins as related to parthenocarpy, economic importance

(4) Vegative reproduction

(b) Structure and physiology of the sporophyte

(1) Root, leaf, and stem of a typical herbaceous plant

(2) Water and mineral absorption, movement

(3) Food translocation and storage

(4) Growth from the seed and maturation to include primary and secondary tissues; cell enlargement, cell differentiation

(5) Irritability - tropisms and other movements, relationship of auxins

G. Invertebrates - structure, function, and distribution

1. Protozoa: to be studied as simple organisms solving fundamental problems of existence, free-living and parasitic forms to be considered

2. Coelenterate: tissue grade of organization, cell specialization, regeneration, nerve-net structure

3. Platyhelminthes: bilateral symmetrý, cephalization, organ-systems, mesodermal structures, free-living versus parasitic forms

4. Echinodermata: phylogenetic relationships to chordata

5. Annelida: general body plan, trochophore larva, schizo-coel, segmentation

6. Arthropoda: general body plan, adaptations to a land environment, respiratory mechanisms of the various classes, hormones affecting the metamorphosis of insects, economic importance

NOTE: The invertebrate phyla listed above have been selected on the basis of phylogenetic significance. Molusca, Porifera, and Nematoda should also be studied.

H. Chordates: structure, function, reproduction, development, classification, evolution, and distribution
Laboratory study of the structure and function of organ systems of some vertebrate such as a frog, rat, or fetal pig. The candidate is expected to have acquired some familiarity with the invertebrate chordates, the notochord of invertebrate chordates and of vertebrates, and various vertebrate classes.

1. Digestive system: structure, enzymes, nervous and hormonal control, absorption

2. Respiratory system: the breathing mechanism in a fish, in an amphibian, and in a mammal; gaseous exchange in lungs, gills, and skin; relationship to cellular respiration

3. Circulatory system: composition and functions of blood and lymph, immunity, homeostatic control of blood composition, patterns of circulation in an amphibian and in a mammal, renal and hepatic portal systems

4. Excretory system: general structure; detailed structure of a nephric unit and functions performed in each part; relationship of the kidney to homeostasis; sweat glands; the liver as an excretory organ, including urea formation

5. Skeletal and muscular system: the basic structural plan of the skeleton and the relation of muscles to skeletal movements, ligaments, tendons, antagonistic action of muscles, muscle physiology

6. Integrative systems

   (a) Central nervous system: the five major divisions of the brain, functions of parts of the brain and spinal cord, cranial and spinal nerves, types and structure of neurons, nature of the nerve impulse, synaptic transmission, reflex arc, conditioned reflex

   (b) Autonomic nervous system: structure, function, and neurohumors of sympathetic and parasympathetic divisions; relationship of the sympathetic division to the adrenal medulla

   (c) Endocrine glands: pituitary, thyroid, islets of Langerhans (alpha and beta cells), parathyroids, gonads, adrenals, hormones affecting the digestive glands, relationship of the pituitary to the brain

7. Reproductive system

   (a) Structure

   (b) Details of oogenesis and spermatogenesis

(c) Hormonal control of sperm and egg production and uterine development in mammals

(d) Fertilization in land and water organisms

(e) Natural and artificial methods of parthenogenesis

8. Development of an animal embryo

(a) Effects of yolk upon embryological development

(b) Early embryology of a homolecithal egg

(c) Early embryology of an amphibian egg through the neurula stage

(d) Germ layer origins of organ systems

(e) Formation and function of four extra-embryonic membranes of a reptile or bird

(f) Formation of the placenta and umbilical cord and their functions

(g) Pattern of circulation in a mammalian embryo and the changes occurring at birth

III. CONTINUITY OF LIVING THINGS

A. Genetics: plant, animal, and human examples should be considered

1. Meiosis: phases, synapsis and crossing-over, tetrad formation, animal and vegetal poles

2. Classical genetics and the development of the gene theory

(a) Mendel's work and principles

(b) Sutton's hypothesis - relating Mendelian laws to chromosomes

(c) Morgan's experiments establishing genes as portions of chromosomes

(d) Lethal factors

(e) Multiple alleles - blood types

(f) Factor interaction resulting in modified two-factor ratios

(g) Multiple factors - relation to the normal probability curve

(h) Mechanisms of sex determination (XY, WZ, XO, monoploid-diploid)

(i) Sex linkage in humans and in fruit flies

(j) Techniques of mapping the chromosomes: percentage of crossing-over

3. Mutations: genic and chromosomal (deletions, duplications, translocations, inversions), ploidy, induction of mutations, relationship to evolution

4. Mechanism of gene action: experiments with neurospora, gene-enzyme relationships with illustrations in humans (phenylketonuric, alkaptonuria, sickle-cell anemia)

5. Experiments that indicate the relationships between DNA and genes: bacterial transformations, bacterial viruses

6. Genetic code: experiments to illustrate the techniques employed, relation to protein synthesis

7. Examples of cytoplasmic inheritance

8. Population genetics: Hardy-Weinberg Principle and its relation to natural selection and genetic drift (see Evolution)

B. Evolution

1. Theories of the origin of life

2. Criteria for determining the nature of a species

3. Evidence for evolution from biochemistry, morphology, embryology, physiology, paleontology, and geographical distribution

4. Theories of the mechanism of evolution

(a) Lamarck's theory of use and disuse

(b) Darwin's theory of natural selection

(c) DeVries and mutations

(d) Modern concepts

5. Factors influencing natural selection and speciation: population genetics (size, isolation, genetic drift), adaptive radiation (suggested example - Darwin's Finches on the Galapagos)

6. The evolution of man

IV. ECOLOGICAL RELATIONSHIPS AMONG LIVING THINGS
It is assumed that the relationship between the organism and its environment has received attention throughout the course. The purpose of this section is to summarize the information thought desirable.

A. Physical (Abiotic) factors: soil, water, temperature, light, atmosphere, radiation

B. Biotic factors

1. Cycle of the elements (especially carbon and nitrogen)

2. Food chains - relationships with regard to numbers, mass, size, energy flow

3. Symbiosis: mutualism, parasitism, commensalism

4. Succession

5. Social relationships (ants, bees, birds, deer)

HOW TO TAKE A TEST

You have studied hard, long, and conscientiously.

With your official admission card in hand, and your heart pounding, you have been admitted to the examination room.

You note that there are several hundred other applicants in the examination room waiting to take the same test.

They all appear to be equally well prepared.

You know that nothing but your best effort will suffice. The "moment of truth" is at hand: you now have to demonstrate objectively, in writing, your knowledge of content and your understanding of subject matter.

You are fighting the most important battle of your life — to pass and/or score high on an examination which will determine your career and provide the economic basis for your livelihood.

What extra, special things should you know and should you do in taking the examination?

BEFORE THE TEST

YOUR PHYSICAL CONDITION IS IMPORTANT

If you are not well, you can't do your best work on tests. If you are half asleep, you can't do your best either. Here are some tips:

1. Get about the same amount of sleep you usually get. Don't stay up all night before the test, either partying or worrying — DON'T DO IT.
2. If you wear glasses, be sure to wear them when you go to take the test. This goes for hearing aids, too.
3. If you have any physical problems that may keep you from doing your best, be sure to tell the person giving the test. If you are sick or in poor health, you really cannot do your best on any test. You can always come back and take the test some other time.

AT THE TEST

EXAMINATION TECHNIQUES

1. Read the *general* instructions carefully. These are usually printed on the first page of the examination booklet. As a rule, these instructions refer to the timing of the examination; the fact that you should not start work until the signal and must stop work at a signal, etc. If there are any *special* instructions, such as a choice of questions to be answered, make sure that you note this instruction carefully.

2. When you are ready to start work on the examination, that is as soon as the signal has been given, read the instructions to each question booklet, underline any key words or phrases, such as *least*, *best*, *outline*, *describe*, and the like. In this way you will tend to answer as requested rather than discover on reviewing your paper that you *listed without describing*, that you selected the *worst* choice rather than the *best* choice, etc.

3. If the examination is of the objective or so-called multiple-choice type, that is, each question will also give a series of possible answers: A, B, C, or D, and you are called upon to select the best answer and write the letter next to that answer on your answer paper, it is advisable to start answering each question in turn. There may be anywhere from 50 to 100 such questions in the three or four hours allotted and you can see how much time would be taken if you read through all the questions before beginning to answer any. Furthermore, if you come across a question or a group of questions which you know would be difficult to answer, it would undoubtedly affect your handling of all the other questions.

4. If the examination is of the essay-type and contains but a few questions, it is a moot point as to whether you should read all the questions before starting to answer any one. Of course if you are given a choice, say five out of seven and the like, then it is essential to read all the questions so you can eliminate the two which are most difficult. If, however, you are asked to answer all the questions, there may be danger in trying to answer the easiest one first because you may find that you will spend too much time on it. The best technique is to answer the first question, then proceed to the second, etc.

5. Time your answers. Before the examination begins, write down the time it started, then add the time allowed for the examination and write down the time it must be completed, then divide the time available somewhat as follows:

    a. If 3 ½ hours are allowed, that would be 210 minutes. If you have 80 objective-type questions, that would be an average of about 2 ½ minutes per question. Allow yourself no more than 2 minutes per question, or a total of 160 minutes, which will permit about 50 minutes to review.

    b. If for the time allotment of 210 minutes, there are 7 essay questions to answer, that would average about 30 minutes a question. Give yourself only 25 minutes per question so that you have about 35 minutes to review.

6. The most important instruction is *to read each question* and make sure you know what is wanted. The second most important instruction is to *time yourself properly* so that you answer every question. The third most important instruction is to *answer every question.* Guess if you have to but include something for each question, Remember that you will receive no credit for a blank and will probably receive some credit if you write something in answer to an essay question. If you guess a letter, say "B" for a multiple-choice question, you may have guessed right. If you leave a blank as the answer to a multiple-choice question, the examiners may respect your feelings but it will not add a point to your score. Some exams may penalize you for wrong answers, so in such cases *only*, you may not want to guess unless you have some basis for your answer.

7. Suggestions

   a. Objective-Type Questions

      (1) Examine the question booklet for proper sequence of pages and questions.

      (2) Read all instructions carefully.

      (3) Skip any question which seems too difficult; return to it after all other questions have been answered.

      (4) Apportion your time properly; do not spend too much time on any single question or group of questions.

      (5) Note and underline key words—*all, most, fewest, least, best, worst, same, opposite.*

      (6) Pay particular attention to negatives.

      (7) Note unusual option, e.g., unduly long, short, complex, different or similar in content to the body of the question.

      (8) Observe the use of "hedging" words—*probably, may, most likely, etc.*

      (9) Make sure that your answer is put next to the same number as the question.

      (10) Do not second guess unless you have good reason to believe the second answer is definitely more correct.

      (11) Cross out original answer if you decide another answer is more accurate; do not erase, *until* you are ready to hand your paper in.

      (12) Answer all questions; guess unless instructed otherwise.

      (13) Leave time for review.

b. Essay-Type Questions

(1) Read each question carefully.
(2) Determine exactly what is wanted. Underline key words or phrases.
(3) Decide on outline or paragraph answer.
(4) Include many different points and elements unless asked to develop any one or two points or elements.
(5) Show impartiality by giving pros and cons unless directed to select one side only.
(6) Make and write down any assumptions you find necessary to answer the question.
(7) Watch your English, grammar, punctuation, choice of words.
(8) Time your answers; don't crowd material.

8. Answering the Essay Question

Most essay questions can be answered by framing the specific response around several key words or ideas. Here are a few such key words or ideas:

M's: manpower, materials, methods, money, management

P's: purpose, program, policy, plan, procedure, practice, problems, pitfalls, personnel, public relations

a. Six basic steps in handling problems:

(1) preliminary plan and background development
(2) collect information, data and facts
(3) analyze and interpret information, data and facts
(4) analyze and develop solutions as well as make recommendations
(5) prepare report and sell recommendations
(6) install recommendations and follow up effectiveness

b. Pitfalls to Avoid

(1) *Taking Things for Granted*
A statement of the situation does not necessarily imply that each of the elements is necessarily true; for example, a complaint may be invalid and biased so that all that can be taken for granted is that a complaint has been registered

(2) *Considering only one side of a situation*
Wherever possible, indicate several alternatives and then point out the reasons you selected the best one.

(3) *Failing to indicate follow up*
Whenever your answer indicates action on your part, make certain that you will take proper follow-up action to see how successful your recommendations, procedures, or actions turn out to be.

(4) *Taking too long in answering any single question*
Remember to time your answers properly.

EXAMINATION SECTION

EXAMINATION SECTION

TEST 1

DIRECTIONS: Each question or incomplete statement is followed by several suggested answers or completions. Select the one that BEST answers the question or completes the statement. *PRINT THE LETTER OF THE CORRECT ANSWER IN THE SPACE AT THE RIGHT.*

1. Only during a certain period of development in the early embryo is a specific area of cells able to react to organizer substance. 1.___
This area is said to be
A. competent B. determined
C. available D. trophic

2. A metabolic axial gradient was described by Child as extending in a diminishing ratio from the 2.___
A. animal pole to the vegetal pole
B. vegetal pole to the animal pole
C. yolk to the nucleus
D. centrosome to equatorial plate

3. Of the following, the embryonic membrane in the developing chick that serves as an exchange for gases in respiration is the 3.___
A. amnion B. allantois
C. chorion D. chorioallantois

4. In the development of the vertebrate embryo, the liver is a derivative of which one of the following? 4.___
A. Fore-gut B. Lateral mesoderm
C. Mid-gut D. Splanchnic mesoderm

5. To obtain frog's eggs in the laboratory out of season, female frogs can be injected with which one of the following? 5.___
A. Pituitary gland B. Thyroid gland
C. Testosterone D. Adrenalin

6. Which one of the following is characteristic of the human umbilical cord? 6.___
_____ vein(s) and _____ artery(ies).
A. One; one B. One; two C. Two; one D. Two; two

7. Gynandromorphs arise MAINLY as a result of which one of the following? 7.___
A. Hormone imbalance
B. Irregular distribution of chromosomes
C. An extra X chromosome
D. An extra Y chromosome

8. Modern taxonomic studies indicate that bacteria are MOST closely related to which one of the following groups? 8.___
A. Slime molds
B. Protozoa
C. Fungi
D. Blue-green algae

9. With which one of the following is adaptive radiation MOST closely associated? 9.___
A. Ecological opportunity
B. Geological development
C. Oceanic variation
D. Natural barriers

10. Photosynthesis may be considered as a process that provides a reserve supply of which one of the following? 10.___
A. FMN
B. DNA
C. ATP
D. PGAL

11. Of the following, the one group that belongs to the same phylum as sea urchins is that of the 11.___
A. tunicates
B. sea lilies
C. sea anemones
D. king crabs

12. Segmentation is characteristic of the phyla Annelida, Arthropoda, and which one of the following? 12.___
A. Echinodermata
B. Chordata
C. Mollusca
D. Platyhelminthes

13. Of the following, the present-day mammals that MOST clearly show reptilian characteristics are the 13.___
A. marsupials
B. placentals
C. monotremes
D. Chiroptera

14. Of the following, the relationship between Sacculina and a crab is BEST described as 14.___
A. commensalism
B. mutualism
C. association
D. parasitism

15. Metamorphosis of the Cecropia moth has been shown to be controlled by which one of the following? 15.___
A. A rise in temperature
B. A fall in temperature
C. Endocrine glands
D. The availability of suitable foods

16. Color vision in man requires the functioning principally of which one of the following parts of the eye? 16.___
A. Rods
B. Choroid coat
C. Cones
D. Iris

17. The effective rhythm and sequence of the contractions of the four chambers of the heart are initiated in an area found in which one of the following? 17.___
A. Right auricle
B. Left ventricle
C. Aorta
D. Medulla

18. Of the following, the organ or tissue that develops from a triploid nucleus is the 18.___
  A. pollen grain B. sporophyte embryo
  C. seed leaves D. endosperm tissue

19. Which one of the following represents the number of types of gametes that can be produced by a triple heterozygote? 19.___
  A. 3 B. 4 C. 6 D. 8

20. Pollen tubes form a path through the style to the ovary by means of which one of the following processes? 20.___
  A. Chemotaxis B. Digestion
  C. Geotropism D. Assimilation

21. The familiar fern plants represent the generation known as the 21.___
  A. thallophyte B. gametophyte
  C. sporophyte D. bryophyte

22. During the process of fertilization of the egg, the 22.___
  A. sperm penetrates the egg by boring through the membrane
  B. egg engulfs the sperm
  C. chromosomes become haploid
  D. tail of the sperm stimulates the formation of the fertilization membrane

23. Meiosis is MOST closely associated with which one of the following? 23.___
  A. Maturation of gametes B. Fertilization
  C. Cleavage D. Differentiation

24. In the development of vertebrates, the blastopore marks the region of the future 24.___
  A. mouth B. nostrils
  C. anus D. salivary glands

25. In a large number of crosses of two heterozygous round-seeded, yellow-seeded pea plants, the fraction of offspring that would PROBABLY appear wrinkled and green is 25.___
  A. 1/16 B. 3/16 C. 6/16 D. 9/16

26. Of the following, gene maps can BEST be constructed on the basis of the study of 26.___
  A. dominance B. independent assortment
  C. percentages of crossover D. segregation

27. The concept of *one gene, one enzyme* was based MAINLY on studies of which one of the following? 27.___
  A. Drosophila B. Neurospora
  C. Garden peas D. Mice

28. The rare appearance of a white-eyed female or a red-eyed male in a cross between a white-eyed female Drosophila and a red-eyed male may BEST be attributed to which one of the following? 28.___
   A. Segregation
   B. Independent assortment
   C. Nondisjunction
   D. Linkage

29. Of the following, which one is characteristic of the life cycle of yeast cells? 29.___
   A. The cells are always monoploid.
   B. The cells are always diploid.
   C. The cells may be either monoploid or diploid.
   D. Sexual reproduction does not occur.

30. Which one of the following was demonstrated by the experiments of Lederberg and Tatum? 30.___
   A. Anaerobic bacteria can develop into aerobic forms.
   B. *Wild type* bacteria can be caused to synthesize a variety of necessary nutrients.
   C. Asexual reproduction slows down the process of bacterial evolution.
   D. Bacteria can reproduce sexually.

31. The study of which one of the following organisms depends upon the observation of the formation of plaques? 31.___
   A. Gram positive bacteria
   B. Gram negative bacteria
   C. All viruses
   D. Bacteriophage

32. Although not permanent, *complete remission* of leukemia symptoms has been achieved by means of which one of the following? 32.___
   A. Radiation treatments
   B. *Mustard gas-like chemicals*
   C. Newly developed antibiotics
   D. Splenectomy

33. Of the following, the chemotherapeutic action of sulfanilamide depends upon its 33.___
   A. ability to make the bacterial cell membrane more permeable
   B. ability to disrupt the functioning of the bacterial nucleoproteins
   C. toxicity to some types of bacteria
   D. competitive inhibition of the availability of PABA to the bacteria

34. All of the following diseases are caused by Rickettsia EXCEPT 34.___
   A. Q-fever
   B. tsut sugamushi disease
   C. herpes zoster
   D. epidemic typhus

35. Of the following, the statement that is TRUE about infectious myxomatosis is that it is a disease that has been 35.___
   A. increasing since there has been an increase in air travel
   B. decreasing since the increased practice of pasteurizing milk
   C. intentionally introduced to control a rodent population explosion
   D. decreasing since the increased use of garbage disposal plants

36. Which one of the following has stimulated renewed interest in Rous sarcoma? 36.___
   A. The new knowledge about the role of DNA
   B. Spectrophotometric studies of cancer cells
   C. The development of chemicals that are effective against cancer cells
   D. Discoveries that viruses are associated with several kinds of tumors

37. Barr bodies and *drumsticks* are cellular structures that are 37.___
   A. used as cellular indicators of sex
   B. related to the production of specific enzymes by certain regions of the DNA macromolecule
   C. frequently observed in irradiated cells
   D. always found outside the cell nucleus

38. Ninhydrin is MOST likely to be used in a study of which one of the following? 38.___
   A. Changes in chromosomes after irradiation
   B. Fate of different germ layers during ontogeny
   C. Identification of amino acids in unknown solutions
   D. pH changes in a culture of protozoa

39. Among the following, the reason that the mitochondria of cells play an important role in metabolism is that they 39.___
   A. produce pyruvic acid out of carbohydrates
   B. are the site of the citric acid cycle
   C. release free energy available to the organism
   D. control the combination of cell fuels with oxygen

40. The contraction of a myofibril of striated muscle results from which one of the following? 40.___
   A. An interaction of actin, myosin, water, inorganic ions, and ATP
   B. The contraction of the myosin independent of any other substance
   C. The contraction of actin when activated by an electrochemical impulse
   D. The contraction of the sarcolemma which squeezes the actomysin together

41. The one term among the following that BEST describes birds which are hatched almost naked and later acquire their first coat of feathers is 41.___

A. precocial
B. juvenile
C. altricial
D. depilated

42. Of the following groups, the one that includes some local trees that have opposite leaves is 42.___

A. maples, oaks, beeches
B. ashes, sycamores, hickories
C. maples, ashes, horse chestnuts
D. chestnuts, sweetgums, maples

43. It is currently theorized that before the ancient atmosphere was modified by a product of photosynthesis, the atmosphere of the earth consisted MAINLY of 43.___

A. water, ammonia, nitrogen
B. ammonia, water, carbon dioxide
C. cyanide, ammonia, hydrogen
D. nitrogen, water, carbon dioxide

44. Among the following, the MAIN role of vitamins in respiration is that they 44.___

A. control the formation of ATP from ADP
B. control the permeability of cell membranes
C. contribute to the composition of various coenzymes
D. contribute directly to the building of energy-rich bonds

45. Of the following, the fact that is TRUE is that in anaerobic respiration 45.___

A. oxygen acts as a hydrogen acceptor
B. there are no available hydrogen acceptors
C. the only products formed are alcohol and CO_2
D. pyruvic acid acts as a hydrogen acceptor

46. Among the following, the group in the presence of which the clotting of blood will take place is 46.___

A. thrombokinase, prothrombin, fibrinogen, chloride ions
B. platelets, erythrocytes, prothrombin, phosphate ions
C. torn blood vessels, erythrocytes, fibrinogen, calcium ions
D. thrombokinase, prothrombin, fibrinogen, calcium ions

47. Increased resistance to malarial infection by some populations has been found to be associated with which one of the following? 47.___

A. A highly nutritious diet
B. Freedom from encroachment by *civilizing* influences
C. A high incidence of sickle-cell anemia
D. DDT-induced mutations in mosquitoes

48. The chloride shift refers to an exchange of ions in which one of the following situations? 48.___
A. Urea is formed when ammonia is combined with CO_2
B. Hydrochloric acid is formed in the gastric glands
C. Bicarbonate ions diffuse into and out of red corpuscles
D. A marine organism adapts to life in fresh water

49. The significance of the Hill reaction was that it demonstrated which one of the following? 49.___
A. Water supplies its oxygen to carbohydrate manufacture.
B. The function of light and chlorophyll in photosynthesis is to promote the splitting of water.
C. Photolysis of water can sometimes occur without light.
D. The most important part of photosynthesis is the *light reaction*.

50. Before molecules of glucose can be diffused through the membranes of cells, the molecules must be 50.___
A. digested
B. phosphorylated
C. oxidized
D. charged opposite to the charge on the membrane

KEY (CORRECT ANSWERS)

1. A	11. B	21. C	31. D	41. C
2. A	12. B	22. B	32. C	42. C
3. D	13. B	23. A	33. D	43. B
4. A	14. D	24. C	34. C	44. C
5. A	15. C	25. A	35. C	45. D
6. B	16. C	26. C	36. D	46. D
7. B	17. A	27. B	37. A	47. C
8. D	18. D	28. C	38. C	48. C
9. A	19. D	29. C	39. B	49. B
10. C	20. B	30. D	40. A	50. B

TEST 2

DIRECTIONS: Each question or incomplete statement is followed by several suggested answers or completions. Select the one that BEST answers the question or completes the statement. *PRINT THE LETTER OF THE CORRECT ANSWER IN THE SPACE AT THE RIGHT.*

1. Migration of the salmon to its natural spawning grounds seems to depend MAINLY on the sensitivity of its 1.____
   A. lateral line B. taste buds
   C. nose D. eyes

2. The chemical substance hirudin is made by which one of the following? 2.____
   A. Molds B. Soil bacteria
   C. Leeches D. Earthworms

3. Of the following, the one which is an organism that remains larval in appearance throughout life is 3.____
   A. amoeba B. alligator C. eel D. axolotl

4. Food particles are prevented from entering the larynx by the presence of the 4.____
   A. uvula B. pharynx
   C. soft palate D. epiglottis

5. Contraction of the extensor muscle of the upper arm tends to do which one of the following? 5.____
   A. Straighten the arm B. Bend the arm at the elbow
   C. Close the fingers D. Rotate the lower arm

6. Of the following, the one which is a hormone produced by the posterior lobe of the pituitary gland is 6.____
   A. pitressin B. prolactin
   C. thyrotrophic hormone D. corticotrophic hormone

7. The Pavlov pouch is used MAINLY in the study of which one of the following? 7.____
   A. Conditioning B. Reflex behavior
   C. Gastric secretion D. Salivation

8. The MOST obvious effect of insulin is that it increases the 8.____
   A. transformation of glycogen to glucose
   B. transformation of blood glucose to glycogen
   C. activity of the Islands of Langerhans
   D. effects of glucagon

9. Blood RICHEST in oxygen is found in which one of the following? 9.____
   A. Pulmonary artery B. Pulmonary vein
   C. Portal vein D. Renal artery

10. Ecdysis is a process concerned with which one of the following? 10.___
A. Ecology B. Evolution C. Molting D. Division

11. The margins of the sternum articulate with the cartilages of only the _____ pairs of rib. 11.___
A. first five B. first seven
C. last five D. last seven

12. The phase of the heart's action in which blood is forced out of the ventricles is called 12.___
A. expansion B. diastole C. systole D. relaxation

13. Fontanelles are normally found in which one of the following? 13.___
A. Inferior meatus B. Skull of an infant
C. Infundibulum D. Jugular foramen

14. The LARGEST of the lymphoid organs in the human adult is the 14.___
A. tonsil B. thymus C. liver D. spleen

15. The deficiency of cones in the retinas of dogs results in 15.___
A. night blindness B. astigmatism
C. color blindness D. poor peripheral vision

16. Which one of the following crosses would result in a genotype ratio of 1:2:1? 16.___
A. Yg x gg B. Yg x Yg C. Yg x YY D. YY x gg

17. Which one of the following may cause a lilac bush to produce both purple and white blossoms during a given season? 17.___
A. Grafting B. Hybridization
C. Cross-pollination D. Changes in pH of the soil

18. Development of unfertilized daphnia eggs is an example of which one of the following? 18.___
A. Maturation B. Metamorphosis
C. Ontogeny D. Parthenogenesis

19. Sickle-cell anemia is due to 19.___
A. a virus B. iron deficiency
C. high altitude D. gene action

20. The number of different kinds of gametes that can be produced by an individual with the genotype Aa Bb Cc is 20.___
A. 2 B. 4 C. 6 D. 8

21. In connection with the sex-linked inheritance of red eyes and white eyes in Drosophila, the result that may be expected from a cross of a red-eyed, hybrid female and a white-eyed male is 21.___
A. red eyes for all male offspring
B. red eyes for all female offspring
C. red eyes for half of the male offspring
D. the hybrid condition for all female offspring

22. Which one of the following is still regarded as being essentially CORRECT? 22.___
   A. Darwin's hypothesis of pangenesis
   B. Swammerdam's theory of preformation
   C. Bonnet's theory of encasement
   D. Wolff's idea of epigenesis

23. After the birth of a human child, all of the following normally atrophy EXCEPT the 23.___
   A. left umbilical vein
   B. ductus ateriosus
   C. ductus venosus
   D. left hepatic vein

24. During the embryonic development of the eye, the 24.___
   A. optic vesicle is the organizer for the lens
   B. lens if the organizer for the optic vesicle
   C. optic vesicle and lens develop simultaneously
   D. optic vesicle and lens develop independently of each other

25. The bird embryo is to primitive streak as the frog embryo is to 25.___
   A. blastopore
   B. stomodeal invagination
   C. archenteron
   D. neural groove

26. The ducts of Cuvier are part of the embryonic _____ system. 26.___
   A. circulatory
   B. respiratory
   C. excretory
   D. digestive

27. The morula MOST directly results from which one of the following? 27.___
   A. Cleavage
   B. Differentiation
   C. Assimilation
   D. Invagination

28. Tetrad formation is GENERALLY characteristic of which one of the following? 28.___
   A. Mitosis
   B. Fertilization
   C. Meiosis
   D. Cleavage

29. The cavity inside the double-walled gastrula becomes in the adult the 29.___
   A. nerve cord
   B. alimentary canal
   C. heart
   D. lungs

30. Treponema pallidum is the cause of which one of the following? 30.___
   A. Rocky mountain spotted fever
   B. Blood-poisoning
   C. Food-poisoning
   D. Syphilis

31. All of the following diseases are caused by viruses EXCEPT 31.___
   A. rabies
   B. yellow fever
   C. psittacosis
   D. typhus fever

32. Which one of the following BEST describes the shape of a vibrio bacterium? 32.___
A. Ovoid B. Cylindrical
C. Spherical D. Spiral

33. The FIRST scientist to describe the three principal bacterial shapes was 33.___
A. Pasteur B. Leeuwenhoek
C. Hooke D. Koch

34. BERGEY'S MANUAL is useful in identifying 34.___
A. trees and shrubs of the U.S.A.
B. ferns
C. flowers of North America
D. bacteria

35. The use of sonic apparatus to destroy bacteria is limited PRINCIPALLY because 35.___
A. sonic waves do not cause mechanical rupture
B. sonic waves produce their effect only where large quantities of bacteria are exposed
C. great pressure of from 400 to 500 atmospheres is required to cause mechanical rupture
D. the amount of material that can be exposed to sonic energy at one time is limited in volume

36. Sulfonamides are effective because they 36.___
A. form salts with nucleic acid
B. compete with PABA
C. coagulate proteins
D. disrupt cell membranes

37. The tissue in which Nissl bodies are MOST likely to be found is 37.___
A. adipose B. bone
C. cardiac muscle D. nerve

38. Concerning mitochondria, it is CORRECT to say that they 38.___
A. are major centers for producing energy
B. serve as generating centers for cilia
C. have no internal morphology
D. are the major parts of the microsomes

39. Lampbrush chrcmosomes are found in 39.___
A. amphibian oocytes
B. avian spermatocytes
C. dipteran salivary gland cells
D. dipteran oocytes

40. DNA is to Crick as RNA polymerase is to 40.___
A. Kornberg B. Calvin C. Kendrew D. Ochoa

41. The electron microscope has shown that the 41.___
   A. cytoplasm is more differentiated than the nucleus
   B. nucleus is more differentiated than the cytoplasm
   C. nucleus and cytoplasm are equally differentiated
   D. nucleus and cytoplasm are both homogeneous

42. Cilia and flagella of plants and animals appear to have common evolutionary origin because both 42.___
   A. are long and thin, resembling primitive proteins
   B. have a helical structure like DNA
   C. perform similar functions
   D. have nearly identical ultra-structures

43. Which one of the following statements is NOT true of tunicates? 43.___
   A. They have actively swimming larvae possessing a notochord.
   B. Adults discard filtered water through the excurrent pore.
   C. They synthesize cellulose.
   D. They are unisexual.

44. Which one of the following is a characteristic of the Coelenterata? 44.___
   A. The polyp is a free floating form.
   B. The medusa is a sessile form.
   C. There is a single opening into the gastrovascular cavity.
   D. Alternation of haploid and diploid generations occurs.

45. Saccharomyces cerevisiae is the scientific name for 45.___
   A. sumac
   B. sugar cane
   C. baker's yeast
   D. black rot

46. Which one of the following is an example of a deciduous conifer? 46.___
   A. Magnolia
   B. Oak
   C. Spruce
   D. Larch

47. Of the following groups, which one has the GREATEST number of species? 47.___
   A. Conifers
   B. Club mosses
   C. True fungi
   D. Slime molds

48. Of the following, a type of organism which disappeared during the Mesozoic Era is the 48.___
   A. brachiopod
   B. ammonite
   C. trilobite
   D. chain corals

49. Embryological development indicates that the echinoderms are derived from the evolutionary stem that later gave rise to the 49.___
   A. arthropods
   B. vertebrates
   C. coelenterata
   D. porifera

50. Evidence from Sinanthropus fossils indicates that this form was 50.___
   A. tree-dwelling
   B. cannibalistic
   C. more ape-like than Gigantopithecus
   D. lacking in supraorbital ridges

KEY (CORRECT ANSWERS)

1. C	11. B	21. C	31. D	41. A
2. C	12. C	22. D	32. D	42. D
3. D	13. B	23. D	33. B	43. D
4. D	14. D	24. A	34. D	44. C
5. A	15. C	25. A	35. D	45. C
6. A	16. B	26. A	36. B	46. D
7. C	17. A	27. A	37. D	47. C
8. B	18. D	28. C	38. A	48. C
9. B	19. D	29. B	39. A	49. B
10. C	20. D	30. D	40. D	50. B

TEST 3

DIRECTIONS: Each question or incomplete statement is followed by several suggested answers or completions. Select the one that BEST answers the question or completes the statement. *PRINT THE LETTER OF THE CORRECT ANSWER IN THE SPACE AT THE RIGHT.*

1. The Dutch elm disease is caused by a 1.____
   A. fungus B. beetle C. virus D. bacterium

2. An example of seaweed is 2.____
   A. fucus B. vallisneria
   C. vaucheria D. elodea

3. A blood cell resembling the ameba is the 3.____
   A. erythrocyte B. saprophyte
   C. cocyte D. leucocyte

4. The bile duct empties into the 4.____
   A. gall bladder B. small intestine
   C. spleen D. large intestine

5. The malleus, incus, and stapes are 5.____
   A. muscles B. bones
   C. nerves D. blood vessels

6. Glucose is converted to glycogen MAINLY in the 6.____
   A. liver B. small intestine
   C. pancreas D. thyroid gland

7. Paramecia eliminate solid matter at the 7.____
   A. contractile vacuole B. pellicle
   C. food vacuoles D. anal spot

8. THE ORIGIN OF SPECIES BY MEANS OF NATURAL SELECTION was written by 8.____
   A. Lamarck B. Morgan C. deVries D. Darwin

9. A dog learns to salivate at the sound of a bell. This type of behavior is MOST closely associated with the research of 9.____
   A. Lysenko B. Watson C. Pavlov D. Dewey

10. In mammals, accommodation of the lens of the eye is a 10.____
    A. tropism B. reflex
    C. voluntary act D. habit

11. Explosions of nuclear devices have increased the danger of damage to human bone tissue by substituting for one of the elements in normal bone a radioactive isotope of 11.____
    A. iodine B. calcium C. strontium D. phosphorus

12. Starch is changed to sugar in the mouth by the action of 12.___
A. pepsin B. rennin C. steapsin D. ptyalin

13. The heart is in a state of contraction during 13.___
A. diastole B. metastasis
C. systole D. syncope

14. $C_{15}H_{11}O_4NI_4$ is the chemical formula of the hormone 14.___
A. thyroxin B. testosterone
C. insulin D. adrenin

15. A structure which NORMALLY serves as a common passageway for both food and air is the 15.___
A. pharynx B. glottis C. trachea D. larynx

16. A type of blood bank from which reserves of red blood corpuscles may be quickly mobilized when needed by the body is the 16.___
A. liver B. bone marrow
C. intestinal mesentery D. spleen

17. In a given sample of blood, clumping occurred with both A serum and B serum.
The blood type was 17.___
A. A B. B C. AB D. O

18. Independent assortment does not always occur in dihybrid crosses.
This may be the result of 18.___
A. recessiveness B. linkage
C. dominance D. segregation

19. Elastic tissue is of the type known as 19.___
A. connective B. muscular
C. nerve D. epithelial

20. A vitamin that contains cobalt as part of its chemical structure is vitamin 20.___
A. A B. B_2 C. B_{12} D. C

21. The relationship between cells and tissues is paralleled by that between 21.___
A. organs and systems B. enzymes and substrates
C. carbohydrates and fats D. ectoderm and endoderm

22. The circulatory mechanism characteristic of all organisms is 22.___
A. the xylem-phloem mechanism
B. the gastrovascular mechanism
C. the flame cell system
D. diffusion

23. A colorblind male, both of whose parents had normal vision and whose maternal and paternal grandparents had normal vision, PROBABLY inherited the gene for colorblindness from his 23.___
A. maternal or paternal grandmother
B. maternal or paternal grandfather
C. father
D. mother

24. The *pacemaker* of heart action refers to the 24.___
A. chordae tendinae B. mitral valve
C. Purkinje network D. sino-auricular node

25. The PRINCIPAL purpose of the reactions of the Krebs cycle is to regenerate 25.___
A. ATP B. TPN C. RNA D. DNA

26. The sphincter located at the juncture of the stomach and the small intestine is called 26.___
A. cardiac B. duodenal C. ileocolic D. pyloric

27. The Feulgen reaction is a specific test for identifying 27.___
A. cellulose B. glycogen
C. nucleo-protein D. lipids

28. During mitosis, the process that occurs FIRST is 28.___
A. chromosome movement along the spindle
B. constriction of the cell membrane
C. formation of equatorial plate
D. separation of the centrosomes

29. The optic nerve is to the retina as the auditory nerve is to the 29.___
A. cochlear window B. Eustachian tube
C. organ of Corti D. stapes

30. Protective mimicry is illustrated by 30.___
A. aphids and ants
B. hermit crab and sea anemone
C. monarch and viceroy butterflies
D. pilot fish and shark

31. Mites and ticks are MOST closely related to 31.___
A. true bugs B. click beetles
C. silverfish D. spiders

32. Bowman's capsule surrounds a 32.___
A. glomerulus B. Golgi body
C. gonad D. Graafian follicle

33. The CORRECT sequence of structures through which air passes as it enters the lungs is 33.___
A. larynx, pharynx, trachea
B. bronchus, bronchiole, alveolus
C. alveolus, trachea, bronchus
D. larynx, bronchiole, pharynx

34. Similar adaptations for seed dispersal are found in 34.___
A. ash and maple
B. elm and oak
C. poppy and milkweed
D. goldenrod and jimson weed

35. A drug used to relieve high blood pressure is 35.___
A. actomyosin
B. hirudin
C. pitressin
D. reserpine

36. A bean seed differs from a corn seed in regard to the number of 36.___
A. cotyledons
B. hypocytyls
C. micropyles
D. plumules

37. The waxy substance found on the outer surface of the leaf epidermis is called 37.___
A. chitin B. cutin C. lignin D. suberin

38. An inherited condition in human beings that is sex-linked is 38.___
A. syphilis
B. polydactylism
C. feeblemindedness
D. hemophilia

39. The radius is found in the 39.___
A. upper arm
B. forearm
C. cervical vertebrae
D. pelvic girdle

40. Nightcrawlers are 40.___
A. crayfish
B. eel larvae
C. earthworms
D. moth larvae

41. The Salk polio vaccine contains 41.___
A. killed polio virus
B. weak polio virus
C. antibodies
D. strong virus

42. The study of fossils is known as 42.___
A. ecology
B. paleontology
C. ontogeny
D. conchology

43. Fan-shaped leaves, fleshy fruit, and edible nuts are characteristic of the 43.___
A. Gingko
B. Boston fern
C. box-elder
D. larch

44. Peristalsis MOST commonly occurs in the 44.___
A. arteries
B. kidneys
C. esophagus
D. liver

45. Blood leaving the left side of the human heart passes next through the 45.___
A. venae cavae
B. aorta
C. pulmonary arteries
D. pulmonary veins

46. A living egg-laying mammal is the 46.___
A. porpoise B. platypus C. wallaby D. grampus

47. Of the following, the one that is NOT a hormone is
A. pancreatin B. cortin
C. insulin D. adrenalin
47.___

48. A disease which may be prevented by the use of a toxoid is
A. pneumonia B. smallpox
C. tetanus D. typhoid
48.___

49. The metabolism of calcium in the body is MOST directly controlled by the
A. pituitary gland B. bone marrow
C. parathyroid gland D. spleen
49.___

50. Metacarpals are found in the
A. vertebral column B. feet
C. hands D. pelvic girdle
50.___

KEY (CORRECT ANSWERS)

1. A	11. C	21. A	31. D	41. A
2. A	12. D	22. D	32. A	42. B
3. D	13. C	23. D	33. B	43. A
4. B	14. A	24. D	34. A	44. C
5. B	15. A	25. A	35. D	45. B
6. A	16. D	26. D	36. A	46. B
7. D	17. C	27. C	37. B	47. A
8. D	18. B	28. D	38. D	48. C
9. C	19. A	29. C	39. B	49. C
10. B	20. C	30. C	40. C	50. C

TEST 4

DIRECTIONS: Each question or incomplete statement is followed by several suggested answers or completions. Select the one that BEST answers the question or completes the statement. *PRINT THE LETTER OF THE CORRECT ANSWER IN THE SPACE AT THE RIGHT.*

1. The theory of Use and Disuse was proposed by 1.___
   A. DeVries B. La Farge C. Lamarck D. Thales

2. ACTH is a(n) 2.___
   A. autacoid B. enzyme C. hormone D. vitamin

3. A recently discovered hoax was _____ man. 3.___
   A. Java
   B. Neanderthal
   C. Piltdown
   D. Texepan

4. To discover whether a trait in an organism is dominant, the organism should be crossed with a 4.___
   A. hybrid dominant
   B. hybrid recessive
   C. pure dominant
   D. pure recessive

5. Chromosomes do NOT occur in pairs in 5.___
   A. body cells
   B. fertilized eggs
   C. gametes
   D. zygotes

6. Chemotherapy (the use of chemicals in the treatment of disease) had its inception with 6.___
   A. Ehrlich
   B. Madame Curie
   C. Paracelsus
   D. Park

7. The gland which produces insulin is to be found in the 7.___
   A. liver B. pancreas C. pituitary D. thymus

8. Deoxygenrated blood enters the heart at the 8.___
   A. left auricle
   B. left ventricle
   C. right auricle
   D. right ventricle

9. Of the following, the item which is NOT properly grouped with the remaining three is 9.___
   A. chromosome
   B. centrosome
   C. spindle fiber
   D. muscle fiber

10. In tracer studies, radioiodine would be concentrated in the 10.___
    A. adrenals B. liver C. pituitary D. thyroid

11. The sex chromosome combination of a human male is 11.___
    A. XO B. XX C. XY D. YY

12. MOST plant and animal cells are similar in that they both have 12.___
    A. cytoplasm and cellulose
    B. cytoplasm and contractile vacuole
    C. cytoplasm and nucleus
    D. membrane and cell wall

13. Saponification in the small intestine is the direct result of the action of 13.___
    A. bile B. lacteals C. secretin D. villein

14. Of the following *men*, the one with the LARGEST brain case was 14.___
    A. Cro-Magnon B. Heidelberg
    C. Java D. Peking

15. Of the following, the one non-antibiotic is 15.___
    A. gramicidin B. streptomycin
    C. sympathin D. terramycin

16. Among the following, the SMALLEST in size is the 16.___
    A. bacillus B. coccus
    C. Rickettsia D. virus

17. Of the following, the item which is NOT properly grouped with the remaining three is 17.___
    A. thrombin B. fibrin
    C. vitamin K D. vitamin B_2

18. Tx x Tt in which T is the dominant will result in a 18.___
    A. 1:1 ratio B. 3:1 ratio
    C. 9:3:3:1 ratio D. 100% of the dominant

19. In general, the size of an animal's egg depends on the 19.___
    A. amount of cytoplasm B. amount of yolk
    C. rate of development D. size of nucleus

20. A *blue baby* may result from the mating of an Rh ______ male and Rh ______ female. 20.___
    A. positive; positive B. negative; positive
    C. positive; negative D. negative; negative

21. Since barbiturates cause a paralysis of skeletal muscle, they must block impulses moving from 21.___
    A. the autonomic nervous sytem to muscles
    B. the central nervous system to muscles
    C. muscles to the autonomic nervous system
    D. muscles to the central nervous system

22. A drop of human blood which does NOT clump in either anti A or anti B serum is 22.___
    A. A B. B C. AB D. O

23. If the chromosome number of a frog is 26, the number of chromosomes contained in its sperms is 23.___
A. 13 B. 26 C. 39 D. 52

24. The MOST effective farming method for returning minerals to the soil is 24.___
A. contour plowing
B. crop rotation
C. strip farming
D. terracing

25. The essential parts of a flower are 25.___
A. ovary and petals
B. ovary and sepals
C. pistils and stamens
D. stamens and stigmas

26. The hormone cortisone is produced by the 26.___
A. anterior pituitary
B. cortex of the adrenals
C. medulla of the adrenals
D. posterior pituitary

27. From among the following, the CLOSEST definition of an instinct is a 27.___
A. conditioned reflex
B. habit
C. series of reflexes
D. none of the above

28. The vitamin which functions in the elaboration of prothrombin in the liver is 28.___
A. A B. B_{12} C. C D. K

29. Gamma globulins used in the protection against measles and polio contain 29.___
A. antibodies
B. dead viruses
C. toxoids
D. weakened viruses

30. The cattalo is superior in size and strength to either its cow or bison parent.
This superiority is a result of 30.___
A. hybridization
B. inbreeding
C. mutation
D. selection

31. The MOST highly oxygenated blood in the body is found in the 31.___
A. aorta
B. carotid artery
C. pulmonary artery
D. pulmonary vein

32. An example of symbiotic relationship is the 32.___
A. dodder
B. earthworm
C. lichen
D. tapeworm

33. Foods are irradiated in order to increase their content of vitamin 33.___
A. A B. B C. C D. D

34. Giantism is the result of _____ gland(s). 34.___
A. oversecretion of adrenal
B. oversecretion of pituitary
C. undersecretion of thyroid
D. undersecretion of parathyroid

35. In order to reduce the incidence of dental caries, the ingredient added to drinking water is 35._
A. bromides B. chlorides C. fluorides D. iodides

36. A *disease* which may be prevented by wearing shoes is caused by 36._
A. hookworm B. mealy worm
C. tapeworm D. trichina worm

37. The end products of protein digestion are 37._
A. amino acids B. glucose
C. glycerol D. none of the above

38. Blinking in response to bright light is an example of 38._
A. a habit B. an instinct
C. phototropism D. a reflex

39. Of the following, the man who made discoveries in genetics as of most recent date is 39._
A. Mendel B. Metchnikoff
C. Morgan D. Muller

40. The chromosome number of the fruitfly is normally 8. It might be 16 if it were NOT kept down by the process of 40._
A. conjugation B. maturation
C. mitosis D. parthenogenesis

41. A structure of the paramecium which enables it to get rid of wastes is the 41._
A. cell membrane B. chondriosome
C. gullet D. trichocyst

42. Muller is known for his work in producing mutations MAINLY in 42._
A. corn B. fruitflies
C. Neurospora D. planaria

43. A T.B. drug is 43._
A. isobutanol B. isoniazid
C. isonicotinic acid D. niacin

44. In the United States, the GREATEST percentage of the population is of blood type 44._
A. A B. B C. AB D. Rh positive

45. Pancreatic juice acts in the presence of 45._
A. HCl B. H_2CO_3 C. Na_2CO_3 D. NaCl

46. In the process of fermentation of yeast, the products formed are 46._
A. carbon dioxide and alcohol
B. carbon dioxide and water
C. oxygen and alcohol
D. oxygen and glucose

47. A Nobel Prize in medicine was shared by Lippman and 47.___
A. DuBois B. Houssay C. Krebs D. Marshall

48. Typhus is caused by 48.___
A. bacteria B. protozoa
C. Rickettsiae D. viruses

49. After birth, the body is MOST limited in forming new _____ cells. 49.___
A. blood B. bone C. nerve D. skin

50. A large mammal now extinct is the 50.___
A. Archeopteryx B. Brontosaurus
C. mammoth D. platypus

KEY (CORRECT ANSWERS)

1. C	11. C	21. B	31. D	41. A
2. C	12. C	22. D	32. C	42. B
3. C	13. A	23. A	33. D	43. B
4. D	14. A	24. B	34. B	44. D
5. C	15. C	25. C	35. C	45. C
6. A	16. D	26. B	36. A	46. A
7. B	17. D	27. C	37. A	47. C
8. C	18. B	28. D	38. D	48. C
9. D	19. B	29. A	39. D	49. C
10. D	20. C	30. A	40. B	50. C

EXAMINATION SECTION

TEST 1

DIRECTIONS: Each question or incomplete statement is followed by several suggested answers or completions. Select the one that BEST answers the question or completes the statement. *PRINT THE LETTER OF THE CORRECT ANSWER IN THE SPACE AT THE RIGHT.*

1. Experiments with radioactive carbon performed on algae show that one of the FIRST carbon compounds formed in photosynthesis is 1.___
   A. phosphoglyceric acid B. fructose
   C. carbonic acid D. glucose

2. In certain insects, the sex formula is XX-XO. In both males and females, there are 22 autosomes. The chromosome number found in sperm cells is 2.___
   A. 11 B. 12 C. 11 and 12 D. 23

3. In drosophila, the sex of a fly of the genotype XY is determined PRIMARILY by genes located on the 3.___
   A. autosomes and Y-chromosomes
   B. Y-chromosome
   C. autosomes
   D. autosomes and X-chromosome

4. A corn grain dropped near a barnyard grew into a large corn plant which, after maturing, had ears with few kernels. The MOST probable explanation for the paucity of kernels is that the 4.___
   A. barnyard fertilizer in high concentration affected kernel development
   B. plant did not receive the same attention given to plants grown in the field
   C. corn grain was probably not of selected seed variety
   D. cross-fertilization did not occur

5. Two black guinea pigs, when mated, may produce a white offspring. This is PROBABLY the result of 5.___
   A. mutation B. heterozygosity
   C. independent assortment D. incomplete dominance

6. Accommodation of the eye for near vision results when the 6.___
   A. tension on the suspensory ligament increases
   B. ciliary muscle contracts
   C. ciliary muscle relaxes
   D. lens becomes flatter and broader as a result of stretching

7. An awareness by a person of the position or location of muscles and bones is attributed to the action of 7.___
   A. chemoreceptors B. proprioreceptors
   C. enteroreceptors D. tactoreceptors

Questions 8-10.

DIRECTIONS: Answer Questions 8 through 10 after studying the following statement:

G is a completely dominant gene necessary for any coat color in the mouse; H is a completely dominant gene responsible for black coat color; hh gives brown coat provided G is present; no sex linkage is involved.

8. All the F_1 generation of a given cross between a black female mouse and a white male were the same. This color MUST have been 8.___
A. black B. brown C. white D. spotted

9. The number of phenotypes resulting from crossing a mouse heterozygous for both pairs of genes with a doubly recessive mouse will be 9.___
A. one B. two C. three D. four

10. A mating between two brown mice of genotypes which will not yield all brown offsprings will yield 10.___
A. 3 brown; 1 white B. 3 white; 1 brown
C. 1 brown; 1 white D. all white

11. Organs are grouped into systems on the basis of 11.___
A. common structure
B. related functions
C. proximity to each other
D. the order of their appearance in the embryo

12. The embryonic organ which meets the absorptive, respiratory, and excretory needs of developing embryos of higher vertebrates is the 12.___
A. allantois B. amnion C. gill D. pronephros

13. The Krebs oxidative cycle appears to be determined largely, if not completely, by organized groups of enzymes derived from the 13.___
A. Golgi bodies B. nuclear membrane
C. nuclear sap D. mitochondria

14. The Feulgen reaction is a chemical aid to the identification of 14.___
A. sex of unborn children
B. growth hormones in plants
C. pregnancy hormones in urine
D. nucleic acid

15. If there are 16 chromosomes in each cell of a fern sporophyte, the number of chromosomes in each cell of the prothallus of this fern would be 15.___
A. 4 B. 8 C. 16 D. 32

Questions 16-20.

DIRECTIONS: For each of the following items (Questions 16 through 20), choose the letter which indicates the state of evolution at which the character described was first introduced.

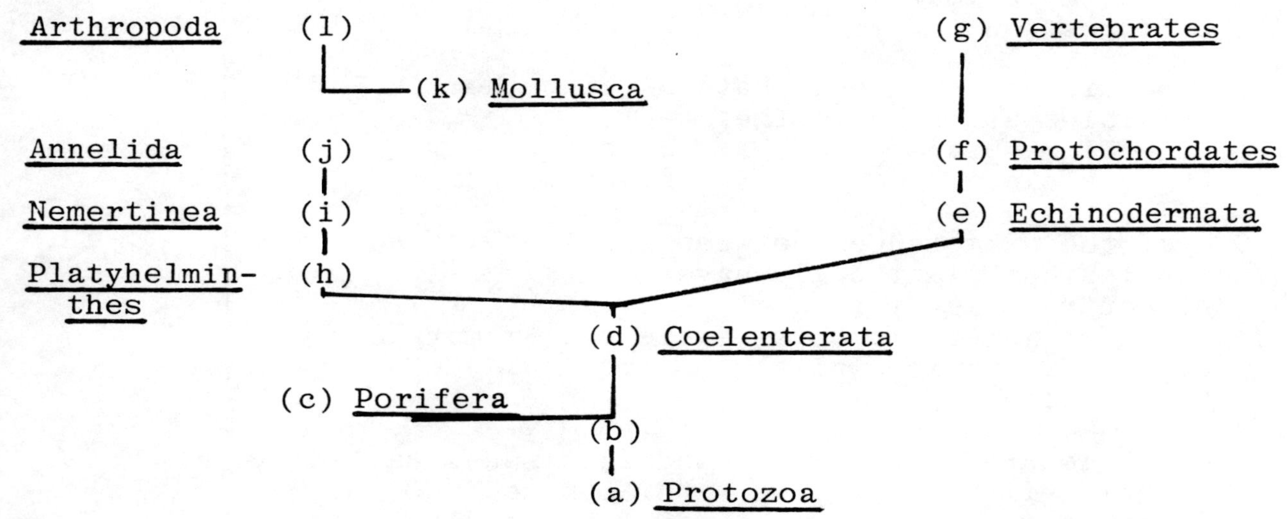

16. An arrangement of the many-celled body such that food intake occurs at one point and the elimination of solid wastes at a different point 16.____
    A. b B. d C. h D. i

17. Loss of autotrophic nutrition 17.____
    A. a B. k C. d D. h

18. Three germ layers, ectoderm, endoderm, and mesoderm 18.____
    A. i B. c C. h D. d

19. A well-defined, closed circulatory system, unconnected with the outside, 19.____
    A. d B. e C. h D. j

20. A body form such that the body can be bisected in only one way to yield halves that are mirror images of each other 20.____
    A. c B. d C. h D. j

21. An animal classified as a carnivore is a 21.____
    A. gopher B. nutria C. skunk D. porcupine

22. Strawberry plants can be used to demonstrate 22.____
    A. corms B. haustoria
    C. stolons D. multiple fruits

23. A flower which has bilateral symmetry is the 23.____
    A. mountain laurel B. evening primrose
    C. snapdragon D. wild geranium

24. All of the following are aquarium plants EXCEPT 24.____
    A. sagittaria B. anacharis
    C. cabomba D. tradescantia

25. A geneticist who won a Nobel Prize for his work on the artificial production of mutations was 25.___
A. McClung B. Morgan C. Muller D. Sturtevant

26. The process of producing polypeptides from amino acids is included in the life function called 26.___
A. assimilation
B. catabolism
C. digestion
D. embolism

27. The portion of an ameba that contains the LARGEST number of visible particles is the 27.___
A. cell membrane
B. ectoplasm
C. pellicle
D. endoplasm

28. One of the differences between plant cells and animal cells is that plant cells have 28.___
A. contractile fibrils
B. inert materials outside the cell membrane
C. polysaccharide walls
D. vacuoles

29. Myofibrils are structures found in tissues called 29.___
A. epithelium
B. muscle
C. squamous
D. yellow elastic

30. In cellular metabolism, mitochondria 30.___
A. form the spindle fibers that are necessary for mitosis
B. store energy in the form of fat
C. convert sugar into glycogen
D. are involved in intra-cellular oxidation

31. During the process of mitosis, the kinetochores of chromosomes become attached to 31.___
A. astral rays
B. middle lamellae
C. neurofibrils
D. spindle fibres

32. The cells in the lacunae near the Haversian canals secrete a large quantity of 32.___
A. calcium phosphate
B. carbohydrates
C. collagen
D. magnesium phosphate

33. The vitamin MOST readily destroyed by heat is 33.___
A. ascorbic acid
B. alpha tocopherol
C. riboflavin
D. thiamin

34. The substance MOST closely associated with calcium metabolism is 34.___
A. adrenin
B. riboflavin
C. vitamin A
D. vitamin D

35. The function that diastase performs in corn grains is performed in mammals by 35.___
A. ptyalin B. pepsin C. rennin D. steapsin

36. The function that is performed by root hairs in plants is performed in the jejunum of a mammal by 36.___
A. circumvallate papillae
B. lacunae
C. Peyer's patches
D. villi

37. During the process of digestion, proteins are finally broken down into 37.____
A. amino acids
B. monosaccharids
C. peptones
D. stearic acids

38. In man, the organ which absorbs MOST of the water in the food is the 38.____
A. large intestine
B. small intestine
C. villi
D. stomach

39. The chemical in normocytes that carries oxygen in a loose bond is 39.____
A. cytochrome
B. glycogen
C. stroma
D. hemoglobin

40. The pacemaker of the heart is located in the 40.____
A. auriculo-ventricular node
B. left auricle
C. mitral valve
D. tricuspid valve

41. The MOST richly oxygenated blood is carried in the 41.____
A. aorta
B. coronary artery
C. internal carotid
D. pulmonary vein

42. The loops of Henle are found in the 42.____
A. adrenal gland
B. intestine
C. kidney
D. pons

43. Of the following, the MOST important function of integumentary glands in humans is 43.____
A. discharge of urea
B. regulation of salt content
C. discharge of excess water
D. regulation of heat

44. The "respiratory center" in the brain is found in the 44.____
A. corpus callosum
B. frontal lobes
C. medulla
D. occipital lobes

45. The space through which an impulse passes from one neuron to another in a vertebrate nervous system is called a 45.____
A. ganglion
B. myelin sheath
C. plexus
D. synapse

46. Mosaic vision is characteristic of the 46.____
A. chameleon
B. dragon fly
C. leopard frog
D. nighthawk

47. The hormone that helps in the conversion of glucose to glycogen is 47.____
A. insulin
B. heparin
C. acetycholine
D. oxytocin

48. Antibodies have been found in relatively large quantities in 48.____
A. gamma globulin
B. heparin
C. lymph
D. thrombin

49. When diphtheria antitoxin is injected, it develops immunity known as 49.____
A. active, required B. natural, acquired
C. permanent D. passive, acquired

50. A type of phagocytic cell found in the blood of mammals is the 50.____
A. polymorph B. platelet
C. normocyte D. reticulocyte

KEY (CORRECT ANSWERS)

1. A	11. B	21. C	31. D	41. D
2. C	12. A	22. C	32. A	42. C
3. D	13. D	23. C	33. A	43. D
4. D	14. D	24. D	34. D	44. C
5. B	15. B	25. C	35. A	45. D
6. B	16. D	26. A	36. D	46. B
7. B	17. A	27. D	37. A	47. A
8. A	18. C	28. C	38. A	48. A
9. C	19. D	29. B	39. D	49. D
10. A	20. C	30. D	40. A	50. A

TEST 2

DIRECTIONS: Each question or incomplete statement is followed by several suggested answers or completions. Select the one that BEST answers the question or completes the statement. *PRINT THE LETTER OF THE CORRECT ANSWER IN THE SPACE AT THE RIGHT.*

1. Many of the physical properties of protoplasm can be explained by considering it to be a(n) 1.____
   A. mixture B. solution
   C. colloidal suspension D. emulsion

2. If the pancreatic ducts of an experimental animal were tied off, the MOST probable consequence would be 2.____
   A. a sudden increase in blood pressure and heart rate
   B. a voracious appetite, with excessive thirst and urination
   C. derangement of the carbohydrate metabolism
   D. stoppage of fat digestion and slowing of digestion of proteins and carbohydrates

3. A structure which normally serves as a common passageway for both food and air is the 3.____
   A. pharynx B. larynx C. glottis D. trachea

4. Deamination of proteins occurs MAINLY in the 4.____
   A. small intestine B. liver
   C. spleen D. pancreas

5. The products of fat digestion are absorbed by the 5.____
   A. capillaries in the villi
   B. lacteals in the villi
   C. capillaries in the stomach walls
   D. gall bladder

6. About 70% of the energy from glucose oxidation is used 6.____
   A. as heat
   B. for contracting muscles
   C. to produce nerve impulses
   D. to cause gland cells to secrete

7. In the process of respiration in a plant, 7.____
   A. potential energy is stored
   B. protein is synthesized
   C. stored food is utilized
   D. chlorophyll is necessary

8. The glomeruli are MOST closely related to the system involved in 8.____
   A. reproduction B. digestion
   C. support and movement D. excretion

9. The liquid which collects in the cavity of Bowman's capsule is 9.___
   A. urine in concentrated form
   B. blood plasma minus plasma proteins
   C. freshly aerated blood
   D. used bile ready for excretion

10. Three of the following are chromosomal aberrations which are important in the origin of species. The one that is NOT is 10.___
   A. duplication
   B. translocation
   C. meiosis
   D. inversion

11. A trait determined by two identical alleles is said to be 11.___
   A. heterozygous
   B. homologous
   C. analagous
   D. homozygous

12. Three of the following responses in plants are brought about by the action of hormones. The response that is NOT brought about is the 12.___
   A. bending of a stem toward light
   B. inhibition of lateral bud development by a terminal bud
   C. growth of pollen tubes through the style
   D. movement of the specialized leaves of the Venus-flytrap

13. The hormone that controls the use of calcium in the body is secreted by the 13.___
   A. thyroid
   B. parathyroids
   C. pancreas
   D. adrenals

14. A *tropic* hormone is one that is secreted by an endocrine gland to 14.___
   A. regulate the temperature of the body
   B. regulate the metabolism of the body
   C. stimulate or inhibit the secretion of another endocrine gland
   D. produce a response to stress known as the general-adaptation syndrome

15. $C_{15}H_{11}O_4NI_4$ is the chemical formula of the hormone 15.___
   A. thyroxin
   B. testosterone
   C. adrenin
   D. insulin

16. The animal phylum that numbers about 723,000 species is the 16.___
   A. mollusca
   B. arthropeda
   C. protozoa
   D. chordata

17. Flatworms are USUALLY found in ponds or streams 17.___
   A. on the underside of objects
   B. free-swimming
   C. on the upper side of objects
   D. on the north side of objects

18. Of the following, three are larval stages in the life history of the liver fluke. The one that is NOT is the 18.____
A. redia B. cercaria
C. trocophore D. miracidium

19. The outer of the two membranes surrounding the embryo and fetus of mammals is the 19.____
A. chorion B. placenta C. amnion D. coelom

20. In the life cycle of the wheat rust, the spores that settle and germinate on the leaves of barberry bushes are known as 20.____
A. uredospores B. teliospores
C. basidiospores D. aeciospores

21. Plants whose leaves are generally fleshy and waterproofed are known as 21.____
A. hydrophytes B. bryophytes
C. mesophytes D. zerophytes

22. Under anaerobic conditions, yeast obtains energy through the process of 22.____
A. oxidation B. glycogenolysis
C. fermentation D. digestion

23. Antibodies that act on bacteria in such a way that phagocytes may more easily ingest them are known as 23.____
A. opsonins B. antitoxins
C. lysins D. agglutinins

24. Commensalism is the type of association between organisms which may be 24.____
A. helpful to both
B. helpful to one and harmful to the other
C. helpful to one and indifferent to the other
D. harmful to both

25. Gill slits in the embryos of mammals are regarded as evidence of the fact that the 25.____
A. embryo uses gills to breathe
B. adult mammals use gills to breathe
C. ancestors of mammals used gills to breathe
D. mammals of the future will develop gills

26. A shrub that flowers normally in the late fall is the 26.____
A. blueberry B. high bush cranberry
C. mock orange D. witch hazel

27. To secure epithelial cells from the inside of the cheek use 27.____
A. a sterilized needle
B. a sterilized coverslip
C. the blunt edge of a sterile scalpel
D. the blunt edge of a toothpick

28. In mounting butterflies, the pin is USUALLY inserted 28.___
A. between the head and thorax
B. near the bottom end of the abdomen
C. through the center of the thorax
D. through the right wing

29. To separate female drosophila for crossing, choose flies which have a ____ abdomen. 29.___
A. black-tipped B. broad-spotted
C. broad-striped D. small-spotted

30. A good place to get a supply of paramecia for culturing in the laboratory is in 30.___
A. a running stream B. a stagnant pond
C. brackish water D. the Hudson River

31. To obtain conjugation in the common bread mold (Rhizopus), it is necessary to have 31.___
A. asexual spores from different hyphae
B. plus and minus strains
C. two groups of sporangia
D. two mycelia

32. An adhesive which will affix paraffin sections or micro-organisms to slides is COMMONLY made from 32.___
A. egg albumin B. rubber cement
C. flour and water D. starch paste

33. Hay is USUALLY used in a medium for culturing 33.___
A. fruit flies B. protozoa
C. planaria D. molds

34. Wrinkled paraffin sections of tissues may be flattened by 34.___
A. adding alcohol
B. adding xylol
C. placing them on a warming table
D. using a detergent

35. To show the effect of an enzyme, one could use milk and 35.___
A. HCl B. pepsin C. rennin D. secretin

36. Cuttings which develop roots MOST quickly are those of 36.___
A. elm B. maple C. oak D. willow

37. In testing for glucose, one of the following is useful: 37.___
A. Benedict's solution B. Lugol's solution
C. nitric acid D. sucrose

38. The number of smooth peas to use with one wrinkled pea in a Riker mount which is to illustrate the mating of hybrids (smooth dominant, wrinkled recessive) is 38.___
A. one B. two C. three D. four

39. The species which has leaves lacking toothlike points is the 39.___
A. red oak B. white oak
C. American elm D. sugar maple

40. From an infusion of unwashed grapes in water, one may USUALLY get a good culture of 40.___
   A. euglena B. mixed ciliates
   C. paramecia D. yeast

41. To get a number of small plants from a leaf, one would use the leaf of 41.___
   A. Bryophyllum B. butter-and-eggs (Linaria)
   C. geranium D. ragweed

42. Of the following, the leaves which BEST show variation in form are 42.___
   A. elm B. flowering dogwood
   C. Norway maple D. sassafras

43. A coplin jar is GENERALLY used for 43.___
   A. copper-plating B. culturing protozoa
   C. staining slides D. storing preserved animals

44. A characteristic by which the male dog can be distinguished from the female is 44.___
   A. red tongue B. spot on the head
   C. very thick thumbs D. web-feet

45. The organ of Corti is found in the 45.___
   A. adrenal gland B. ear
   C. eye D. liver

46. A chemical used to dehydrate and clear specimens is 46.___
   A. alcohol B. methyl green
   C. nigrosin D. xylol

47. A camera lucida is a device that is helpful in 47.___
   A. clearing objects for microscopic study
   B. making drawings of microscopic objects
   C. making lantern slide transparencies
   D. taking photomicrographs

48. The motion of small cocci in a sealed hanging drop is GENERALLY due to 48.___
   A. amoeboid motion B. action of flagellae
   C. Brownian movement D. ciliary movement

49. For demonstrating centrosomes and spindles, a laboratory assistant should make available slides of 49.___
   A. early cleavage stages of whitefish eggs
   B. human cheek epithelial cells
   C. mitosis in onion root tips
   D. pollen mother cells in sections of anthers

50. A substance that is NOT used in the modern treatment of severe burns is 50.___
   A. blood B. cortisone
   C. penicillin D. tannic acid

KEY (CORRECT ANSWERS)

1. C	11. D	21. D	31. B	41. A
2. D	12. D	22. C	32. A	42. D
3. A	13. B	23. A	33. B	43. C
4. B	14. C	24. C	34. C	44. C
5. B	15. A	25. C	35. C	45. B
6. A	16. B	26. D	36. D	46. D
7. C	17. A	27. D	37. A	47. B
8. D	18. C	28. C	38. C	48. C
9. B	19. A	29. C	39. B	49. A
10. C	20. C	30. B	40. D	50. D

TEST 3

DIRECTIONS: Each question or incomplete statement is followed by several suggested answers or completions. Select the one that BEST answers the question or completes the statement. *PRINT THE LETTER OF THE CORRECT ANSWER IN THE SPACE AT THE RIGHT.*

1. Which one of the following genuses was the result of a hoax? 1.____
   A. Eoanthropus B. Pithecanthropus
   C. Dryopithecus D. Sinanthropus

2. Enucleate erythrocytes are characteristic of which one of the following? 2.____
   A. Reptiles B. Fish
   C. Amphibians D. Mammals

3. Beta particles are 3.____
   A. protons B. neutrons
   C. electrons D. neutrons and protons

4. Hiccups are a result of spasmodic, involuntary contractions of the 4.____
   A. stomach muscles B. diaphragm
   C. abdominal muscles D. rib muscles

5. Genes are composed PRINCIPALLY of 5.____
   A. DNA B. ATP C. 2-4D D. hormones

6. The type of kidney found in fully matured reptiles, birds, and mammals is the 6.____
   A. mesonephros B. ananephros
   C. metanephros D. pronephros

7. The taiga is practically absent in the 7.____
   A. southern hemisphere B. northern part of Siberia
   C. mountains of India D. Burmese jungle

8. Variations in the colors of wheat kernels are BEST ascribed to the effects of 8.____
   A. xenia B. maternal inheritance
   C. multiple alleles D. photoperidism

9. The actual incidence of hemophilia is less than the theoretically predictable level because 9.____
   A. hemophilia is sex-linked
   B. of adverse marriage selection pressure against hemophiliacs
   C. the gene for hemophilia is recessive
   D. homozygosity is seldom found in the female

10. The frequency of crossing-over of genes tends to vary 10.___
A. inversely with the distance between genes in allelic chromosomes
B. inversely with the number of genes near the centromere
C. directly with the character of the gene
D. inversely with the increasing complexity of the organism

11. Certain ultraviolet radiations are an effective agent for mutations PRINCIPALLY because 11.___
A. they produce thermal effects
B. they can be easily administered
C. nucleoproteins absorb some ultraviolet radiations
D. they may produce hemolysis

12. Of the following diseases, the one that is seriously affecting the rabbit population is 12.___
A. glanders
B. malta fever
C. elephantiasis
D. myxomatosis

13. The human embryo's placenta is derived from the 13.___
A. decidua vera
B. chorion
C. amnion
D. corpus luteum

14. The structures that produce sex cells in the prothallium are 14.___
A. anthers and archegonia
B. ovaries and anthers
C. testes and archegonia
D. antheridia and archegonia

15. The thyrotrophic hormone is produced by the 15.___
A. thyroid
B. thymus
C. pituitary
D. adrenal

16. Smooth muscle cells are innervated by the 16.___
A. peripheral nervous system
B. parasympathetic nerves
C. central nervous system
D. autonomic nervous system

17. Of the following, the one which is a hormone which acts to produce secondary sex characteristics of the male is 17.___
A. pitocin
B. gonadotrophin II
C. androsterone
D. estradiol

18. Meiosis occurs in the spirogyra 18.___
A. as the zygospore germinates
B. in preparation for conjugation
C. during the vegetative stage
D. as the protoplasmic bridges form

19. Egestion in planaria takes place through the 19.___
A. anus
B. flame cells
C. mouth
D. collar cells

20. Experimental evidence shows that the replication of DNA molecules occurs essentially during the 20.___
A. interphase
B. late prophase
C. metaphase
D. early anaphase

21. Striated muscle tissue is called a syncytium because the fibers contain many 21.___
   A. myofibrils B. light and dark bands
   C. transverse stripes D. nuclei

22. The basic chemical formula for starch is 22.___
   A. $(C_6H_{10}O_5)n$ B. $(C_6H_{12}O_6)n$
   C. $C_{12}H_{22}O_{11}$ D. $C_6H_{12}O_6$

23. Of the following, an animal with an evertible alimentary structure is the 23.___
   A. hydra B. dogfish C. amphioxus D. molgula

24. The branched type of gastrovascular cavity is well-exemplified by a 24.___
   A. planaria B. hydra C. sponge D. tapeworm

25. The sexual generation of obelia is the 25.___
   A. zooid B. planula C. hydrotheca D. medusa

26. Chlorophyll may be extracted from leaves by boiling the leaves in 26.___
   A. alcohol B. benzene
   C. dilute acetic acid D. water

27. To dehydrate a specimen, it is BEST to use 27.___
   A. absolute alcohol B. gum arabic
   C. turpentine D. xylol

28. To destroy sucking insects on laboratory plants, it is BEST to use 28.___
   A. flit B. rotenone
   C. soap solution D. 2-4D

29. The thoracic duct is part of the 29.___
   A. heart B. lymphatic system
   C. respiratory system D. umbilical cord

30. Of the following, the substance which should NOT be used to slow down the activity of paramecia on a microscope slide is 30.___
   A. absorbent cotton B. ether
   C. lens paper D. methyl cellulose

31. The oil used with an oil-immersion microscope is 31.___
   A. cedarwood B. clove
   C. light machine D. olive

32. Frogs may be prepared for dissection by 32.___
   A. boiling them gently B. etherizing them
   C. freezing them D. soaking in formaldehyde

33. Nitrogen-fixing bacteria may be found on the roots of 33.___
   A. clover B. geranium
   C. sunflower D. timothy

34. Of the following, the BEST substance to use to reveal the cell membrane in onion cells is 34.___
A. concentrated saline B. ink
C. iodine stain D. Wright's stain

35. Chloroplasts may be seen by setting up a microscope demonstration of 35.___
A. elodea cells B. leaf epidermis cells
C. onion skin cells D. paramecia

36. Scarification is used in 36.___
A. planting seeds
B. pollinating flowers
C. preparing seeds for planting
D. preparing the seed bed

37. To demonstrate the movement of cytoplasmic structures, one might BEST use cells of 37.___
A. elodea B. geranium C. potato D. the cheek

38. Of the following, the plant which would be a POOR choice for a freshwater aquarium is 38.___
A. cabomba B. elodea C. fucus D. vallismeria

39. To pith a frog, 39.___
A. cut off its head
B. insert a needle in its brain
C. rub mild acid on its leg
D. stimulate with an electric current

40. Crowded cultures in which the food supply has diminished USUALLY result in cannibalism in 40.___
A. amoeba B. blepharisma
C. paramecium D. vorticella

41. Zugospores can be demonstrated in 41.___
A. amphioxus B. bacillus subtilis
C. paramecium D. spirogyra

42. Pure agar contains sufficient nutrient material to culture 42.___
A. few, if any, organisms B. most algae
C. most bacteria D. most molds

43. An example of a motile unicellular plant is a 43.___
A. coccus B. desmid C. diatom D. yeast

44. A good loop for bacteriological work may be made of 44.___
A. copper B. catgut C. invar D. nichrome

45. Petri dishes may BEST be sterilized before use in 45.___
A. the Arnold sterilizer B. the autoclave
C. the hot air oven D. lysol

46. In order to demonstrate protoplasmic movement, it is good practice, before placing a slide of elodea under the microscope, to 46.___

A. add a few drops of a paramecium culture
B. expose the plant to an electric light
C. keep the plant at a low temperature
D. keep the plant in the dark

47. Under similar conditions, the SLOWEST moving protozoan in the following group would be 47.___
A. ameba B. blepharisma
C. colpoda D. paramecium

48. Radiocarbon 14 dating provides a timetable that covers the last ____ years. 48.___
A. few thousand B. few hundred thousand
C. million D. ten million

49. Bacteria GENERALLY reproduce by 49.___
A. conjugation B. fertilization
C. fission D. vegetative propagation

50. The gland whose removal prevents metamorphosis in the frog is the 50.___
A. adrenal B. pancreas C. pineal D. thyroid

KEY (CORRECT ANSWERS)

1. A	11. C	21. D	31. A	41. D
2. D	12. D	22. A	32. B	42. A
3. C	13. B	23. B	33. A	43. C
4. B	14. D	24. A	34. A	44. D
5. A	15. C	25. D	35. A	45. C
6. C	16. D	26. A	36. C	46. B
7. A	17. C	27. A	37. A	47. A
8. C	18. A	28. B	38. C	48. A
9. B	19. C	29. B	39. B	49. C
10. A	20. A	30. B	40. B	50. D

TEST 4

DIRECTIONS: Each question or incomplete statement is followed by several suggested answers or completions. Select the one that BEST answers the question or completes the statement. *PRINT THE LETTER OF THE CORRECT ANSWER IN THE SPACE AT THE RIGHT.*

1. Pollen grains may be made to germinate on a slide containing 1.___
   A. auxin B. hydroponic solution
   C. sugar solution D. thyroxin

2. After use, the oil-immersion lens of a microscope should be cleaned gently with 2.___
   A. xylol B. dilute sodium hydroxide
   C. dilute sulfuric acid D. glycerine

3. When cheek cells are to be removed from microscopic study in the laboratory, one should employ a(n) 3.___
   A. dissecting needle B. sharp scalpel
   C. toothpick D. microtome

4. A slide of plant cells may be made readily by using 4.___
   A. carrot B. corn stalk
   C. onion D. potato

5. Bread mold will grow MOST satisfactorily if the bread is 5.___
   A. kept dry B. kept moist
   C. sterilized D. kept in the sun

6. In a biology demonstration, sterile petri dishes are exposed. One dish is left unexposed in order to 6.___
   A. reduce the cost of the demonstration
   B. conserve materials
   C. have a control
   D. have a spare dish in the event of emergency

7. Of the following, the one that is NOT used as a general stain is 7.___
   A. Lugol's solution B. methylene blue
   C. gentian violet D. Benedict's solution

8. In sterilizing agar, an autoclave is heated to 15 pounds pressure for *approximately* 8.___
   A. 2 minutes B. 20 minutes C. 2 hours D. 20 hours

9. A bell jar model of the lungs can be made to demonstrate inhalation by _____ the rubber sheet. 9.___
   A. heating B. lowering C. piercing D. raising

10. Three substances found in gastric juices are 10.___
   A. H_2O, pepsin, HCl B. H_2O, pepsin, H_2SO_4
   C. H_2O, ptyalin, HCl D. H_2O, ptyalin, H_2SO_4

11. Emulsification of fat in the intestine is aided by a liquid called 11.____
    A. chyme B. chyle C. bile D. lacteal

12. In demonstrating the presence of starch in foods, the one substance that would NOT be suitable is 12.____
    A. eggplant B. asparagus
    C. macaroni D. potato

13. In a demonstration of photosynthesis, one leaf of a geranium plant is covered with black paper in order to 13.____
    A. protect the leaf from injury
    B. show the importance of light
    C. transmit monochromatic light
    D. show that the plant is healthy

14. Digestion of starch in a test tube can be demonstrated by adding 14.____
    A. albumin B. glucose
    C. artificial gastric juice D. saliva

15. Capillary circulation of blood may be demonstrated readily by using a 15.____
    A. white rat's tail
    B. goldfish tail
    C. drosophila fly's wing
    D. lens of a frog's eye

16. Plants that are kept under a bell jar 16.____
    A. need extra minerals
    B. need additional oxygen
    C. do not need to be watered frequently
    D. shrink in size

17. In the laboratory, live frogs are BEST kept in healthy condition by housing them in 17.____
    A. a moist chamber B. a hot-air oven
    C. agar agar solution D. an autoclave

18. In testing for the presence of simple sugar, one should use 18.____
    A. ACTH B. Benedict's solution
    C. isotonic solution D. cortisone

19. The movement of protozoa on a microscope slide may be slowed down satisfactorily by using 19.____
    A. Duco cement B. ammonia solution
    C. strong salt solution D. teased lens paper

20. Among angiosperms, the male gametophytes are MOST closely associated with 20.____
    A. carpels B. the nucellus
    C. pollen grains D. sporophylls

21. Of the following, the one with the MOST dominant sporophyte generation is 21.____
    A. Spirogyra B. the bird moss
    C. the Christmas fern D. the white pine

22. The part of the microscope that controls the amount of entering light is called the 22.___
A. diaphragm B. eyepiece C. nosepiece D. stage

23. The gland that controls the other ductless glands in the body is the 23.___
A. adrenal B. parathyroid
C. pituitary D. thyroid

24. Even after being blown over on its side, a plant will grow upward. This is an example of behavior known as 24.___
A. negative geotropism B. negative heliotropism
C. positive geotropism D. a reflex act

25. The scientist who experimented with conditioned reflexes was 25.___
A. von Behring B. Hooke
C. Pavlov D. Lamarck

26. An insectivorous water plant is the 26.___
A. bladderwort B. liverwort
C. spleenwort D. spiderwort

27. An example of a fruit is a 27.___
A. corn kernel B. chestnut
C. pea D. peach pit

28. According to recent studies, the oxygen given off during photosynthesis is derived from the oxygen contained in 28.___
A. chlorophyll B. carbon dioxide
C. glyceric acid D. water

29. A branch root starts its formation in the 29.___
A. cork cambium B. cortex
C. endodermis D. pericycle

30. Three of the following plants produce archegonia during reproduction. The plant that does NOT is 30.___
A. Marchantia B. Pinus
C. Polytrichum D. Pisum

31. An example of close interdependence in a biotic environment is exhibited by 31.___
A. oak and moth B. corn and cornborer
C. maple and bee D. termite and protozoa

32. Thin leaves, lack of xylem, and lack of root hairs are characteristics of an ecological group of plants called 32.___
A. hydrophytes B. mesophytes
C. pteriodophytes D. xerophytes

33. Colchicine applied to plants may produce variations in offspring as a result of induced 33.___
A. chiasmata B. translocation
C. polyploidy D. diploidy

34. The *one-gene, one-enzyme, one-action* hypothesis is supported by the artificial production of mutants in a mold called 34.____
   A. Aneurin B. Neurolemma
   C. Neuroptera D. Neurospora

35. The superior size and vigor of a mule are results of a biological effect called 35.____
   A. heterosis B. hybridization
   C. natural selection D. poikilothermia

36. A pubic symphysis is found in three of the following animals. It is NOT found in the 36.____
   A. cat B. toad C. pigeon D. lizard

37. A water vascular system and tube feet are found in an animal called the 37.____
   A. sea cucumber B. sea anemone
   C. cod D. squid

38. Two men who held opposing points of view regarding the theory of spontaneous generation were 38.____
   A. Redi and Spallanzani B. Pasteur and Pouchet
   C. Koch and Tyndall D. Schwann and Schulze

39. Aerobic bacteria that can also live in the absence of air are said to be 39.____
   A. anomalous B. facultative
   C. involutional D. pleomorphic

40. The organism which causes tuberculosis is MOST closely related to the organism which causes 40.____
   A. bacillary dysentery B. bubonic plague
   C. leprosy D. whooping cough

Questions 41-45.

DIRECTIONS: After reading and studying the statement that follows, answer Questions 41 through 45, inclusive.

Chemical investigations show that during muscle contraction, the store of organic phosphates in the muscle fibers is altered as energy is released. In doing so, the organic phosphates (chiefly adenosine triphosphate and phospho-creatine) are transformed anaerobically to organic compounds plus phosphates. As soon as the organic phosphates begin to break down in muscle contraction, the glycogen in the muscle fibers also transforms into lactic acid plus free energy; this energy the muscle fiber uses to return the organic compounds plus phosphates into high-energy organic phosphates ready for another contraction. In the presence of oxygen, the lactic acid from the glycogen decomposition is changed also. About one-fifth of it is oxidized to form water and carbon dioxide and to yield another supply of energy. This time the energy is used to transform the remaining four-fifths of the lactic acid into glycogen again.

41. The energy for muscle contraction comes directly from the 41.____
A. breakdown of the organic phosphates
B. resynthesis of adenosine triphosphate
C. breakdown of glycogen into lactic acid
D. oxidation of lactic acid

42. Lactic acid does NOT accumulate in a muscle that 42.____
A. is in a state of lacking oxygen
B. has an ample supply of oxygen
C. is in a state of fatigue
D. is repeatedly being stimulated

43. The energy for the resynthesis of adenosine triphosphate and phosphocreatine comes from the 43.____
A. oxidation of lactic acid
B. synthesis of organic phosphates
C. change from glycogen to lactic acid
D. resynthesis of glycogen

44. The energy for the resynthesis of glycogen comes from the 44.____
A. breakdown of organic phosphates
B. resynthesis of organic phosphates
C. change occurring in one-fifth of the lactic acid
D. change occurring in four-fifths of the lactic acid

45. The breakdown of the organic phosphates into organic compounds plus phosphates is an ____ reaction. 45.____
A. anabolic reaction
B. aerobic
C. endothermic
D. anaerobic

Questions 46-50.

DIRECTIONS: In each of the following Questions 46 through 50, three terms are correctly associated and one term is incorrectly associated with the word(s) or phrases that follow. In each case, select the term that is INCORRECTLY associated with the word(s) or phrase that follows it.

46. A. hilum - seed scar B. hypocotyl - endosperm 46.____
C. plumule - embryo leaves D. testa - seed coat

47. A. thallophyte - chlorella B. bryophyte - club moss 47.____
C. spermatophyte-bloodroot D. pteridophyte - bracken

48. A. bulb - Easter lily B. tuber - hyacinth 48.____
C. leaf cutting-bryophyllum D. rhizome - lily of the valley

49. A. scarlet fever-Dick test B. syphilis - Kahn test 49.____
B. typhoid fever-Widal test D. yellow fever - Biuret test

50. A. drupe - apple B. berry - tomato 50.____
C. legume - locust tree D. samara - ash

KEY (CORRECT ANSWERS)

1. C	11. C	21. D	31. D	41. A
2. A	12. B	22. A	32. A	42. B
3. C	13. B	23. C	33. C	43. C
4. C	14. D	24. A	34. D	44. C
5. B	15. B	25. C	35. A	45. D
6. C	16. C	26. A	36. C	46. B
7. D	17. A	27. A	37. A	47. B
8. B	18. B	28. D	38. B	48. B
9. B	19. D	29. D	39. B	49. D
10. A	20. C	30. D	40. C	50. A

TEST 5

DIRECTIONS: Each question or incomplete statement is followed by several suggested answers or completions. Select the one that BEST answers the question or completes the statement. *PRINT THE LETTER OF THE CORRECT ANSWER IN THE SPACE AT THE RIGHT.*

1. Which one of the following FIRST proposed the side chain theory of immunity? 1.____
   A. Koch B. Ehrlich
   C. Von Behring D. Park

2. Which one of the following is caused by the toxin found MAINLY in preserved foods, either home or commercially prepared? 2.____
   A. Undulant fever B. Botulism
   C. Ptomaine poisoning D. Bacillary dysentery

3. The vaccine known as BCG is used to produce immunity against 3.____
   A. tuberculosis B. typhoid
   C. malaria D. mumps

4. Which one of the following diseases is water-borne? 4.____
   A. Undulant fever B. Cholera
   C. Malaria D. Bubonic plague

5. A toxoid is used to produce immunity to which one of the following? 5.____
   A. Smallpox B. Poliomyelitis
   C. Tuberculosis D. Diphtheria

6. Of the following, the discovery which contributed MOST directly to the success of Salk's work was that involving 6.____
   A. successful tissue culture techniques
   B. crystallization of tobacco mosaic
   C. successful use of electrophoresis
   D. passing viruses through a porcelain filter

7. The human fetus depends for MOST of its existence on a type of nutrition called 7.____
   A. trophoblastic B. hemotrophic
   C. embryotrophic D. blastocystic

8. From which one of the following embryonic tissues are the kidneys developed? 8.____
   A. Blastopore B. Ectoderm
   C. Mesoderm D. Endoderm

9. Which one of the following is used to identify the Fuelgen reaction? 9.____
   A. Xanthophylls B. DNA proteins
   C. Grana D. Lipids

10. In which part of the *skull* is the middle lamella found? 10.___
  A. Nucleoplasm B. Cell wall
  C. Cytoplasm D. Cell membrane

11. Of the following, a plant which may play an important role in space travel is the 11.___
  A. spirogyra B. oedogonium
  C. chlamydomonas D. chlorella

12. Recently, a prize in medicine for discoveries concerning the physical mechanisms of stimulation within the cochlea was awarded to 12.___
  A. Lederberg B. Von Bekesy
  C. Tatum D. Calvin

13. A common mold that is used to show the effects of genes on enzyme production is the 13.___
  A. saprolegnia B. ergot
  C. aspergillus D. neurospora

14. Human mutations caused by radiation from nuclear fall-out are expected to be produced MAINLY through the action of 14.___
  A. phosphorus P^{32} B. iodine I^{131}
  C. strontium Sr^{90} D. carbon C^{14}

15. Which one of the following is the CHIEF agent of erosion? 15.___
  A. Running water B. Air
  C. Animals D. Plants

16. Of the following, the MOST effective method of returning minerals to the soil is 16.___
  A. stripping B. terracing
  C. contour plowing D. crop rotation

17. Which one of the following organic compounds is NOT a polysaccharide? 17.___
  A. Maltose B. Starch
  C. Cellulose D. Glycogen

18. The process of building up complex carbohydrates from simple sugars is known as 18.___
  A. hydrolysis B. condensation
  C. peptide linkage D. induction

19. Which one of the following statements does NOT apply to the tracheophytes? 19.___
  A. They possess vascular tissue.
  B. The sporphyte generation is dominant over the gametophyte.
  C. The embryo forms in an archegonium.
  D. They are made up of mosses and ferns.

20. The body of a complex fungus such as Rhizopus nigricans is called a 20.___
  A. rhizoid B. mycelium C. hypha D. stolon

21. Cyclosis may be demonstrated by using fresh slides of which one of the following? 21.____
   A. Paramecium   B. Onion epidermis
   C. Elodea leaf   D. Root tips

22. Which one of the following movements of plants illustrates the behavior of plant hormones? 22.____
   A. Rapid drooping of a mimosa plant
   B. "Sleep movements" of a clover
   C. Leaf-closing movements of a Venus' flytrap
   D. Turning of geranium leaves toward light

23. The parasympathetic system 23.____
   A. speeds up the heartbeat
   B. is composed of chains of ganglia parallel to the spinal cord
   C. produces cholinesterase to stimulate muscle contraction
   D. opposes the action of the sympathetic system

24. Of the following, the one which is a hormone produced in the pituitary gland that plays a role in growth is 24.____
   A. luteotropin   B. somatotropin
   C. oxytocin   D. vasopressin

25. Which of the following instruments can measure the activities of the cerebral cortex? 25.____
   A. Electroencephalograph   B. Sphygmomanometer
   C. Pneumograph   D. Electrocardiograph

26. Assume that the diploid number of chromosomes is 48 in humans, and that there is tetrad formation in human oogenesis. 26.____
   The number of tetrads that form in the metaphase of the first maturation division will be
   A. 12   B. 24   C. 48   D. 96

Questions 27-29.

DIRECTIONS: After reading the statement that follows, answer Questions 27 through 29, respectively.

In peas, yellow (Y) is dominant over green (y)
Tall (T) is dominant over short (t)
Red (R) is dominant over white (r)

27. If a pea plant of genotype YyRRTt is self-pollinated, the number of types of gametes formed is 27.____
   A. 2   B. 4   C. 6   D. 8

28. The expected proportion of offspring with phenotype Yellow, Red, Tall would be 28.____
   A. 1/4   B. 9/16   C. 27/64   D. 9/64

29. The possible production of a phenotype green, red, short, is expected from the genetic principle called 29.____
   A. the gene theory   B. incomplete dominance
   C. independent assortment   D. linkage

30. In a Himalayan rabbit, the nose, ears, tail, and paws are black. The rest of the fur is white. This is PROBABLY due to the fact that 30.____
   A. these parts are too cool for gene action to produce melanin
   B. peripheral circulation is poor
   C. in most of the skin there is an absence of tyrosinase that is needed to produce pigment
   D. the general skin temperature is too high for production of pigment

31. A flower of genotype CcRr is self-pollinated. The offspring produce phenotypes in the ratio of 9 colored and 7 white. 31.____
This indicates
   A. that the law of dominance does not work in this flower
   B. that colored is incompletely dominant over white
   C. Morgan's "single chain" theory of gene loci applies
   D. that both dominant genes must be present to produce colored phenotypes

32. Embryonic structures destined to give rise to muscles are known as 32.____
   A. myeloblasts B. myelocytes
   C. myonemes D. myotomes

33. The two MOST closely related birds are 33.____
   A. blue jay and grackle B. flicker and sandpiper
   C. hermit thrush and veery D. crow and ovenbird

34. Of the following pairs, the ONLY correct association between the organism and its color is 34.____
   A. blepharisma - pink B. vorticella - blue
   C. chilomonas - green D. stentor - yellow

35. Of the following fossils, the one that is MOST closely related to the Cro-Magnon man is 35.____
   A. Ecanthropus B. Pithecanthropus
   C. Homo neanderthalenis D. Sinanthropus

36. A recently discovered living *link* between fish and land animals was a crossopterygian fish called 36.____
   A. latimeria B. pelicosaur
   C. lungfish D. ornithorhyncus

37. Reptiles were the dominant forms of life during the period called 37.____
   A. Carboniferous B. Cenozoic
   C. Cretaceous D. Permian

38. The similar shapes and adaptations of a pyterodactyl and a pigeon are examples of 38.____
   A. acquired characteristics
   B. analogous skeletal structures
   C. convergent evolution
   D. microevolution

39. An example of morphological isogamy associated with physiological heterogamy occurs in 39.____
   A. Elodea B. Ulothrix
   C. Spirogyra D. Polytrichum

40. The epididymis 40.____
   A. is a passageway for sperm from testes to vas deferens
   B. causes precipitation of calcium by osteoblasts
   C. secretes a fluid necessary for the inactivation of flagellae
   D. causes growth of endometrial lining following menstruation

41. Of the following, the BEST example of a cleodoic egg is the egg of a 41.____
   A. frog B. guppy C. mouse D. sparrow

42. The primary *organizer* in amphibian development is found near the 42.____
   A. animal pole B. dorsal lip of the blastopore
   C. myelencephalon D. optic vesicle

43. A structure formed during the development of seals, turtles, and robins but NOT in salamanders is a(n) 43.____
   A. amnion B. optic vesicle
   C. pronephros D. telencephalon

44. An early stage in the development of primate embryos is the formation of an inner cell mass in a structure called a 44.____
   A. blastocoel B. blastocyst
   C. blastula D. neurula

45. The cytosine-guanine and thymine-adenine linkages form important *rungs* in the ladder-like construction of nuclear material called 45.____
   A. adenosine triphosphate
   B. adenosine diphosphate
   C. desoxyribose nucleic acid
   D. para-amino salicylic acid

46. An epiphytic plant is the 46.____
   A. cactus B. date palm
   C. pineapple D. tropical orchid

47. A fungus that grows CHIEFLY on trees and logs rather than in soil is the 47.____
   A. coral fungus B. deadly Amanita
   C. puffball D. sulphur mushroom

48. The physiological relationship between a fungus mycelium and the roots of the white pine is called 48.____
   A. ascolichen B. mycorrhiza
   C. myxomycete D. rhizobium

49. In the broad-leaved forest areas of the eastern United States, the phenomenon known as succession ends with the climax trees 49.___
   A. elm, cottonwood
   B. beech, maple
   C. ash, oak
   D. hickory, sycamore

50. The plant that blooms EARLIEST in the year is 50.___
   A. Indian Tobacco
   B. Jack-in-the-Pulpit
   C. skunk cabbage
   D. wild cucumber

KEY (CORRECT ANSWERS)

1. B	11. D	21. C	31. D	41. D
2. B	12. B	22. D	32. D	42. B
3. A	13. D	23. D	33. C	43. A
4. B	14. C	24. B	34. A	44. B
5. D	15. A	25. A	35. C	45. C
6. A	16. D	26. B	36. A	46. D
7. C	17. A	27. B	37. C	47. D
8. C	18. B	28. B	38. C	48. B
9. B	19. D	29. C	39. C	49. B
10. B	20. B	30. D	40. A	50. C

EXAMINATION SECTION
TEST 1

DIRECTIONS: Each question or incomplete statement is followed by several suggested answers or completions. Select the one that BEST answers the question or completes the statement. *PRINT THE LETTER OF THE CORRECT ANSWER IN THE SPACE AT THE RIGHT.*

1. Genetical experiments with Neurospora have shown that 1.___
   A. heterosis is based upon enzymes
   B. pure line selection minimizes variations
   C. inbreeding is generally harmful
   D. genes control the production of many enzymes

2. Severing the vagus nerve 2.___
   A. augments the flow of gastric juices
   B. completely stops the flow of gastric juices
   C. reduces the flow of gastric juices
   D. stops the production of gastrin

3. From the ovary, the egg of the mammal next goes into the 3.___
   A. follicle B. abdominal cavity
   C. oviduct D. uterus

4. All of the following may be caused by virus EXCEPT 4.___
   A. poliomyelitis B. influenza
   C. malaria D. smallpox

5. The female drosophila can be distinguished from the male by noting that the 5.___
   A. female possesses a fringe of black bristles in the uppermost joint of the first pair of legs
   B. tip of the abdomen in the female is elongated and more rounded
   C. first pair of legs in the male is longer than in the female
   D. female has dark bristles in the third pair of legs

6. Lichens are composites, consisting of fungi and 6.___
   A. bacteria B. algae C. mosses D. protozoa

7. The MAIN tissue in the pyloric sphincter is 7.___
   A. muscle B. epithelium
   C. connective D. nerve

8. The crayfish is a member of the class 8.___
   A. chilopoda B. arachnida
   C. arthropoda D. crustacea

9. The structure in a mammal that carries sperm cells for the testes to the urethra is the organ called 9.___
   A. seminiferous tubule B. urachis
   C. ureter D. vas deferens

10. The tubercle bacillus is BEST stained with 10.___
   A. hematoxylin B. acid fast stain
   C. chromic acid D. glacial acetic acid

11. Stock cultures of drosophila should be kept in rooms which have no greater range in temperature than from 11.___
   A. 15-20°C B. 20-25°C C. 25-30°C D. 35-40°C

12. The flagella of collar cells waft small particles of food into the collars whence the food passes into gastric vacuoles in the individual cells of the 12.___
   A. hydra B. planaria C. starfish D. sponge

13. Of the following, the one NEVER found in invertebrates is 13.___
   A. coelom B. triploblastic embryo
   C. dorsal nerve cord D. red blood corpuscles

14. Enzymes can BEST be classified as which one of the following? 14.___
   A. Carbohydrates B. Inorganic trace elements
   C. Proteins D. Phospholipid-nucleic acids

15. Antocatalysis in cytology refers to 15.___
   A. protein digestion B. hormonal activity
   C. bacterial disintegration D. gene duplication

16. In passing to the lungs, air passes in order through the 16.___
   A. larynx, pharynx, bronchioles, and bronchi
   B. pharynx, larynx, bronchi, and bronchioles
   C. pharynx, larynx, bronchioles, and bronchi
   D. larynx, pharynx, bronchi, and bronchioles

17. Of the following larvae, the one which may pass through snail and fish before entering the human body are those of the 17.___
   A. Chinese liver fluke B. trichina
   C. hookworm D. tapeworm

18. Bread mold illustrates the type of nutrition which is 18.___
   A. holophytic B. parasitic
   C. xerophytic D. saprophytic

19. The ciliary muscle is used for the process of 19.___
   A. locomotion B. food transportation
   C. accommodation D. dust removal

20. Infection may be spread rapidly in the mastoid bone because of which one of the following characteristics? 20.___
   A. Spongy in texture
   B. Close to the cerebrum
   C. Unable to circulate antibodies
   D. Essentially non-living in composition

21. Haversian systems are found in 21.___
A. fibrous cartilage
B. elastic cartilage
C. bone
D. areolar tissue

22. Of the following, an example of evolutionary stagnation is/are 22.___
A. crossopterygians
B. lungfish
C. archaeopteryx
D. Cro-Magnon man

23. In the chemical expression, A - Ⓟ~Ⓟ, the symbol ~ represents 23.___
A. release of gases
B. precipitation
C. high energy bond
D. low energy bond

24. Phage is parasitic on 24.___
A. bacteria
B. virus
C. molds
D. rickettsia

25. Pasteur's famous experiment with two groups of sheep and other cattle demonstrated the success of his vaccine against 25.___
A. rabies
B. cholera
C. tuberculosis
D. anthrax

26. The study of living things in relation to their environment is known as 26.___
A. demography
B. ecology
C. paleontology
D. phylogeny

27. The MOST likely sequence of communities is 27.___
A. evergreens, grass, sand, beech-maple
B. grass, evergreens, beech-maple, sand
C. sand, grass, evergreens, beech-maple
D. sand, evergreens, grass, beech-maple

28. The relation of termites and their intestinal flagellates is a classic example of 28.___
A. amensalism
B. commensalism
C. parasitism
D. symbiosis

29. The evolution of man is essentially a story of the period known as 29.___
A. Devonian
B. Miocene
C. Eocene
D. Pleistocene

30. A fossil man formerly accepted by MOST anthropologists and shown to be a scientific hoax is the _____ man. 30.___
A. Peking
B. Java
C. Neanderthal
D. Piltdown

31. The age of the earth is commonly and accurately estimated by means of the 31.___
A. thickness of earth's crust
B. amount of salt in the sea
C. rate of deposition of sedimentary rock
D. uranium-lead ratio

32. Fossils are USUALLY found in rocks classified as 32.___
A. metamorphic
B. igneous
C. conglomerate
D. sedimentary

33. A microscope whose ocular is marked 5x and whose objective is marked 10x produces a magnification of 33.___
A. 7.5
B. 15
C. 50
D. 500

34. In making an electrical connection for the use of film projectors, the BEST procedure to use is 34.___
A. either heavy plastic or heavy rubber wall plugs
B. only heavy plastic plugs
C. only heavy rubber plugs
D. whatever plugs are available

35. When liquids are heated in soft glass test tubes, the tube should be _____ on the outside and kept _____ in the flame. 35.___
A. dry; in motion
B. kept wet; in motion
C. kept dry; fixed
D. kept wet; fixed

36. When inserting a thistle tube through a rubber stopper, it is MOST advisable to grasp the thistle tube by the 36.___
A. bowl and use leverage to push it through the dry stopper
B. stem close to the stopper and push it through the dry stopper in a straight line motion
C. stem close to the stopper and push it through the wet stopper in a straight line motion
D. stem close to the stopper and push it through the wet stopper in a rotary motion

37. When a bunsen burner suddenly *strikes back*, the acceptable procedure is to 37.___
A. decrease the air supply
B. increase the air supply
C. increase the gas supply
D. turn off the gas

38. The malleus, incus, and stapes are 38.___
A. blood vessels
B. bones
C. muscles
D. nerves

39. Large storage bottles of dangerous acids should 39.___
A. be kept on the floor
B. contain only the diluted acids
C. be kept on the highest shelves out of reach
D. not be kept in stock

40. In preparing dilute sulphuric acid, prepare 40.___
A. large quantities at one time by adding the acid to the water
B. large quantities at one time by adding water to the concentrated acid
C. small quantities by adding the water to the acid, stirring all the while
D. the smallest quantity needed by adding the concentrated acid in small quantities to the water

41. Special precautions must be observed in handling all of the following acids EXCEPT 41.___
   A. citric
   B. nitric
   C. glacial acetic
   D. concentrated sulfuric

42. White phosphorus should 42.___
   A. be kept in stick form submerged in sand
   B. be immersed in kerosene in a stoppered bottle set in a tin of sand
   C. be kept under water in a stoppered bottle set in a tin of sand
   D. never be stored in a laboratory

Questions 43-50.

DIRECTIONS: In Questions 43 through 50, select the demonstration or laboratory exercise which utilizes ALL the materials listed to best advantage.

43. Microscopes, slides, cover slips, clover plants, jars of water, filter paper, dilute carbol fuchsin 43.___
   A. To become acquainted with the parts of the microscope
   B. To learn a technique in bacteriology
   C. To demonstrate root hairs
   D. To show the relationship between nitrogen-fixing bacteria and the host plant

44. Toothpicks, dilute methylene blue solution, microscopes, slides, cover slips 44.___
   A. To develop an interest in the use of the microscope
   B. To study the structure of an epithelial cell
   C. To study the structure of a smooth muscle cell
   D. To study the structure of a striated muscle cell

45. Microscopes, elodea leaves, slides, cover slips, 5% salt solution 45.___
   A. To show cytoplasmic streaming
   B. To show cytolsis
   C. To study mitosis
   D. To show plasmolysis

46. Test tubes, straws, phenolphthalein-sodium hydroxide mixture, watches 46.___
   A. To show effect of exercise upon the rate of oxidation
   B. To demonstrate osmosis
   C. To show rate of production of oxygen
   D. To show that CO_2 turns lime-water milky

47. Lima beans, rulers, large test tubes, test tube racks 47.___
To show
   A. Mendelian segregation
   B. that variation exhibits a normal range of distribution
   C. mechanics of grafting
   D. the law of chance

48. Bron-thymol blue, elodea, test tubes, rack, test tube holders, bunsen burner, matches, corks for test tubes
To show that plants
A. absorb carbon dioxide during photosynthesis
B. transpire excess water
C. absorb water during photosynthesis
D. give off oxygen

48.___

49. Orange juice, carrot juice, water, 2,6 dichlorophenolindophenol, test tubes, medicine droppers
To test for vitamin
A. A B. B C. C D. D

49.___

50. Ungerminated corn grains, germinating corn seedlings, iodine solution, Benedict's solution, bunsen burner, test tubes, test tube holder, knife, matches
A. To show that plants carry on digestion
B. To test corn grains for starch
C. To test corn grains for sugar
D. To test corn seedlings for sugar

50.___

KEY (CORRECT ANSWERS)

1. D	11. A	21. C	31. D	41. A
2. C	12. D	22. B	32. D	42. C
3. B	13. C	23. C	33. C	43. D
4. C	14. C	24. A	34. C	44. B
5. B	15. D	25. D	35. A	45. D
6. B	16. B	26. B	36. D	46. A
7. A	17. A	27. C	37. D	47. B
8. D	18. D	28. D	38. B	48. A
9. D	19. C	29. D	39. A	49. C
10. B	20. A	30. D	40. D	50. A

TEST 2

DIRECTIONS: Each question or incomplete statement is followed by several suggested answers or completions. Select the one that BEST answers the question or completes the statement. *PRINT THE LETTER OF THE CORRECT ANSWER IN THE SPACE AT THE RIGHT.*

1. Addison's disease may result from tubercular infection of the 1.___
   A. adrenal glands B. bones
   C. lymph nodes D. spleen

2. In a nearsighted person, the 2.___
   A. image is in focus behind the eyeball
   B. retina is too close to the lens
   C. lens is too concave
   D. eyeball is too long from lens to retina

3. The rods of the retina are MOST closely associated with 3.___
   A. the blind spot B. bright light vision
   C. color vision D. twilight vision

4. Plasmolysis refers to 4.___
   A. destruction of the plasma membrane
   B. increase of quantity of blood plasma
   C. loss of plasma from the blood
   D. shrinkage of protoplasm due to loss of water

5. The *anvil*, *hammer*, and *stirrup* refer to 5.___
   A. adaptations for pollination
   B. bones of the middle ear
   C. reflex arcs
   D. theory of immunity

6. Albinism in corn is an example of 6.___
   A. chimera B. inversion
   C. lethal character D. sex-linked character

7. The Archeopteryx possessed 7.___
   A. a toothless beak
   B. clawless wings
   C. tail feathers, but not a true tail
   D. a true tail with feathers on it

8. The stage in embryology at which the primitive gut is well-formed is called the 8.___
   A. blastula B. fistula C. gastrula D. morula

9. Diabetes insipidus is caused by 9.___
   A. insufficient secretion of insulin
   B. oversecretion of insulin
   C. insufficient secretion of vasopressin
   D. insufficient secretion of renin

10. The MOST conclusive line of evidence that biological evolution has actually occurred is 10.___
   A. common ancestry of vertebrates
   B. fossil records
   C. geographic isolation
   D. comparative anatomy

Questions 11-25.

DIRECTIONS: In each of Questions 11 through 25, there are two statements, I and II. You are to decide whether
   A. I and II are correct
   B. I and II are incorrect
   C. I is correct and II is incorrect
   D. I is incorrect and II is correct.
Of the four (4) choices below, each pair of sentences identifies the CORRECT combination. The plus sign (+) signifies a correct statement, the minus sign (-) an incorrect statement.

11. I. The gene for color blindness in man is located on the X chromosome. 11.___
   II. The gene for hemophilia in man is located on the Y chromosome.
   A. A+B+ B. A-B- C. A+B- D. A-B+

12. I. Angiosperms are more primitive than gymnosperms. 12.___
   II. Bryophytes are more primitive than pteridophytes.
   A. A+B+ B. A-B- C. A+B- D. A-B+

13. I. A cell plate is formed in dividing animal cells. 13.___
   II. Centrosomes have never been found in plant cells.
   A. A+B+ B. A-B- C. A+B- D. A-B+

14. I. The endosperm cells of a ripe corn seed have the diploid number of chromosomes. 14.___
   II. The embryo cells of a ripe corn have the diploid number of chromosomes.
   A. A+B+ B. A-B- C. A+B- D. A-B+

15. I. Drone bees develop parthenogenetically. 15.___
   II. Worker bees are sterile females.
   A. A+B+ B. A-B- C. A+B- D. A-B+

16. I. The excretory system of man develops from the ecto-derm. 16.___
   II. The nervous system of man develops from the mesoderm.
   A. A+B+ B. A-B- C. A+B- D. A-B+

17. I. Red corpuscles will burst when placed in a hypotonic solution. 17.___
   II. Red corpuscles will shrink when placed in an isotonic solution.
   A. A+B+ B. A-B- C. A+B- D. A-B+

18. I. Auricles have thinner walls than ventricles.
II. The right ventricle has thinner walls than the left ventricle.
A. A+B+ B. A-B- C. A+B- D. A-B+ 18.____

19. I. The union of isogametes is a type of asexual reproduction.
II. The union of heterogametes is a type of sexual reproduction.
A. A+B+ B. A-B- C. A+B- D. A-B+ 19.____

20. I. The part of a microscope on which the slide is placed for observation is called the base.
II. The lenses in the eyepiece usually have greater magnifying power than the lenses in the objectives.
A. A+B+ B. A-B- C. A+B- D. A-B+ 20.____

21. I. The life process by which the protoplasm of a cell increases is called absorption.
II. The sum total of the chemical and physical processes going on in a cell is called anabolism.
A. A+B+ B. A-B- C. A+B- D. A-B+ 21.____

22. I. The lichen is a parasite.
II. Nitrogen-fixing bacteria are saprophytes.
A. A+B+ B. A-B- C. A+B- D. A-B+ 22.____

23. I. The drooping of the leaves of the mimosa plant is effected by auxins.
II. The upward growth of a stem is an example of negative geotropism.
A. A+B+ B. A-B- C. A+B- D. A-B+ 23.____

24. I. It is more difficult to obtain a pure breed of animals with a dominant mutation than one with a recessive mutation.
II. In most instances, a mutation is beneficial to the organism in which it occurs.
A. A+B+ B. A-B- C. A+B- D. A-B+ 24.____

25. I. Bone is a type of connective tissue.
II. Glands are composed of epithelial tissue.
A. A+B+ B. A-B- C. A+B- D. A-B+ 25.____

26. Most scientific names of plants and animals have two parts, of which the second is the
A. variety B. genus C. species D. family 26.____

27. A working muscle under anaerobic conditions does NOT 27.____
A. use up glycogen reserves rapidly
B. accumulate lactic acid rapidly
C. accumulate inorganic phosphates
D. convert lactic acid into glycogen

28. Somatortraphin is the hormone of the pituitary gland which influences 28.___
A. use of sugar by cells
B. growth of the skeleton
C. maturing of the gonads
D. water content of the skeleton

29. Chordate animals display three unique features at some stage in their development - a notochord, a dorsal nerve cord, and 29.___
A. gill clefts
B. diaphragm
C. a closed circulatory system
D. a dorsally situated heart

30. The excretory organs (green glands) of the crayfish are located CLOSEST to which one of the following? 30.___
A. Midgut B. Heart C. Eyes D. Gonads

31. The relationship which exists between the shark and remora is 31.___
A. symbiosis B. commensalism
C. parasitism D. mutualism

32. Which one of the following is deposited in the cell wall of diatoms? 32.___
A. Silicon B. Lime C. Chitin D. Gelatin

33. Peyer's patches are located in the 33.___
A. pancreas B. nasopharynx
C. ileum D. hypothalamus

34. Secretin is produced by cells of the 34.___
A. liver B. ileum C. jejunum D. duodenum

35. A cephalothorax is characteristic of which one of the following? 35.___
A. Grasshopper B. Crayfish
C. Scorpion D. Centipede

36. Grana are constituents of 36.___
A. cytoplasmic granules B. chromatin granules
C. reticulocytes D. chloroplasts

37. Sucrose, during digestion, is broken down into 37.___
A. glucose and fructose B. galactose and glucose
C. galactose and fructose D. maltose and glucose

38. The structural formula shown at the right represents a(n) 38.___
A. lipoid
B. coenzyme
C. protein
D. amino acid

$$\begin{array}{c} \quad\quad COOH \\ \quad\quad | \\ H_2H - C - H \\ \quad\quad | \\ \quad\quad R \end{array}$$

39. Cell turgor is increased when the external medium is 39.___
A. hypertonic
B. isotonic
C. hypotonic
D. isoelectrically equivalent

40. Which one of the following is an evolutionary link between reptiles and birds? 40.___
A. Chrondricytes
B. Archaeopteryx
C. Pterodactyl
D. Didelphys

41. A hormone which regulates the use of calcium by bones is produced by the 41.___
A. thymus
B. parathyroid
C. thyroid
D. pituitary

42. A Sonoran habitat would MOST likely be found at which one of the following? 42.___
A. Seashore
B. Mouth of a river
C. Base of mountains
D. Peaks of foothills or on mountains

43. Among vertebrates, the embryonic ectoderm gives rise to which one of the following? 43.___
_____ system.
A. Nervous
B. Digestive
C. Skeletal
D. Respiratory

44. A diet inadequate with respect to iodine will PROBABLY result in 44.___
A. exophthalmic goiter
B. Basedow's disease
C. endemic goiter
D. Graves' disease

45. The MAIN extensor muscle of the arm is the 45.___
A. pectoralis major
B. triceps
C. biceps
D. gastrocnemius

46. Pioneer studies on the effects of deuterium on intermediary metabolism were performed by 46.___
A. Schoenheimer
B. Urey
C. Fermi
D. Oppenheimer

47. The vegetation of dry plains, semideserts, and true deserts is composed of 47.___
A. hydrophytes B. parasites
C. saprophytes D. xerophytes

48. The color of certain Hydrangea flowers may be changed to blue by the addition to the soil of 48.___
A. SO_2 B. Al C. CO D. CaO

49. The INCORRECT sequence in the following groups of food chains is: 49.___
A. Insect - spider - frog - fish - otter
B. Algae - protozoa - aquatic insects - black bass-pickerel
C. Grass - cricket - frog - snake - hawk
D. Protozoa - aquatic insect larvae - diatoms - copepods - bass - raccoon

50. A successful graft of an apple scion on a pear stock would result in 50.___
A. genetic resistance
B. clonal selection
C. growth of apples on the scion
D. growth of pears on the scion

KEY (CORRECT ANSWERS)

1. A	11. C	21. B	31. B	41. B
2. D	12. B	22. B	32. A	42. D
3. D	13. B	23. D	33. C	43. A
4. D	14. D	24. C	34. D	44. C
5. B	15. A	25. A	35. B	45. B
6. C	16. B	26. C	36. D	46. A
7. D	17. C	27. D	37. A	47. D
8. C	18. C	28. B	38. D	48. B
9. C	19. D	29. A	39. C	49. D
10. B	20. B	30. C	40. B	50. C

TEST 3

DIRECTIONS: Each question or incomplete statement is followed by several suggested answers or completions. Select the one that BEST answers the question or completes the statement. *PRINT THE LETTER OF THE CORRECT ANSWER IN THE SPACE AT THE RIGHT.*

1. The blood constituent MOST likely to provide antibodies is 1.___
   A. albumin B. fibrinogen
   C. globulin D. heparin

2. The tricuspid valve is between the 2.___
   A. left auricle and left ventricle
   B. right auricle and right ventricle
   C. right ventricle and pulmonary artery
   D. aorta and left ventricle

3. The ability to taste PTC paper is 3.___
   A. acquired
   B. inherited as a recessive trait
   C. inherited as a dominant trait
   D. sex-linked among the Mongoloids

4. The body obtains important coenzymes from foods containing which one of the following? 4.___
   A. Vitamins B. Lipoids
   C. Steroids D. Amino acids

5. A micron is equal to _____ mm. 5.___
   A. .1 B. .01 C. .001 D. .0001

6. The cells that are MAINLY responsible for regeneration in the hydra are 6.___
   A. endodermal B. neuromuscular
   C. mesenchymal D. epidermal

7. A sphygmomanometer is used to measure 7.___
   A. basal metabolism B. sedimentation rate
   C. clotting time D. blood pressure

8. Of the following systems, the one to which the tonsils belong is the 8.___
   A. respiratory B. lymphatic
   C. digestive D. circulatory

9. The skeleton of a shark is made of 9.___
   A. bone B. chitin
   C. cartilage D. calcareous plates

10. Of the following organisms, the two which probably existed during the same period are 10.___
   A. Pelycosaurs and flowering plants
   B. Pterosaurs and giant dragon flies
   C. Cycads and Gingkos
   D. Australopithecines and Trilobites

11. Viruses and chloroplasts behave alike in that they 11.___
   A. replicate in living cells only
   B. are essentially made up of DNA
   C. are saprophytic
   D. reproduce in a cell-free medium

12. Liverworts are MOST closely related to which one of the following? 12.___
   A. Ferns B. Algae C. Lichens D. Mosses

13. Studies in which one of the following fields led MOST directly to the conception that ontogeny recapitulates phylogeny? 13.___
   A. Paleontology B. Embryology
   C. Comparative anatomy D. Taxonomy

14. The relationship between termites and ciliates is known as 14.___
   A. mutualism B. parasitism
   C. commensalism D. holophytism

15. Molds are to spores as green plants are to 15.___
   A. stems B. leaves C. roots D. seeds

16. To insure a satisfactory classroom demonstration of the *scratch* reflex in the frog, the instructor should destroy the frog's 16.___
   A. brain B. spinal cord
   C. brain and spinal cord D. sciatic nerve

17. The hammer, anvil, and stirrup bones lie in the 17.___
   A. outer ear B. middle ear
   C. inner ear D. semicircular canals

18. The cellular structure that helps to regulate turgor is the 18.___
   A. Golgi apparatus B. reticular apparatus
   C. tonoplast D. mitochondrion

19. Clams, snails, and octopi are similar in that they possess 19.___
   A. conspicuous shell and foot
   B. conspicuous shell and mantle
   C. gills and foot
   D. gills and mantle

20. The phylum to which the leech belongs is the 20.___
A. platyhelminthes B. nematoda
C. arthropoda D. annelida

21. The Salk polio vaccine is produced from viruses grown in tissue from which one of the following? 21.___
A. Rabbits B. Sheep
C. Monkeys D. Guinea pigs

22. Which one of the following is NOT found in the skull? 22.___
A. Turbinals B. Hyoid C. Mastoid D. Parietal

23. In vascular plants, the stele is surrounded by 23.___
A. collenchyma B. meristem
C. endodermis D. phellogen

24. Which one of the following is NOT associated with the others in the performance of a related function? 24.___
A. Calcium ion B. Fibrinogen
C. Monocytes D. Platelets

25. Erythroblasts are found normally only in the 25.___
A. blood B. spleen
C. liver D. bone marrow

26. Of the following, a condition NOT usually considered to be associated with heavy cigarette smoking is 26.___
A. shorter life span B. slowing of the heartbeat
C. cancer of the lung D. heart disease

27. The number of *senses* in man is 27.___
A. less than five B. five
C. seven D. more than seven

28. Damage to the cerebellum would interfere MAINLY with which one of the following? 28.___
A. Memory B. Voluntary acts
C. Sensation D. Equilibrium

29. The center which maintains the rhythm of breathing is located in the 29.___
A. cerebellum B. medulla
C. cerebrum D. spinal cord

30. The MAJOR function of bile is 30.___
A. digestion B. emulsification
C. absorption D. lubrication

31. The surgical removal of the stomach would interfere MAINLY with the functioning in the body of which one of the following? 31.___
A. Enzyme secretion B. Fat digestion
C. Food storage D. Protein absorption

32. The liquid portion of whole blood is called 32.___
A. serum B. lymph C. plasma D. water

33. Failure of lymph to circulate would MOST directly affect which one of the following? 33.___
A. Fat digestion
B. Transport between the body cells and blood
C. Production of red blood cells
D. Circulation of blood platelets

34. If in a given sample of blood, clumping occurred with both A serum and B serum, the blood type was 34.___
A. A B. B C. AB D. O

35. Recent work indicates that the commonest normal human diploid chromosome number is 35.___
A. 45 B. 46 C. 47 D. 48

36. The glomeruli are MOST closely related to the system involved in 36.___
A. reproduction B. support and movement
C. digestion D. excretion

37. Of the following, the area in whose functions the effects of alcohol are first observed is the 37.___
A. cerebrum B. cerebellum
C. medulla D. spinal cord

38. Inhalation in man is caused by _____ the ribs and _____ the diaphragm. 38.___
A. lowering; raising B. raising; raising
C. lowering; lowering D. raising; lowering

39. In man, diffusion of carbon dioxide and oxygen occurs MAINLY in the 39.___
A. pharynx B. alveoli C. bronchi D. glottis

40. Of the following, a structure which normally serves as a common passageway for both food and air is the 40.___
A. glottis B. pharynx C. trachea D. larynx

41. The kidney is to renal corpuscles as the skin is to 41.___
A. oil glands B. sweat glands
C. pores D. epidermis

42. Deamination of proteins occurs MAINLY in the 42.___
A. small intestine B. spleen
C. pancreas D. liver

43. Of the following, the one which is a final waste product of protein metabolism is 43.___
A. pepsinogen B. amino acid
C. urea D. urine

44. The LOWEST concentration of nitrogenous waste may be found in blood passing through the 44.____
A. pulmonary artery B. renal artery
C. hepatic vein D. renal vein

45. The liquid which collects in the cavity of Bowman's capsule is 45.____
A. urine in concentrated form
B. blood plasma minus plasma proteins
C. freshly aerated blood
D. used bile ready for excretion

46. Of the following, which one MOST closely indicates the approximate number of calories required by an average man who does office work? 46.____
A. 1500-1800 B. 2000-2200 C. 2400-2700 D. 3000-3300

47. Of the following vitamins, the one which can MOST readily be manufactured in our bodies is 47.____
A. A B. B_1 C. C D. D

48. The CHIEF function of roughage is to 48.____
A. build muscle tissue
B. provide quick energy
C. provide certain vitamins
D. stimulate peristalsis

49. The passage of food into the larynx is normally prevented by the 49.____
A. pharynx B. trachea
C. epiglottis D. hard palate

50. If an organism has 2n chromosomes in each of its body cells, the mature sperm will contain the number of chromosomes represented by 50.____
A. 2n B. n C. n/2 D. 4n

KEY (CORRECT ANSWERS)

1. C	11. A	21. C	31. C	41. B
2. B	12. D	22. B	32. C	42. D
3. C	13. B	23. C	33. B	43. C
4. A	14. A	24. C	34. C	44. D
5. C	15. D	25. D	35. B	45. B
6. C	16. A	26. B	36. D	46. C
7. D	17. B	27. B	37. A	47. D
8. B	18. C	28. D	38. D	48. D
9. C	19. D	29. B	39. B	49. C
10. C	20. D	30. B	40. B	50. B

EXAMINATION SECTION

TEST 1

DIRECTIONS: Each question or incomplete statement is followed by several suggested answers or completions. Select the one that BEST answers the question or completes the statement. *PRINT THE LETTER OF THE CORRECT ANSWER IN THE SPACE AT THE RIGHT.*

1. In an Ameba, materials are taken from its environment and then moved throughout its cytoplasm. 1.___
   These processes are known as
   A. absorption and circulation
   B. food processing and energy release
   C. energy release and synthesis
   D. coordination and regulation

2. In which kingdom is an organism classified if it lacks a membrane separating MOST of its genetic material from its cytoplasm? 2.___
   A. Protist B. Monera C. Plant D. Animal

3. Which is TRUE of organisms that are classified in the same genus? 3.___
   They must be
   A. in the same phylum but may be of different species
   B. of the same species but may be in different phyla
   C. in the same phylum but may be in different kingdoms
   D. in the same kingdom but may be in different phyla

4. According to the cell theory, which statement is CORRECT? 4.___
   A. Viruses are true cells.
   B. Cells are basically unlike in structure.
   C. Mitochondria are found only in plant cells.
   D. Cells come from pre-existing cells.

5. To transplant a nucleus from one cell to another cell, a scientist would use 5.___
   A. an electron microscope
   B. an ultracentrifuge
   C. microdissection instruments
   D. staining techniques

6. A student using a compound microscope measured the diameter of several red blood cells and found that the average cell length was 0.008 millimeter. 6.___
   What is the AVERAGE length of a single red blood cell in micrometers?
   A. 0.8 B. 8 C. 80 D. 800

7. MOST cellular respiration in plants takes place in organelles known as 7.___
   A. chloroplasts B. stomates
   C. ribosomes D. mitochondria

8. Which organic compound is CORRECTLY matched with the subunit that composes it? 8.___
   A. Maltose - amino acid
   B. Starch - glucose
   C. Protein - fatty acid
   D. Lipid - sucrose

9. A fruit fly is classified as a heterotroph, rather than as an autotroph, because it is unable to 9.___
   A. transport needed materials through the body
   B. release energy from organic molecules
   C. manufacture its own food
   D. divide its cells mitotically

10. The diagram at the right illustrates phases of a specific life activity being carried on by a cell. Which process is occurring at phase 3? 10.___
   A. Intracellular digestion
   B. Extracellular digestion
   C. Ingestion
   D. Excretion

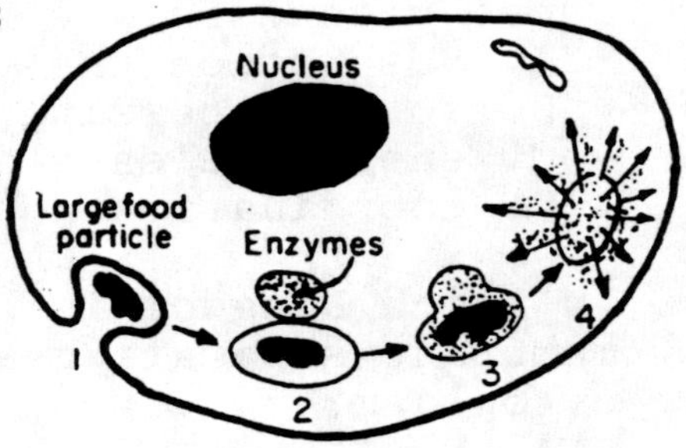

Nucleus
Large food particle
Enzymes
1
2
3
4

11. At optimum light intensity, which atmospheric gas MOST directly influences the rate of photosynthesis? 11.___
   A. Nitrogen
   B. Oxygen
   C. Carbon dioxide
   D. Hydrogen

12. Which physical factor associated with upward movement in vascular plants is MOST affected when leaves are shed in the autumn? 12.___
   A. Transpirational pull
   B. Capillary action
   C. Root pressure
   D. Active transport

13. A red blood cell placed in distilled water will swell and burst due to the diffusion of 13.___
   A. salt from the red blood cell into the water
   B. water into the red blood cell
   C. water from the blood cell into its environment
   D. salts from the water into the red blood cell

14. Carbohydrate molecules A and B come in contact with the cell membrane of the same cell. Molecule A passes through the membrane readily, but molecule B does not. It is MOST likely that molecule A is a(n) 14.___
   A. protein and B is a lipid
   B. polysaccharide and B is a monosaccharide
   C. amino acid and B is a monosaccharide
   D. monosaccharide and B is a polysaccharide

15. Most animals make energy available for cell activity by transferring the potential energy of glucose to ATP. This process occurs during 15.___
   A. aerobic respiration *only*
   B. anaerobic respiration *only*
   C. both aerobic and anaerobic respiration
   D. neither aerobic nor anaerobic respiration

16. Nitrogenous waste products are produced from the complete metabolism of 16.___
   A. water B. sugars C. starches D. proteins

17. What do the tracheal tubes of the grasshopper and the air spaces of a geranium leaf have in common? 17.___
They
   A. regulate the flow of urea into and out of the organism
   B. are the major sites for the ingestion of nutrients
   C. contain enzymes that convert light energy to chemical bond energy
   D. are surrounded by moist internal surfaces where gas exchange occurs

18. Which of the following processes releases the GREATEST amount of energy? 18.___
The
   A. oxidation of one glucose molecule to lactic acid molecules
   B. oxidation of one glucose molecule to carbon dioxide and water molecules
   C. conversion of two glucose molecules to a maltose molecule
   D. conversion of one glucose molecule to alcohol and carbon dioxide molecules

19. Which organism is CORRECTLY paired with its excretory structure? 19.___
   A. Earthworm - nephridium B. Ameba - skin
   C. Grasshopper - nephron D. Hydra - Malpighian tube

20. 20.___

In the diagram of two neurons shown above, at which point would a substance that interferes with the action of a neurotransmitter be MOST effective?
   A. 1 B. 2 C. 3 D. 4

21. The structure and function of the nervous system of the earthworm are MOST similar to those of the 21.___
   A. Ameba B. Hydra
   C. grasshopper D. Paramecium

22. Tropisms in plants MOST directly result from the 22.___
   A. unequal distribution of auxins
   B. transpirational pull of water
   C. transmission of impulses by acetylcholine
   D. excitation of chlorophyll molecules by light

23. 23.___

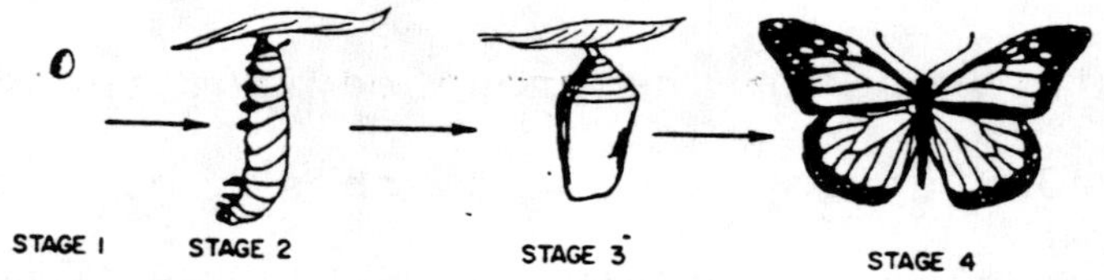

STAGE 1 STAGE 2 STAGE 3 STAGE 4

The above diagram represents four stages of development in an arthropod.
Which substances MOST directly regulate the process illustrated in the diagram?
   A. Auxins B. Hormones C. Vitamins D. Minerals

24. Which life function is MOST closely associated with structure A in the cross-sectional diagram of an earthworm shown at the right? 24.___
   A. Locomotion
   B. Respiration
   C. Transport
   D. Excretion

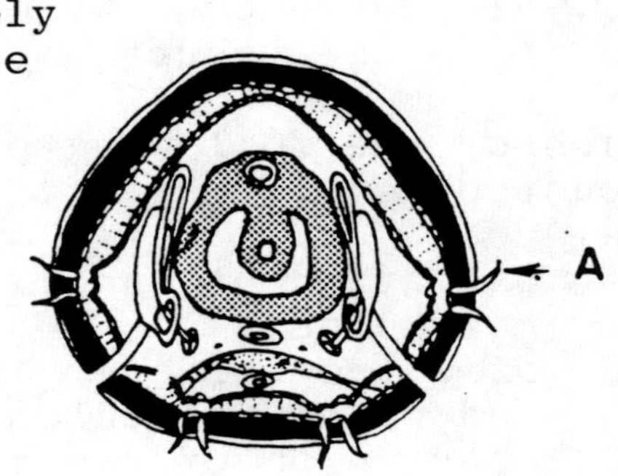

A

25. Which two organisms are able to move due to the interaction of muscular and skeletal systems? 25.___
   A. Earthworm and human B. Grasshopper and Hydra
   C. Hydra and earthworm D. Grasshopper and human

26. Which is NOT a major function of cartilage tissues in a human adult? 26.___
   A. Giving pliable support to body structures
   B. Cushioning joint areas
   C. Adding flexibility to joints
   D. Providing skeletal levers

27. Which is a CORRECT route of an impulse in a reflex arc? 27.___
   A. Receptor → sensory neuron → interneuron → motor neuron → effector
   B. Effector → receptor → motor neuron → sensory neuron → interneuron
   C. Sensory neuron → effector → motor neuron → receptor → interneuron
   D. Motor neuron → sensory neuron → interneuron → effector

28. In addition to water, the PRINCIPAL components of urine are 28.___
A. amino acids and fatty acids
B. urea and salts
C. ammonia and bile
D. hydrochloric acid and bases

29. MOST carbon dioxide is carried in the plasma in the form of 29.___
A. hydrogen ions
B. bicarbonate ions
C. lactic acid
D. oxyhemoglobin

30. Which cells are able to carry on the process of phagocytosis? 30.___
_____ cells.
A. Nerve
B. Epidermal
C. Red blood
D. White blood

KEY (CORRECT ANSWERS)

1. A	11. C	21. C
2. B	12. A	22. A
3. A	13. B	23. B
4. D	14. D	24. A
5. C	15. C	25. D
6. B	16. D	26. D
7. D	17. D	27. A
8. B	18. B	28. B
9. C	19. A	29. B
10. A	20. C	30. D

TEST 2

DIRECTIONS: Each question or incomplete statement is followed by several suggested answers or completions. Select the one that BEST answers the question or completes the statement. *PRINT THE LETTER OF THE CORRECT ANSWER IN THE SPACE AT THE RIGHT.*

1. The thin-walled vessels of the circulatory system where most oxygen and carbon dioxide are exchanged are 1.___
   A. alveoli B. arteries
   C. capillaries D. veins

2. Small lymphatic vessels which extend into the villi are 2.___
   A. veins B. lacteals
   C. nodes D. capillaries

3. 3.___

Which process is represented by the above diagram?
   A. Emulsification B. Excretion
   C. Absorption D. Peristalsis

4. The following list describes some of the events associated with normal cell division: 4.___
   A - Nuclear membrane formation around each set of newly formed chromosomes
   B - Separation of centromeres
   C - Replication of each chromosome
   D - Movement of single-stranded chromosomes to opposite ends of the spindle

   What is the NORMAL sequence in which these events occur?
   A. A → B → C → D B. C → B → D → A
   C. C → D → B → A D. D → C → A → B

5. 5.___

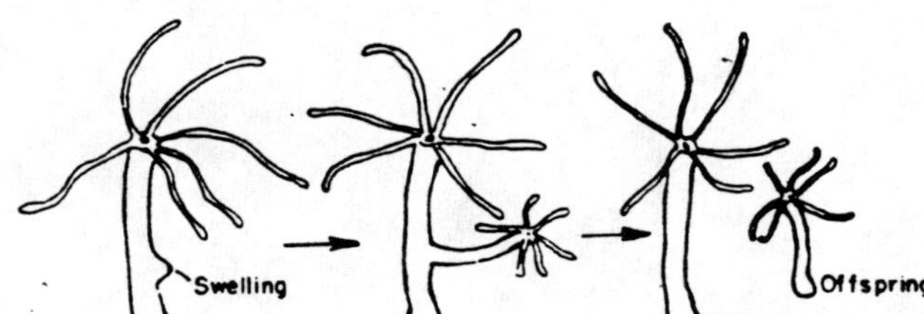

Which process, carried out by a Hydra, is illustrated by the series of above drawings?
   A. Binary fission B. Budding
   C. Vegetative propagation D. Spore formation

6. During the normal meiotic division of a diploid cell, the change in chromosome number that occurs is represented as 6.___
   A. $4n \rightarrow n$ B. $2n \rightarrow 4n$ D. $2n \rightarrow n$ D. $n \rightarrow \frac{1}{2}n$

7. In animals, polar bodies are formed as a result of _____ cell division in _____. 7.___
   A. meiotic; females B. meiotic; males
   C. mitotic; females D. mitotic; males

8. In mammals, the placenta is essential to the embryo for 8.___
   A. nutrition, reproduction, and growth
   B. nutrition, respiration, and excretion
   C. locomotion, respiration, and excretion
   D. nutrition, reproduction, and excretion

9. The diagram at the right illustrates the important stages in the life cycle of an organism that reproduces sexually. 9.___ 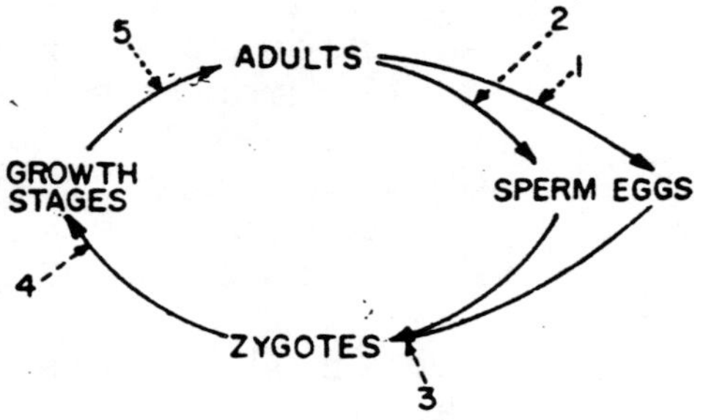
   Which processes result in the formation of cells with the monoploid number of chromosomes?
   A. 1 and 2
   B. 2 and 3
   C. 3 and 4
   D. 4 and 5

10. In a flowering plant, the ovule develops within a part of the 10.___
    A. style B. anther C. pistil D. stigma

11. Which embryonic structure supplies nutrients to a germinating bean plant? 11.___
    A. Pollen tube B. Hypocotyl
    C. Epicotyl D. Cotyledon

12. Polydactyly is a human characteristic in which a person has six fingers per hand. The trait for polydactyly is dominant over the trait for five fingers. 12.___
    If a man who is heterozygous for this trait marries a woman with the normal number of fingers, what are the chances that their child would be polydactyl?
    A. 0% B. 50% C. 75% D. 100%

13. Which statement describes how two organisms may show the same trait, yet have different genotypes for that phenotype? 13.___
    A. One is homozygous dominant and the other heterozygous.
    B. Both are heterozygous for the dominant trait.
    C. One is homozygous dominant and the other homozygous recessive.
    D. Both are homozygous for the dominant trait.

14. A child with blood type O has a mother with blood type A and a father with blood type B. 14.___
The parental genotypes for blood types must be
A. I^AI^A and I^BI^B B. I^Ai and I^BI^B
C. I^AI^B and I^Bi D. I^Ai and I^Bi

15. Two pea plants, hybrid for a single trait, produce 60 pea plants. 15.___
Approximately how many of the pea plants are expected to exhibit the recessive trait?
A. 15 B. 45 C. 30 D. 60

16. Which statement CORRECTLY describes the normal number and type of chromosomes present in human body cells of a particular sex? 16.___
A. Males have 22 pairs of autosomes and 1 pair of sex chromosomes known as XX.
B. Females have 23 pairs of autosomes.
C. Males have 22 pairs of autosomes and 1 pair of sex chromosomes known as XY.
D. Males have 23 pairs of autosomes.

17. Based on the pattern of inheritance known as sex linkage, if a male is a hemophiliac, how many genes for this trait are present on the sex chromosomes in each of his diploid cells? 17.___
A. 1 B. 2 C. 3 D. 0

18. To help to insure the maintenance of a desirable trait in a particular species of plant, a farmer would make use of 18.___
A. binary fission B. mutagenic agents
C. vegetative propagation D. natural selection

19. Which substances are components of a DNA nucleotide? 19.___
A. Phosphate, deoxyribose, and uracil
B. Phosphate, ribose, and adenine
C. Thymine, deoxyribose, and phosphate
D. Ribose, phosphate, and uracil

20. The diagram at the right represents a section of undisturbed rock and the general location of fossils of several closely related species. 20.___
According to currently accepted evolutionary theory, which is the MOST probable correct assumption to be made concerning species A, B, C, and D?

species C & D
species C
species A & B & C
species A & B
species A

A. A is the ancestor of B, C, and D.
B. B was already extinct when C evolved.
C. C evolved more recently than A, B, and D.
D. D is the ancestor of A, B, and C.

21. If a rabbit is sensitized to human blood, the blood of the rabbit will react to chimpanzee blood very much the way it does to human blood. 21.___
This is an example of which type of evidence supporting the theory of evolution?
Comparative
A. habitat
B. anatomy
C. embryology
D. biochemistry

22. Structures having a similar origin but adapted for different purposes, such as the flipper of a whale and arm of a human, are called _____ structures. 22.___
A. homozygous
B. identical
C. homologous
D. embryological

23. An athlete explains that his muscles have become well-developed through daily activities of weightlifting. He believes that his offspring will inherit this trait of well-developed muscles. 23.___
This belief would be MOST in agreement with the theory set forth by
A. Darwin
B. Lamarck
C. Weismann
D. Mendel

24. Natural selection can BEST be defined as 24.___
A. survival of the strongest organism
B. elimination of the smallest organisms by the largest organisms
C. survival of those organisms genetically best adapted to the environment
D. survival and reproduction of those organisms that occupy the largest area in an environment

25. Many modern evolutionists have accepted much of Darwin's theory of evolution, but have added genetic information that gives a scientific explanation of 25.___
A. overproduction
B. the struggle for existence
C. the survival of the fittest
D. variations

26. As a result of sexual reproduction, the rate of evolutionary change in the plant and animal kingdoms has been greatly speeded up because 26.___
A. the offspring show more diversity than in asexual reproduction
B. characteristics change less frequently than in asexual reproduction
C. environmental changes never affect organisms produced by asexual reproduction
D. two parents have fewer offspring than one parent

27. The heterotroph hypothesis is an attempt to explain 27.___
  A. how the Earth was originally formed
  B. why simple organisms usually evolve into complex organisms
  C. why evolution occurs very slowly
  D. how life originated on the Earth

28. Which sequence shows increasing complexity of levels of ecological organization? 28.___
  A. Biosphere, ecosystem, community
  B. Biosphere, community, ecosystem
  C. Community, ecosystem, biosphere
  D. Ecosystem, biosphere, community

29. In a freshwater pond community, a carp eats decaying material from around the bases of underwater plants, while a snail scrapes algae from the leaves and stems of the same plants. 29.___
They can survive at the same time because they occupy
  A. the same niche, but different habitats
  B. the same habitat, but different niches
  C. the same habitat and the same niche
  D. different habitats and niches

30. Which term describes the bird and the cat in the following pattern of energy flow? 30.___
  sun → grass → grasshopper → bird → cat

  A. Herbivores B. Saprophytes
  C. Predators D. Omnivores

KEY (CORRECT ANSWERS)

1. C	11. D	21. D
2. B	12. B	22. C
3. A	13. A	23. B
4. B	14. D	24. C
5. B	15. A	25. D
6. C	16. C	26. A
7. A	17. A	27. D
8. B	18. C	28. C
9. A	19. C	29. B
10. C	20. A	30. C

TEST 3

DIRECTIONS: Each question or incomplete statement is followed by several suggested answers or completions. Select the one that BEST answers the question or completes the statement. *PRINT THE LETTER OF THE CORRECT ANSWER IN THE SPACE AT THE RIGHT.*

1. Which food chain relationship illustrates the nutritional pattern of a primary consumer? 1.___
   A. Seeds and fruits eaten by a mouse
   B. An earthworm eaten by a mole
   C. A mosquito eaten by a bat
   D. A mold growing on a dead frog

2. The elements stored in living cells of organisms in a community will eventually be returned to the soil for use by other living organisms. 2.___
   The organisms which carry out this process are
   A. producers B. herbivores
   C. carnivores D. decomposers

3. The natural replacement of one community with another until a climax stage is reached is known as 3.___
   A. ecological balance B. organic evolution
   C. dynamic equilibrium D. ecological succession

4. Recent evidence indicates that lakes in large areas of New York State are being affected by acid rain. 4.___
   The MAJOR effect of acid rain in the lakes is
   A. an increase in game fish population levels
   B. the stimulation of a rapid rate of evolution
   C. the elimination of many species of aquatic life
   D. an increase in agricultural productivity

5. Bacillus popilliae is a bacterium which causes *milky disease* in the Japanese beetle. 5.___
   Using bacillus popilliae to decrease a Japanese beetle population is an example of the
   A. abiotic control of insect pests
   B. use of biological control of insect pests
   C. use of artificial insecticides
   D. destruction of the abiotic environment

Questions 6-9.

DIRECTIONS: For each statement in Questions 6 through 9, select the process, chosen from the list below, that is BEST described by that statement.

<u>Biological Processes</u>
A. Anaerobic respiration
B. Aerobic respiration
C. Photochemical reactions of photosynthesis
D. Carbon-fixation reactions of photosynthesis

6. Light energy is absorbed by organic pigment molecules. 6.___

7. The oxidation of a glucose molecule results in the synthesis of ATP, water, and carbon dioxide. 7.___

8. Lactic acid accumulates in the muscle tissues of humans during vigorous activity. 8.___

9. PGAL is synthesized. 9.___

Questions 10-13.

DIRECTIONS: Questions 10 through 13 are to be answered on the basis of the chemical equation below and on your knowledge of biology.

$$\underbrace{H_2N-CH_2-COOH}_{X} + H_2N-CH_2-COOH \longrightarrow H_2N-CH_2-C(=O)\overset{Y}{\downarrow}NH-CH_2-COOH + Z$$

10. The chemical reaction represented by the equation is known as 10.___
    A. hydrolysis
    B. digestion
    C. dehydration synthesis
    D. carbon fixation

11. The substance represented by X is a(n) _____ molecule. 11.___
    A. glucose
    B. amino acid
    C. glycerol
    D. fatty acid

12. Which substance is represented by letter Z? 12.___
    A. Water
    B. Carbon dioxide
    C. Oxygen
    D. Salt

13. Letter Y represents a(n) 13.___
    A. peptide bond
    B. hydrogen bond
    C. polymer
    D. enzyme

14. If the test tubes represented in the diagrams below were allowed to stand at room temperature for several hours, which test tube would MOST likely contain the GREATEST amount of alcohol and carbon dioxide? 14.___

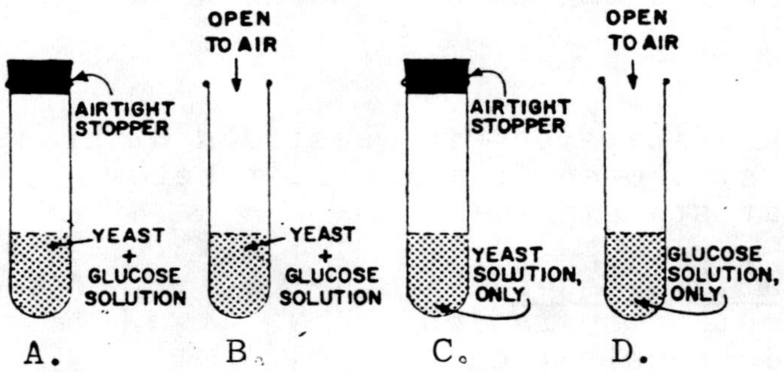

15. Which represents a carbohydrate molecule? 15.___
A. $C_6H_6O_6$ B. $C_{12}H_{12}O_6$ C. $C_6H_{12}O_5$ D. $C_6H_{12}O_6$

Questions 16-19.

DIRECTIONS: For each function in Questions 16 through 19, select the organ, chosen from the list below, which is MOST closely associated with that function. (A letter may be used more than once or not at all.)

<u>Organs</u>

A. Kidney
B. Liver
C. Lung
D. Stomach
E. Skin

16. Removal of CO_2 from the blood. 16.___

17. Extracellular hydrolysis of protein. 17.___

18. Storage of glycogen. 18.___

19. Production of urea. 19.___

20. A type of *heart attack* in which a narrowing of the coronary artery causes an inadequate supply of oxygen to reach the heart muscle is known as 20.___
A. anemia
B. leukemia
C. angina pectoris
D. cerebral palsy

21. In humans, circulation to and from the lungs is known as ______ circulation. 21.___
A. systemic
B. pulmonary
C. coronary
D. lymphatic

22. The somatic nervous system contains nerves that run from the central nervous system to the 22.___
A. muscles of the skeleton
B. heart
C. smooth muscles of the gastrointestinal tract
D. endocrine glands

23. A person who consumes large amounts of saturated fats may increase his or her chances of developing 23.___
A. meningitis
B. hemophilia
C. viral pneumonia
D. cardiovascular disease

24. Which gland does NOT secrete hormones? ______ gland. 24.___
A. Pituitary B. Thyroid C. Sex D. Salivary

25. Which of the following contains the GREATEST amount of skeletal muscle tissue? 25.___
A. Cerebrum B. Small intestine
C. Kidney D. Foot

Questions 26-30.

DIRECTIONS: Questions 26 through 30 are to be answered on the basis of the diagram below which represents some stages in the embryonic development of a specific vertebrate.

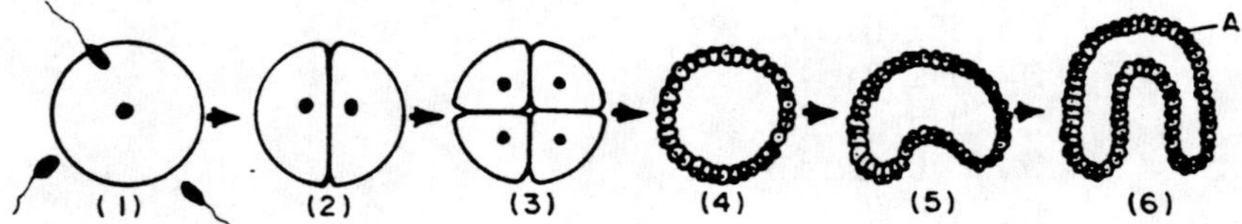

26. In humans, stage 1 NORMALLY occurs in the 26.___
A. ovary B. oviduct C. vagina D. uterus

27. Structures 2 and 3 are formed as a direct result of 27.___
A. meiosis B. gastrulation
C. cleavage D. differentiation

28. The structure in stage 4 represents a 28.___
A. zygote B. blastula C. gastrula D. follicle

29. The cells of layer A give rise to the 29.___
A. digestive system and liver
B. excretory system and muscles
C. circulatory system and gonads
D. nervous system and skin

30. Which cells are NOT represented in the diagrams? 30.___
_____ cells.
A. Endoderm B. Mesoderm
C. Diploid D. Monoploid

KEY (CORRECT ANSWERS)

1. A	11. B	21. B
2. D	12. A	22. A
3. D	13. A	23. D
4. C	14. A	24. D
5. B	15. D	25. D
6. C	16. C	26. B
7. B	17. D	27. C
8. A	18. B	28. B
9. D	19. B	29. D
10. C	20. C	30. B

TEST 4

DIRECTIONS: Each question or incomplete statement is followed by several suggested answers or completions. Select the one that BEST answers the question or completes the statement. *PRINT THE LETTER OF THE CORRECT ANSWER IN THE SPACE AT THE RIGHT.*

Questions 1-3.

DIRECTIONS: For each of the processes in Questions 1 through 3, choose the stage of the human menstrual cycle, chosen from the list below, during which that process occurs. (A letter may be used more than once or not at all.)

Human Menstrual Cycle Stages

A. Ovulation
B. Follicle stage
C. Menstruation
D. Corpus luteum stage

1. The lining of the uterus is shed. 1.___

2. An egg is released from an ovary. 2.___

3. An egg matures in an ovary 3.___

4. Which type of fertilization and development is exhibited by birds and many reptiles? 4.___
_____ fertilization and _____ development.
A. External; external B. Internal; internal
C. External; internal D. Internal; external

5. Which structure is a source of food for embryos which develop externally? 5.___
A. Yolk B. Placenta C. Chorion D. Amnion

Questions 6-9.

DIRECTIONS: For each phrase in Questions 6 through 9, select the type of nucleic acid, chosen from the list below, which is BEST described by that phrase. (A letter may be used more than once or not at all.)

Types of Nucleic Acid

A. DNA
B. Messenger RNA
C. Transfer RNA

6. Genetic material responsible for the individuality of an organism that is passed from parent to offspring. 6.___

7. Carries genetic information from the cell nucleus to the ribosomes. 7.___

8. Contains thymine instead of uracil. 8.___

9. Carries amino acid molecules to the ribosomes. 9.___

10. By which process can a group of genetically identical plants be rapidly produced from the cells of a single plant? 10.___
    A. Screening B. Chromosomal karyotyping
    C. Genetic engineering D. Cloning

11. Which is a genetic disorder in which abnormal hemoglobin leads to fragile red blood cells and obstructed blood vessels? 11.___
    A. Phenylketonuria B. Sickle-cell anemia
    C. Leukemia D. Down's syndrome

12. During the replication of a DNA molecule, separation or *unzipping* of the DNA molecule will normally occur when hydrogen bonds are broken between 12.___
    A. thymine and thymine B. guanine and uracil
    C. adenine and cytosine D. cytosine and guanine

13. Which set of conditions would MOST likely cause a change in gene frequency in a sexually reproducing population? 13.___
    A. Mutations and small populations
    B. Large populations and no migrations
    C. Random matings and large populations
    D. No mutations and no migrations

14. In humans, a gene mutation results from a change in the 14.___
    A. sequence of the nitrogenous bases in DNA
    B. chromosome number in a sperm
    C. chromosome number in an egg
    D. sequence of the sugars and phosphates in DNA

15. The genetic code for one amino acid molecule consists of 15.___
    A. five sugar molecules B. two phosphates
    C. three nucleotides D. four hydrogen bonds

Questions 16-18.

DIRECTIONS: Questions 16 through 18 are to be answered on the basis of the information below.

A scientist studied a river and forest area downstream from a large city with an increasing human population. During the study, the scientist made many observations that could be classified as:

A. Most likely a negative result of human activity
B. Most likely a positive result of human activity
C. Probably not being influenced by human activity to any extent

16. For each observation in Questions 16 through 18, select the phrase, chosen from the list above, which BEST fits that observation. (A letter may be used more than once or not at all.)

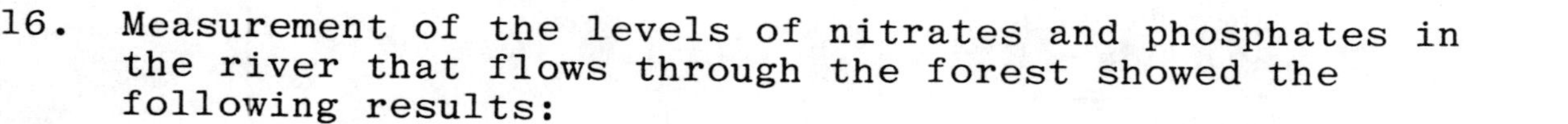

16. Measurement of the levels of nitrates and phosphates in the river that flows through the forest showed the following results: 16.___

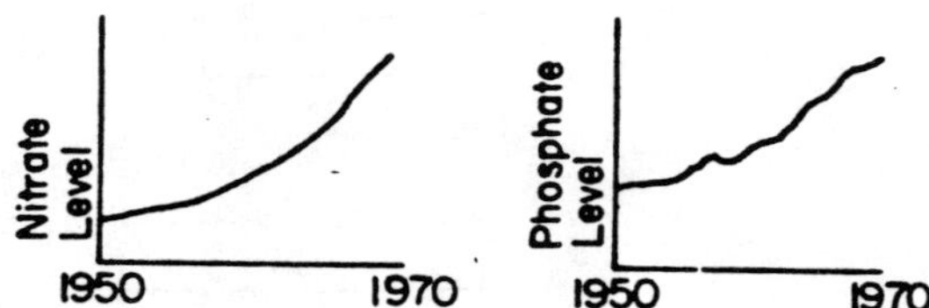

17. After 1970, the concentration of dissolved oxygen in the river increased, while the concentration of suspended particles decreased. 17.___

18. The population of hawks declined, while their food sources increased. High levels of insecticides were found in the reproductive tissues of hawks. 18.___

19. Compared to other organisms, humans have had the GREATEST ecological impact on the biosphere due to their 19.___
   A. internal bony skeleton
   B. homeostatic regulation of metabolism
   C. adaptations for respiration
   D. ability to modify the environment

20. The rapid rise of the human population level over the past few hundred years has been due MAINLY to 20.___
   A. increasing levels of air and water pollution
   B. loss of topsoil from our farmable lands
   C. removal of natural checks on population growth
   D. increasing resistance level of insect species

21. Which land biome is characterized by conifers, which include spruce and fir, as the dominant vegetation? 21.___
   A. Taiga B. Tundra
   C. Desert D. Grassland

22. Which two groups of organisms are MOST likely to be pioneer organisms? 22.___
   A. Songbirds and squirrels B. Lichens and algae
   C. Deer and black bears D. Oak and hickory trees

23. The diagram to the right illustrates some of the essential steps in 23.___
   A. the reproductive cycle
   B. the process of photosynthesis
   C. animal respiration
   D. the nitrogen cycle

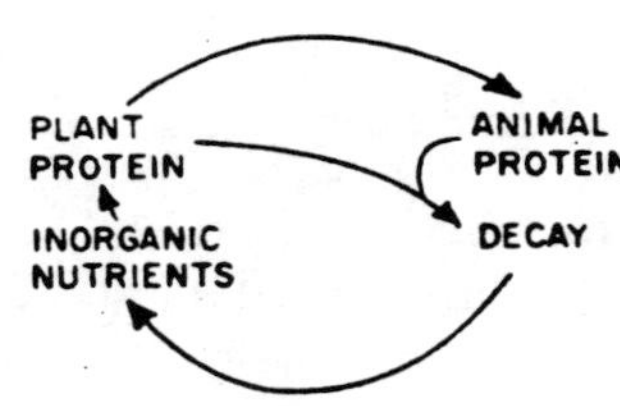

24. Which diagram BEST represents the usual relationships of biomass in a stable community? 24.___

Key:
C - Carnivores
H - Herbivores
P - Producers

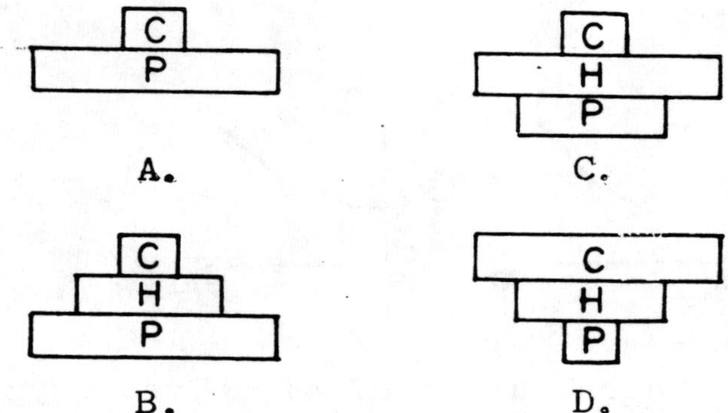

25. Bacteria which live in the human intestine derive their nutrition from digested foods. From these nutrients digested by the human, the bacteria synthesize vitamins usable by the human. 25.___
This relationship demonstrates
A. commensalism
B. saprophytism
C. mutualism
D. parasitism

Questions 26-28.

DIRECTIONS: Questions 26 through 28 are to be answered on the basis of the information and chart below and on your knowledge of biology. The chart shows some indicators that are used in biological work to determine the presence of various substances in chemical compounds. The numbers on the chart represent missing information from Columns I and II. Record the letter of the choice, chosen from the lists below, which provides the information missing from the spaces numbered 26 through 28

<u>Column I Choices</u>

A. Disaccharides
B. Simple sugar
C. Oxygen
D. Starch

<u>Column II Choices</u>

A. Brown color
B. Blue-black color
C. Milky-white color
D. Yellow color

<u>Indicator Chart</u>

Indicator	Column I Test for the Presence of	Column II Positive Result of the Test
Benedict's Solution	26	Red-orange color
Iodine Solution	27	Blue-black color
Bromthymol Blue Solution	Carbon dioxide	28

26.____

27.____

28.____

29. The diagram at the right shows a moss plant and a metric ruler.
How tall is the moss plant in millimeters?
   A. 1.5
   B. 15
   C. 150
   D. 1,500

29.____

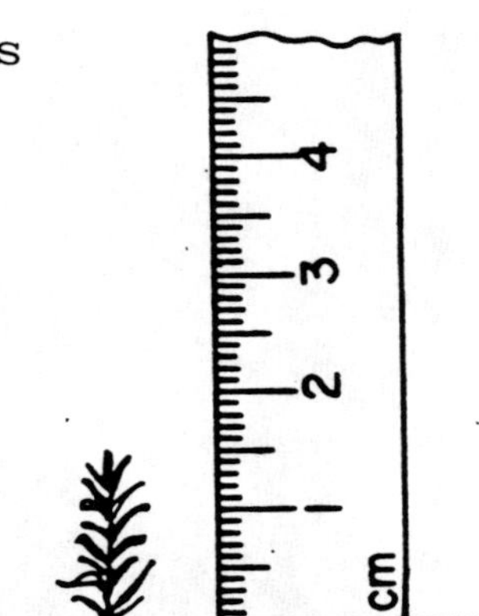

30. Which group of measurement units is CORRECTLY arranged in order of increasing size?
   A. Micrometer, millimeter, centimeter, meter
   B. Millimeter, micrometer, centimeter, meter
   C. Meter, micrometer, centimeter, millimeter
   D. Micrometer, centimeter, millimeter, meter

30.____

KEY (CORRECT ANSWERS)

1. C	11. B	21. A
2. A	12. D	22. B
3. B	13. A	23. D
4. D	14. A	24. B
5. A	15. C	25. C
6. A	16. A	26. B
7. B	17. B	27. D
8. A	18. A	28. D
9. C	19. D	29. B
10. D	20. C	30. A

EXAMINATION SECTION

DIRECTIONS: Each question or incomplete statement is followed by several suggested answers or completions. Select the one that BEST answers the question or completes the statement. *PRINT THE LETTER OF THE CORRECT ANSWER IN THE SPACE AT THE RIGHT.*

1. Perennial plants growing in the desert cope with the lack of water by means of any of the following EXCEPT 1.___
   A. restricted root system
   B. C4 metabolism
   C. succulence
   D. high volume-to-surface ratio
   E. dormancy

2. In which of the following is the group paired with a characteristic that is NOT important to classification in that group? 2.___
   A. Algae - kinds of pigments
   B. Gymnosperms - branching of root systems
   C. Ferns - structure and arrangement of the sporangia
   D. Angiosperms - flower structure
   E. Mosses - structure of the capsule

3. Divergent variation leading to the establishment of two evolutionary lines, and thus ultimately to two taxa, depends PRIMARILY on 3.___
   A. crossing-over
   B. isolation
   C. chromosome number
   D. mutation
   E. pollinating mechanisms

4. When ecologists speak of lake eutrophication, they specifically mean that 4.___
   A. the lake is anoxic
   B. the lake is dead
   C. the rate of production is high
   D. species diversity has declined
   E. pollution in the form of toxic substances has been added

5. Injection of epinephrine (adrenaline) into a human will cause all of the following symptoms EXCEPT 5.___
   A. constriction of the small blood vessels
   B. an increase in blood pressure
   C. an increase in the heartbeat
   D. an increase in peristalsis
   E. an increase in blood sugar

6. Photosynthetic oxygen-producing cells differ from photosynthetic non-oxygen-producing cells in that the former 6.___
   A. produce one ATP, whereas the latter produce two
   B. produce no NADPH, whereas the latter do
   C. reduce ferredoxin, whereas the latter do not
   D. produce elemental sulfur, whereas the latter do not
   E. contain and use both photosystems I and II

Questions 7-8.

DIRECTIONS: Questions 7 and 8 consists of five lettered headings followed by a list of numbered phrases or sentences. For each numbered phrase or sentence, select the one heading that is MOST closely related to it. One heading may be used once, more than once, or not at all.

A. Interspecific competition
B. Intraspecific competition
C. Predation
D. Parasitism
E. Commensalism

7. Which of the population interactions above is involved in the biotic regulation of the following species population? Young barnacles (Balanus balanoides) undercut, displace, and overgrow each other during the first year of colonization on a new site. 7.___

8. Which of the population interactions above is involved in the biotic regulation of the following species population? When they are grown separately, the sequence of intrinsic growth rates in several species of duckweed (Lemna) is: L. minor>L. natans>L. gibba>L. polyrrhiza. When they are grown together in various combinations, the sequence becomes L. natans>L. polyrrhiza>L. gibba>L. minor. 8.___

Questions 9-11.

DIRECTIONS: Questions 9 through 11 consists of five lettered headings followed by a list of numbered phrases or sentences. For each numbered phrase or sentence, select the one heading that is MOST closely related to it. One heading may be used once, more than once, or not at all.

A. Allelopathy
B. Circadian rhythm
C. Photoperiodism
D. Phototropism
E. Vernalization

9. Is characterized by an acceleration of flower formation. 9.___

10. Explains the flowering of certain species at particular times during the year. 10.___

11. Is illustrated by peaks of mitotic activity at certain periods during the day. 11.___

Questions 12-13.

DIRECTIONS: Questions 12 and 13 concern an experimental situation. First study the description of the situation. Then choose the one BEST answer to each question following it.

The ability of bats to avoid obstacles in caves and fly in the forest at night has led to studies of their sensory mechanisms. Bats were tested in the laboratory by having them fly through a barrier of fine wires spaced 30 centimeters apart. Each bat was used as its own control. Flights were recorded as successful if the bats flew through the barrier without striking a wire.

ABILITY OF BATS TO FLY THROUGH A WIRE BARRIER

Experiment	Number of Bats	Experimental Variable	Flights	Success	Control	Flights	Success
I	28	Eyes covered	2,016	76%	Untreated	3,201	70%
II	12	Ears covered	1,047	35%	Untreated	1,297	66%
III	9	Eyes and ears covered	654	31%	Eyes covered	832	75%
IV	8	Closed glass tubes in ears	580	36%	Open glass tubes in ears	636	66%
V	12	Ears covered	853	29%	One ear covered	560	38%
VI	6	Eyes and one ear covered	390	41%	Eyes covered	590	70%
VII	7	Mouth covered	549	35%	Untreated	442	62%

12. Which of the following may NOT be inferred from these data? 12.___
    A. Control flights are generally more successful than are experimental flights.
    B. The three untreated control values (I, II, VII) are similar.
    C. One or both ears closed reduces flight success.
    D. Covered mouth reduces flight success.
    E. Eyesight is essential to flight success, even at low light intensities.

13. The results of which of the following experiments indicate that hearing, especially the bilateral sensory input, is essential for successful flight? 13.___
   A. I *only*   B. VII *only*
   C. II, III   D. I, II, III
   E. II, III, IV, V, VI

14. Radioactive messenger RNA was isolated from reticulocytes and from dividing cells in embryonic liver. When 100 micrograms of RNA from each source was mixed separately with 100 micrograms of DNA under conditions in which DNA-RNA hybrid duplexes formed, the following was observed. 14.___
   I. 0.1 microgram of reticulocyte RNA was bound to 100 micrograms of DNA
   II. 10 micrograms of liver RNA was bound to 100 micrograms of DNA

   Based on the data given above, which of the following statements is plausible?
   A. No RNA made in liver cells exists in reticulocytes.
   B. Liver contains 100 times more RNA per cell than do reticulocytes.
   C. More genes are involved in coding for messenger RNA synthesis in liver cells than in reticulocytes.
   D. All messenger RNA is more stable in liver cells than in reticulocytes.
   E. The rate of RNA synthesis in reticulocytes is 100 times slower than in liver cells.

15. Which of the following conversion reactions does NOT require the energy of ATP in order to proceed? 15.___
   A. Fatty acids to fats
   B. Glucose to cellulose
   C. Glucose to glycogen
   D. Amino acids to proteins
   E. Proteins to amino acids

16. If an animal were exposed to an atmosphere of heavy oxygen ($^{18}O_2$), in which of the following would the heavy oxygen MOST probably FIRST appear? 16.___
   A. Adenosine triphosphate   B. Carbon dioxide
   C. Glucose   D. Urea
   E. Water

17. Which of the following occurs in bacterial transformation? 17.___
   A. Genes are transferred from one cell to another by a bacteriophage.
   B. The genetic information in a messenger RNA molecule directs the amino acid sequence in a protein.
   C. The genetic information in a DNA chain determines the sequences of bases in an RNA chain.

D. The information in a free DNA chain genetically modifies a cell.
E. The genetic information in one cell is transferred to another cell only during cell-to-cell contact.

18. Which of the following is the effect of selection on a quantitative trait in a stable environment? 18.___
A. A Hardy-Weinberg equilibrium
B. Genetic drift
C. Gradual fixation of all alleles
D. An increase in heterosis
E. A tendency to eliminate the extremes of the normal distribution

19. The ultimate fate of energy in an ecosystem is 19.___
A. the conversion of ADP to ATP in organisms
B. an increase in biomass
C. the responses and movements of organisms
D. to be recycled through the ecosystem
E. to be lost from the system as heat

KEY (CORRECT ANSWERS)

1. A	11. B
2. B	12. E
3. B	13. E
4. C	14. C
5. D	15. E
6. E	16. E
7. B	17. D
8. A	18. E
9. E	19. E
10. C	

BIOLOGY NOTES AND RESOURCES

INTRODUCTORY CHEMISTRY

Concepts

1. Matter is composed of atoms.

2. An atom has a nucleus composed of protons and neutrons, surrounded by a large volume of empty space containing electrons.

3. Electromagnetic attraction and repulsion result from interactions between charged particles; like charges repel each other, and unlike charges attract each other.

4. Electrons move around the nucleus of an atom within energy shells; each shell can hold only a limited number of electrons.

5. Atoms are assembled into molecules by chemical bonds between the protons in their nuclei and the electrons surrounding them.

6. A covalent bond is formed when valence electrons are shared between the nuclei of two atoms.

7. Polar covalent bonds are formed when electrons are shared unequally between the nuclei of two atoms.

8. Ionic bonds are the result of electrical attraction between oppositely charged ions, which are formed when an electron is transferred from one atom to another.

9. Hydrogen bonds are weak bonds formed when hydrogen atoms bonded to oxygen or nitrogen are attracted to oxygen or nitrogen in another molecule.

10. Some molecules are also held together by weak interactions.

11. Chemical reactions are interactions between two or more atoms or molecules in which electrons are shared or exchanged, resulting in changes in the chemical properties of the reacting materials.

12. Acids are molecules that donate hydrogen ions to other molecules; bases are molecules that accept hydrogen ions or donate hydroxyl ions to other molecules.

13. The pH of a solution is a measure of the amount of hydrogen ions dissolved in that solution; acids have a pH of less than 7, whereas bases have a pH of greater than 7.

Key Terms

1. An acid is a molecule that donates hydrogen ions to other molecules, especially bases.

2. The atomic mass (sometimes called the atomic weight) is the mass of a typical atom and is approximately equal to the total mass of the particles in that atom's nucleus.

3. The atomic number indicates the number of protons in the nucleus of the atom.

4. Atoms are the smallest particles that retain the chemical properties of a substance.

5. A base is a molecule that accepts hydrogen ions from other molecules, especially acids.

6. A buffer is a material that can maintain the pH of a solution at or near a constant value by either donating or accepting H^+ ions from solution.

7. A chemical bond is a force that binds atoms together in a molecule by means of electromagnetic attractions. A chemical bond is the result of the attraction of the electrons and protons of one atom to the protons and electrons of another atom.

8. A chemical compound is a combination of two or more different elements.

9. A chemical element is a material that has a unique set of characteristics, or chemical properties.

10. A chemical reaction is an interaction between two or more atoms or molecules in which electrons are shared or exchanged, resulting in changes in the chemical properties of the reacting materials.

11. A covalent bond is a chemical bond in which the electrons from two atoms fill each other's valence shell. In a single covalent bond, a pair of electrons is shared by two atoms.

12. Dissociation is the separation of ions in solution in water. Ions tend to float apart from each other in water, because water molecules form a hydration sphere around each ion, blocking their electromagnetic attraction for each other.

13. Electrical charge is a force that can cause positively or negatively charged objects to move.

14. Electromagnetism is either an attractive or repulsive force between electrically charged objects, especially protons and electrons.

15. The electronegativity of an atom is the tendency of the nucleus of that atom to attract the electrons of other atoms. A strongly electronegative atom has a partial negative charge when bonded in a molecule because it attracts the electrons in the molecule.

16. Electrons are small subatomic particles orbiting the nucleus of atoms. Electrons have a negative charge and repel each other, and are attracted to protons.

17. An energy level is a specific distance from an atomic nucleus where electrons same amount of energy are located. Electrons at energy levels closer to the nucleus have less energy than electrons farther away have.

18. A hydrogen bond is a weak attraction holding two molecules containing hydrogen, oxygen, nitrogen, and/or fluorine together. Hydrogen bonds form when hydrogen atoms bonded to nitrogen or oxygen are attracted to a different nitrogen or oxygen.

19. A hydrophobic interaction is a weak attraction between molecules in which parts of molecules are repelled by water and are forced into the lipid soluble interior regions of the molecules.

20. An ionic bond is the attraction holding two ions together when an electron from one atom is permanently donated to another atom rather than being shared with it.

21. Ions are electrically charged atoms, and can move around when exposed to an electromagnetic force. Ions with the same charge repel each other, whereas ions with opposite charges are attracted to each other.

22. A molecule is a structure composed of two or more atoms.

23. A negative charge (symbolized by -) is an electrical charge that repels other negative charges and attracts positive charges.

24. A negative ion is an atom with more electrons than protons, and has a negative charge.

25. Neutrons are large subatomic particles located in the nucleus of an atom. Neutrons have no charge and are therefore electrically neutral.

26. The nucleus of an atom is a dense core that contains almost all of the mass of an atom. An atomic nucleus contains two kinds of particles: protons and neutrons.

27. The pH of a solution is a measurement of the number of hydrogen ions (H^+) dissolved in that solution. The pH of a solution is technically defined as the negative logarithm of the hydrogen ion concentration.

28. A polar covalent bond is a chemical bond in which the electrons from two atoms are shared unequally with an asymmetrical distribution of charge.

29. A positive charge (symbolized by +) is an electrical charge that repels other positive charges and attracts negative charges.

30. A positive ion is an atom with more protons than electrons, and has a positive charge.

31. Protons are large subatomic particles located in the nucleus of an atom. Protons have a positive charge and repel each other, and are attracted to electrons.

32. A solution is a mixture of any material dissolved in a liquid (usually water).

33. Valence electrons are the electrons in the outer shell of an atom, regardless of energy level.

34. The valence shell is the outer shell of electrons of an atom, regardless of energy level.

Review Questions

1. What is matter composed of? What is the structure of a typical atom?

2. What is electromagnetic attraction and repulsion? What causes it?

3. What is chemistry? What are chemical elements? What are chemical compounds? What do the atomic number and atomic weight of an element signify?

4. What are ions? Do different ions of the same element have different chemical properties?

5. What are protons? What are neutrons? What are electrons? How are the electrons of an atom arranged around the nucleus of that atom?

6. What are chemical bonds? What are covalent bonds? What are nonpolar covalent bonds? What are polar covalent bonds? What are ionic bonds? What are hydrogen bonds? What are hydrophobic interactions?

7. What are acids? What are bases? What is the pH scale, and what does it measure?

BIOMOLECULES

Concepts

1. Living organisms are composed primarily of hydrogen, oxygen, nitrogen, and carbon.

2. Hydrogen can form one covalent bond with other atoms; it is part of virtually every biologically important molecule.

3. Oxygen can form a maximum of two covalent bonds with other atoms; it is part of most biomolecules, with the exception of many lipids.

4. Nitrogen can form a maximum of three covalent bonds with other atoms; it is often part of the bonds that hold together monomers in polymeric biomolecules.

5. Carbon can form a maximum of four covalent bonds with other atoms; carbon atoms form the *backbones* of most biomolecules.

6. Water molecules form very strong hydrogen bonds with each other.

7. Water is less dense as a solid than as a liquid.

8. Water has a high heat capacity and high heats of fusion and vaporization.

9. Liquid water has a high surface tension.

10. Water is an excellent solvent for polar and charged materials.

11. Carbohydrates are composed of repeated H-C-OH units.

12. Sugars are carbohydrates containing three to seven carbons; sugars composed of five or six H-C-OH units often form ring-shaped molecules when dissolved in water.

13. Polysaccharides are polymers of two or more monosaccharides.

14. Lipids are primarily composed of H-C-H units.

15. Triglycerides are lipids comprised of three fatty acid molecules bonded to one glycerol molecule.

16. Proteins are polymers of amino acids.

17. The primary sequence of amino acids determines the three-dimensional structure of proteins.

18. The primary structure of proteins is the linear order of amino acids and is held together by peptide covalent bonds.

19. The secondary structure of proteins is alpha helices or beta pleated sheets and is held together by hydrogen bonds.

20. The tertiary structure of proteins is a globular structure held together by disulphide, ionic, hydrogen, hydrophilic, hydrophobic, and van der Waal's interactions.

21. The quaternary structure of proteins is a globular structure composed of two or more chains of amino acids held together by disulphide, ionic, hydrogen, hydrophilic, hydrophobic, and van der Waal's interactions.

22. Nucleic acids are polymers of nucleotides.

23. Nucleotides are composed of a five-carbon sugar, a nitrogenous base, and a phosphate.

Key Terms

1. An aldehyde is a compound containing a carbonyl group located at the end of a chain of carbons.

2. Amino acids are small molecules with a nitrogen-carbon-carbon (N-C-C) skeleton, and which function as the monomers of proteins.

3. An amino group ($-NH_2$) is a functional group formed when an ammonia molecule is added to another molecule.

4. Ammonia (NH_3) is a simple molecule that contains one nitrogen atom polar-covalently bonded to three hydrogen atoms.

5. Calcium is a common element of living organisms, usually found in ionic form as Ca^{++}. Calcium is an important component of rigid and semirigid materials such as bone and chitin.

6. Carbon is an essential element in all biomolecules, and is composed of a nucleus containing six protons (and usually six neutrons) orbited by six electrons.

7. Carbon dioxide (CO_2) is a simple molecule that contains one carbon atom double-covalently bonded to each of two oxygen atoms.

8. A carbohydrate unit is a combination of a carbon atom, a hydrogen atom, and a hydroxyl group arranged as H-C-OH, which can be repeated many times to form very long chains.

9. Carbohydrates are the simplest of the major types of biomolecules, composed of long strings of carbon atoms, most of which are bonded to a hydrogen atom and a hydroxyl group.

10. A carboxyl (-COOH) is a functional group with a carbonyl group and a hydroxyl group at the end of a chain of carbons. Carboxyls usually function as acids in solution in water.

11. Cellulose is a polymer of repeated glucose monomers in which the oxygen bridges that hold the glucose molecules in cellulose together are arranged in zig-zagging linear strands, called cellulose fibers. Cellulose is the principal structural material in plants and photosynthetic protoctists.

12. Dehydration synthesis is a chemical process in which a new molecule is formed by the removal of a water *molecule* from two smaller molecules (dehydration synthesis is sometimes called condensation).

13. Disaccharides are simple polysaccharides composed of two six-carbon monosaccharides held together by a covalent bond.

14. A disulphide bridge is a bond between two sulfur-containing amino acids in a protein, holding together two chains of amino acids in a tertiary structure.

15. Enzymes are globular proteins that function as catalysts in cells, accelerating biochemical reactions.

16. Fats are semisolid lipids used as energy-storage materials by animals.

17. Fatty acids are hydrocarbon chains with a terminal carboxyl group. Fatty acids are one of the two components of oils and fats.

18. Fructose is the six-carbon sugar (monosaccharide) most commonly found in fruits and other plant tissues.

19. A functional group is a part of a molecule that changes the function of the molecule containing the group.

20. Galactose is the six-carbon sugar (monosaccharide) most commonly found in milk.

21. Globular proteins are large tertiary or quaternary proteins that are roughly spherical in shape. Globular proteins usually function as enzymes or regulatory proteins.

22. Glucose is the most common and most stable six-carbon sugar (monosaccharide), and is the immediate source of energy for all living cells.

23. Glycogen (or *animal starch*) is a polymer of glucose monosaccharides bridged by an oxygen atom, found only in animals. In glycogen, the three-dimensional structure of the oxygen bridges results in a twisted helix of polymerized glucose molecules.

24. Heat capacity is the ability of a substance to absorb or release large amounts of heat without changing from solid to liquid or from liquid to gas.

25. Heat of fusion is the heat energy required to cause melting (changing from a solid to a liquid).

26. Heat of vaporization is the heat energy required to cause evaporation or boiling (changing from a liquid to a gas).

27. Hydration spheres are layers of water molecules that adhere to charged (ionic) substances, thereby insulating them from other charged substances.

28. A hydrocarbon unit is a combination of a carbon atom and two hydrogen atoms arranged as

```
  |
H-C-H
  |
```

which can be repeated many times to form very long chains.

29. Hydrogen is the simplest, lightest, and most abundant element in the universe, and is composed of one proton orbited by one electron.

30. Hydrolysis is a chemical reaction in which two monomer units of a polymer are separated from each other by the replacement of the oxygen bridge between them with a hydrogen ion and a hydroxyl group.

31. A hydroxyl group (-OH) is a combination of oxygen and hydrogen often found in alcohols and carbohydrates.

32. Isomers are molecules that have the same molecular formula but different structural arrangements.

33. A ketone is a compound containing a carbonyl group located between two other carbon atoms.

34. Lactose is a disaccharide formed by the dehydration synthesis of a molecule of glucose and a molecule of galactose and is the principal sugar in milk.

35. Lipids are any biomolecules containing carbon and hydrogen, but with relatively little oxygen. Because of their low oxygen content, lipids cannot dissolve in water, but can dissolve in ether, chloroform, or other organic solvents.

36. Maltose is a disaccharide formed by the dehydration synthesis of two molecules of glucose and is the principal sugar polymerized in plants to make starch.

37. Methane (CH_4) is a simple compound composed of a carbon atom and four single covalently bonded hydrogens in a tetrahedral arrangement.

38. A methyl group ($-CH_3$) is a functional group formed when a methane molecule is added to another molecule.

39. Monosaccharides are carbohydrate molecules composed of three to seven H-C-OH units and one or more aldehyde or ketone functional groups.

40. Nitrogen is the most common element in the Earth's atmosphere, and is composed of a nucleus containing seven protons (and usually seven neutrons) orbited by seven electrons.

41. Nucleotides are monomers of nucleic acids, composed of three subunits: a five-carbon sugar, which acts as a structural skeleton; a larger ring-shaped nitrogenous base functional group containing carbon, hydrogen, and nitrogen; and a variable number of phosphates.

42. Oils are liquid lipids used as energy-storage materials by plants.

43. Organic molecules are molecules containing two or more carbon atoms, usually arranged in linear or branched chains.

44. Oxygen is one of the most chemically reactive elements on Earth, and is composed of a nucleus containing eight protons (and usually eight neutrons) orbited by eight electrons.

45. Peptide bonds are covalent bonds joining together the amino acids of proteins. Peptide bonds form between the carboxyl group of one amino acid and the amino group of the next amino acid in a chain.

46. A phospholipid is a triglyceride which has two fatty acid chains (which are not water soluble) and a phosphate-containing functional group (which is water soluble). Phospholipids are common components in cell membranes.

47. Phosphorus is an essential element in nucleic acids, usually forms five covalent bonds (one of which is usually a double bond), and is usually found in association with oxygen.

48. Polypeptides are polymers of amino acids, usually considered to be less than fifty amino acids long.

49. Polysaccharides are chains of two or more monosaccharides.

50. The primary structure of a polypeptide or protein is the linear order of amino acids in the chain.

51. Proteins are large polymers of amino acids, functioning either as structural material (usually in animals) or as enzymes.

52. The quaternary structure of a polypeptide or protein is the globular structure formed by two or more chains of amino acids held together in a single functional unit.

53. R groups (represented in structural formulas by an *R*) are functional groups attached to the central carbon atoms of amino acids, distinguishing the varieties of amino acids from each other and giving them different chemical properties.

54. Ribose sugars are five-carbon sugars, usually found in ring form in solution in water. Ribose sugars are essential structural components of nucleic acids.

55. The secondary structure of a polypeptide or protein is the helical or pleated sheet arrangement formed by the folding of the amino acids of the primary structure.

56. A solute is the solid material that has dissolved in a liquid solution.

57. A solvent is the liquid in which a solute has dissolved.

58. Starch (or amylose) is a polymer of glucose monosaccharides bridged by an oxygen atom, found principally in plants. In amylose, the three-dimensional structure of the oxygen bridges results in a twisted helix of polymerized glucose molecules.

59. Steroids are lipids composed of four hydrocarbon rings, constructed from cholesterol and often functioning as hormones.

60. Structural proteins are proteins composed of long interwoven fibers that support and protect cells.

61. Sucrose is a disaccharide composed of a molecule of glucose attached to a molecule of fructose. Sucrose is a *transportable* form of sugar in plants.

62. Sulfur is a chemical element usually found in proteins, and which has chemical properties similar to those of oxygen.

63. Sugars are carbohydrate molecules (sometimes called monosaccharides) composed of three to seven H-C-OH units and one or more aldehyde or ketone functional groups.

64. Surface tension is the tendency of molecules of a liquid to form a tightly interlocked surface network.

65. The tertiary structure of a polypeptide or protein is the globular arrangement formed by the folding of the alpha helices and/or beta pleated sheets of the secondary structure.

66. Triglycerides are biomolecules composed of three fatty acids covalently bonded to a molecule of glycerol, a three-carbon alcohol.

67. Waxes are solid water-repellent lipids composed of saturated fatty acids bonded to alcohols that have four or more carbons.

Review Questions

1. List and discuss the structures and functions of hydrogen, oxygen, nitrogen, and carbon. How many covalent bonds can each element form?

2. What element forms the *backbone* of nearly all biomolecules? What are the properties of this element, and what kinds of molecules and other structures can it form?

3. What functions do calcium, phosphorus, and sulfur perform in living organisms?

4. Water molecules can form very strong hydrogen bonds with each other. What properties of water result from this special property of water, and how are these properties important to life on Earth?

5. List, give an example, and describe the structures and functions of at least six of the important functional groups in biochemistry.

6. What are the general structures and functions of carbohydrates? What fundamental unit are most carbohydrates composed of?

7. Explain the importance of five- and six-carbon carbohydrates. What is glucose, and why is it so important to living organisms?

8. What are polysaccharides? List and describe at least two disaccharides and two polysaccharides.

9. What are lipids? What special properties do lipids have that other biomolecules do not have? How are these properties related to the functions of lipids?

10. What are proteins? List and describe at least two different types of proteins, and explain how their structures are related to their functions.

11. What are nucleic acids? List and describe the functions of at least three types of nucleic acids.

CELL BIOLOGY

Concepts

1. Organelles are specialized structures that carry out cellular functions.

2. Ribosomes synthesize proteins, and are composed of globular protein molecules held together by RNA molecules.

3. The nucleus of eukaryotic cells protects and confines the genetic material.

4. Eukaryotic chromosomes are composed of DNA molecules wrapped around histone proteins.

5. The eukaryotic nucleolus is the site of ribosome synthesis.

6. The eukaryotic endoplasmic reticulum provides an intracellular synthesis and transportation network for proteins and a storage site for other materials, especially calcium.

7. Eukaryotic golgi bodies process and store proteins and other biomolecules produced in the endoplasmic reticulum.

8. The cytoskeleton, which is composed of microtubules and microfilaments, supports cells and functions in cell movement and locomotion.

9. Mitochondria are endosymbiont-derived organelles that synthesize ATP and other materials within eukaryotic cells.

10. Chloroplasts are endosymbiont-derived organelles that synthesize ATP, carbohydrates, and other materials within some eukaryotic cells.

11. Cell membranes form boundaries around and within cells.

12. Plasma membranes are primarily composed of a phospholipid bilayer.

13. Embedded in plasma membranes are proteins which perform many of the functions of those membranes.

14. Some organisms, especially plants, have cell walls which provide support and protection.

15. Animal cells lack cell walls; they are protected and supported by an extracellular matrix composed primarily of protein.

16. Plasma membranes are semipermeable; they allow the passage of some materials, but prevent the passage of other materials.

17. Particles tend to diffuse through a membrane from where that type of particle is more concentrated to where that type of particle is less concentrated.

18. Osmosis is the diffusion of water through a semipermeable membrane.

19. Active transport is the pumping of materials through membranes against their concentration gradients.

20. Cells can engulf materials from outside themselves by endocytosis, and can eject materials out of themselves by exocytosis.

Key Terms

1. Active transport is the transport of dissolved materials through a membrane against the concentration gradient of that material; active transport requires the expenditure of energy.

2. The cell theory states that all living organisms are composed of cells and that all cells arise from previously existing cells.

3. Chloroplasts are large endosymbiont-derived organelles that carry out photosynthesis. Chloroplasts have multiple membranes and a structural organization similar to that of some bacterial cells. Chloroplasts are found in many protoctist and plant cells, where they synthesize ATP, glucose, and other carbohydrates.

4. A chromatin fiber is a long strand of eukaryotic DNA wrapped around histone units to form chains of nucleosomes.

5. Cilia are multiple undulapodia that beat in unison like the oars of a racing shell, causing coordinated movement that can either cause the cell to move or cause materials to pass over the surface of the cell.

6. The concentration of a material is defined as the number of particles of a specific material per a given volume.

7. A concentration gradient is a change in the concentration of dissolved particles over a distance from an area of high concentration to an area of low concentration.

8. Cytoplasmic streaming is a constant movement of the cytoplasm inside cells, especially plant cells, allowing the contents of the cell to move in response to changes in the cell's external environment.

9. The cytoskeleton is a system of microtubules and microfilaments that forms an internal framework for eukaryotic cells.

10. Diffusion is the movement of specific particles from a volume of high concentration of those particles to a volume of low concentration of those particles.

11. Endocytosis is the process of engulfing large quantities of material into a cell by the formation of a pocket in the membrane.

12. The endoplasmic reticulum (abbreviated ER) is a system of membranes forming a closed network of flattened channels inside eukaryotic cells.

13. The endosymbiont hypothesis for the evolution of endosymbiont-derived organelles states that eukaryotic host cells provided symbiotic bacterial cells with protection, a stable environment, and raw materials, and in exchange, the endosymbiotic bacteria provided their hosts with materials the hosts were unable to synthesize and in some cases, carried out functions that the hosts were unable to perform.

14. Exocytosis is the process of ejecting large quantities of material out of a cell by the fusing of cellular vesicles or vacuoles inside the cell's cytoplasm with the plasma membrane.

15. Facilitated diffusion is the diffusion of large water-soluble or charged materials through protein molecules embedded in cell membranes.

16. Flagella are single undulapodia that are long compared to the length of the cell and beat individually, usually causing the cell to move.

17. Golgi bodies are complex organelles of eukaryotic cells, composed of multiple layers of membranous vesicles, within which proteins and other materials are stored and chemically modified prior to their use.

18. Histones, alkaline proteins associated with eukaryotic DNA, partially neutralize the acidity of DNA, stabilize and protect the DNA, and provide a framework around which the DNA can be spooled.

19. A hypertonic solution is a solution that has more dissolved particles than an equal volume of another solution has.

20. A hypotonic solution is a solution that has fewer dissolved particles than an equal volume of another solution has.

21. Ion channels (sometimes just channels) are permeases that facilitate the passage of charged ions through cell membranes.

22. Isotonic solutions are two solutions that have the same concentration of dissolved particles.

23. Lysosomes are large vesicles filled with digestive enzymes.

24. Membrane proteins are globular proteins embedded in cell membranes like the tiles in a mosaic; membrane proteins function as channels, carriers, and pumps, or act as markers for cell identification.

25. Microfilaments are thread-like structures composed of polymerized globular proteins.

26. Microtubules are hollow, tube-shaped assemblies of globular protein molecules called tubulin subunits.

27. Mitochondria are sausage-shaped or tubular organelles, found in all eukaryotic cells, that synthesize ATP and other energy-containing molecules using oxygen.

28. The nuclear envelope (sometimes called the nuclear membrane) is a double membrane that encloses the nucleus of the cell, forming an internal boundary around the nucleus, protecting the contents of the nucleus, and regulating the flow of materials into and out of the nucleus.

29. Nuclear pores are large holes in the nuclear membrane through which ribosomes and other large objects enter and leave the nucleus.

30. The nucleolus is a region of the nucleus in which the segments of chromosomes that code for ribosomal subunits aggregate and where the two subunits of the ribosomes are synthesized.

31. Organelles are specialized internal cellular structures that carry the functions of a cell.

32. Osmosis is the diffusion of water through a semipermeable membrane.

33. A permeable membrane is a membrane that allows materials to pass through it.

34. Permeases are large globular proteins that span the cell membrane, allowing specific materials to pass through the membrane.

35. Phagocytosis is a type of endocytosis in which a cell engulfs large solid objects by surrounding them with extensions of the plasma membrane called pseudopodia, thereby creating a vacuole.

36. A phospholipid bilayer is part of a cell membrane composed of two layers of phospholipid molecules.

37. Pinocytosis is a process by which a cell engulfs small amounts of liquids by forming coated pits, which then form vesicles inside the cell.

38. Plasmodesmata are very tiny tube-like connections that allow the passage of cytoplasm from plant cell to plant cell.

39. Plastids are membranous organelles that store some of the pigments and products of photosynthesis.

40. A primary cell wall is the outer cell wall of plants, which protects the cell, provides it with some support, and prevents damage to the cell as the result of sudden osmotic changes.

41. The rough endoplasmic reticulum is endoplasmic reticulum with attached ribosomes, which provide a site for the synthesis of proteins for export out of the cell.

42. The secondary cell wall of plant cells is a thick, rigid cell wall located just inside the primary cell wall that provides structural support as well as protection.

43. Secretion is a process by which materials produced inside cells are exported out of cells by secretory vesicles that fuse with the plasma membrane of the cell, expelling their contents by exocytosis.

44. Secretory vesicles are vesicles that transport materials synthesized in the ER and processed in the golgi bodies to the plasma membrane, where they are released.

45. A semipermeable membrane is a membrane that is permeable to some materials but not to others.

46. The smooth endoplasmic reticulum is endoplasmic reticulum without ribosomes, which provides a site for the synthesis of lipids and membrane components for the cell.

47. The sodium-potassium pump is a membrane protein that actively transports sodium out of a cell and potassium into a cell, using energy supplied by the breakdown of ATP.

48. Spindle fibers are specialized microtubules that move eukaryotic chromosomes into the two poles of a dividing cell.

49. A vacuole is a large membrane-bounded organelle that can contain liquid or solid material. Once enclosed in a vacuole, this material may be digested or chemically manipulated by the cell without the material entering (and possibly damaging) the cytoplasm of the cell.

50. A vesicle is a small membrane bubble that is formed from coated pits and is smaller than a vacuole.

Review Questions

1. What is the cytosol? What are organelles? How do they relate to each other?

2. What is chromatin? What are chromosomes? What are histone proteins? How are DNA molecules and histone proteins related?

3. What are ribosomes? What are ribosomes composed of? Where are eukaryotic ribosomes synthesized?

4. What is the cytoskeleton? What is it composed of? What functions does it serve in cells?

5. What is the nucleus of a eukaryotic cell? What is it composed of? What functions does it serve in cells?

6. What is the endoplasmic reticulum? What functions does it perform? What are the differences between rough and smooth endoplasmic reticulum?

7. What are golgi bodies? What functions do golgi bodies perform? How are golgi bodies related to the endoplasmic reticulum, and to secretory vesicles?

8. What are endosymbiont-derived organelles? What evidence is there that they evolved from prokaryotic ancestors?

9. What are mitochondria? What are their functions? What are chloroplasts? What are their functions?

10. List and briefly describe the functions of cell membranes.

11. What are phospholipids? Why are they important components of cell membranes?

12. What are membrane proteins? What functions do these proteins perform?

13. What is diffusion? What factors affect the rate of diffusion through cell membranes?

14. What is active transport? How does active transport differ from diffusion?

15. What is osmosis? What are hypertonic, hypotonic, and isotonic solutions, and how do they affect cells?

Metabolism Poster Part 1

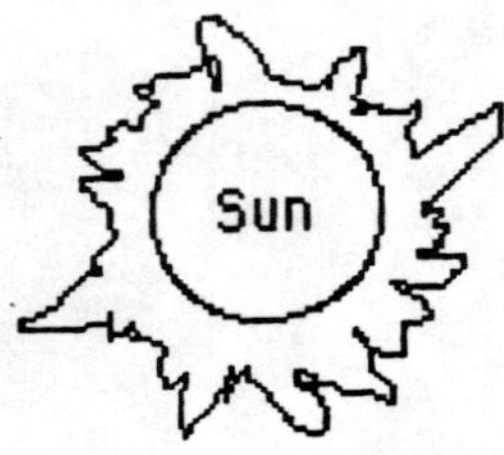

Photophosphorylation

Chloro

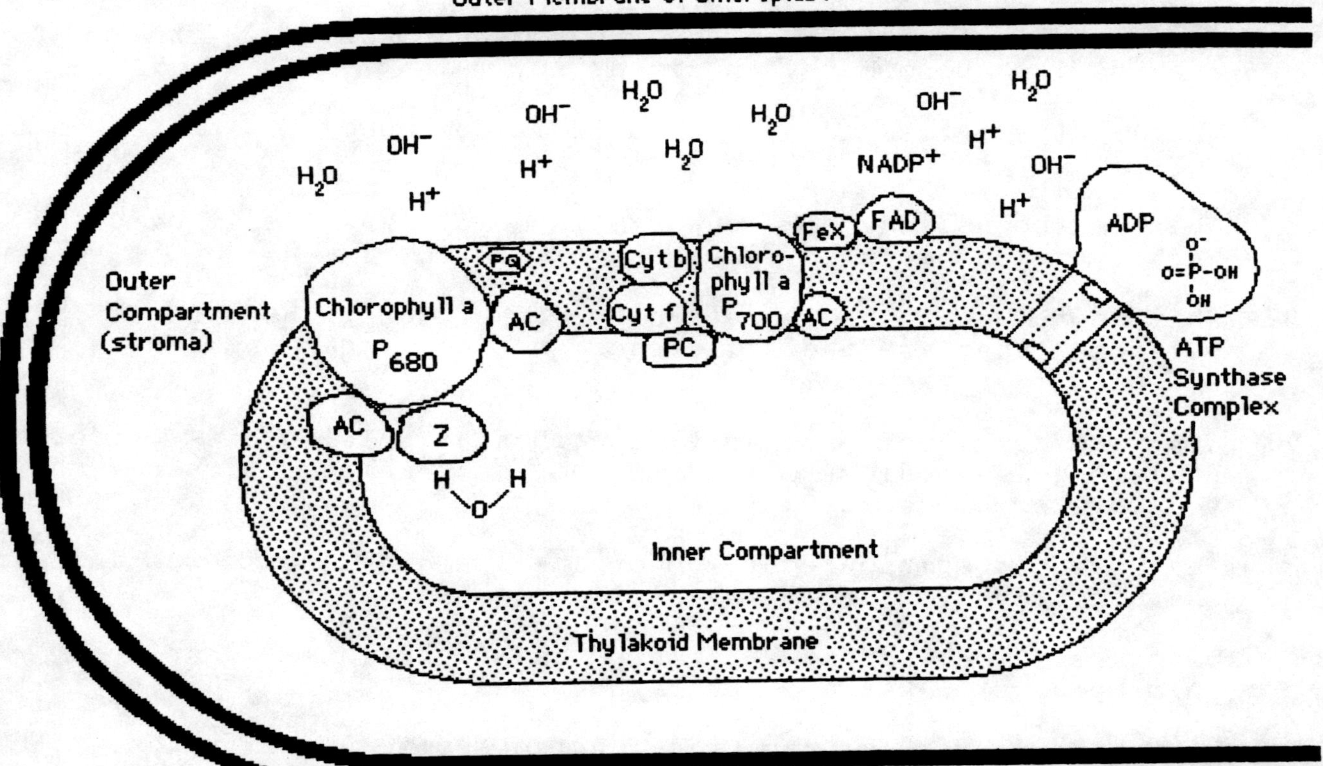

Key:

AC =	antenna complex	**FeX =**	ferredoxin	
Cyt b =	cytochrome b	**NADP+ =**	nicotine-adenine dinucleotide phosphate	
Cyt f =	cytochrome f	**PC =**	plastocyanin (cytochrome)	
FAD =	flavine-adenine dinucleotide	**PQ =**	plastoquinone =	$+ \; 2H^+ \; 2e^- \rightarrow$

oxidized form — reduced form

Notes:

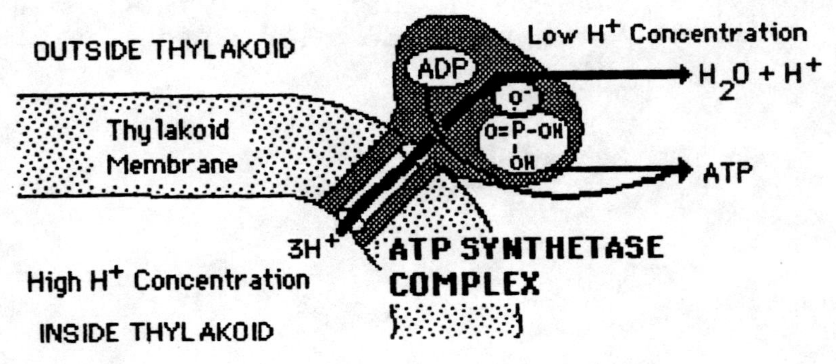

Metabolism Poster Part 2

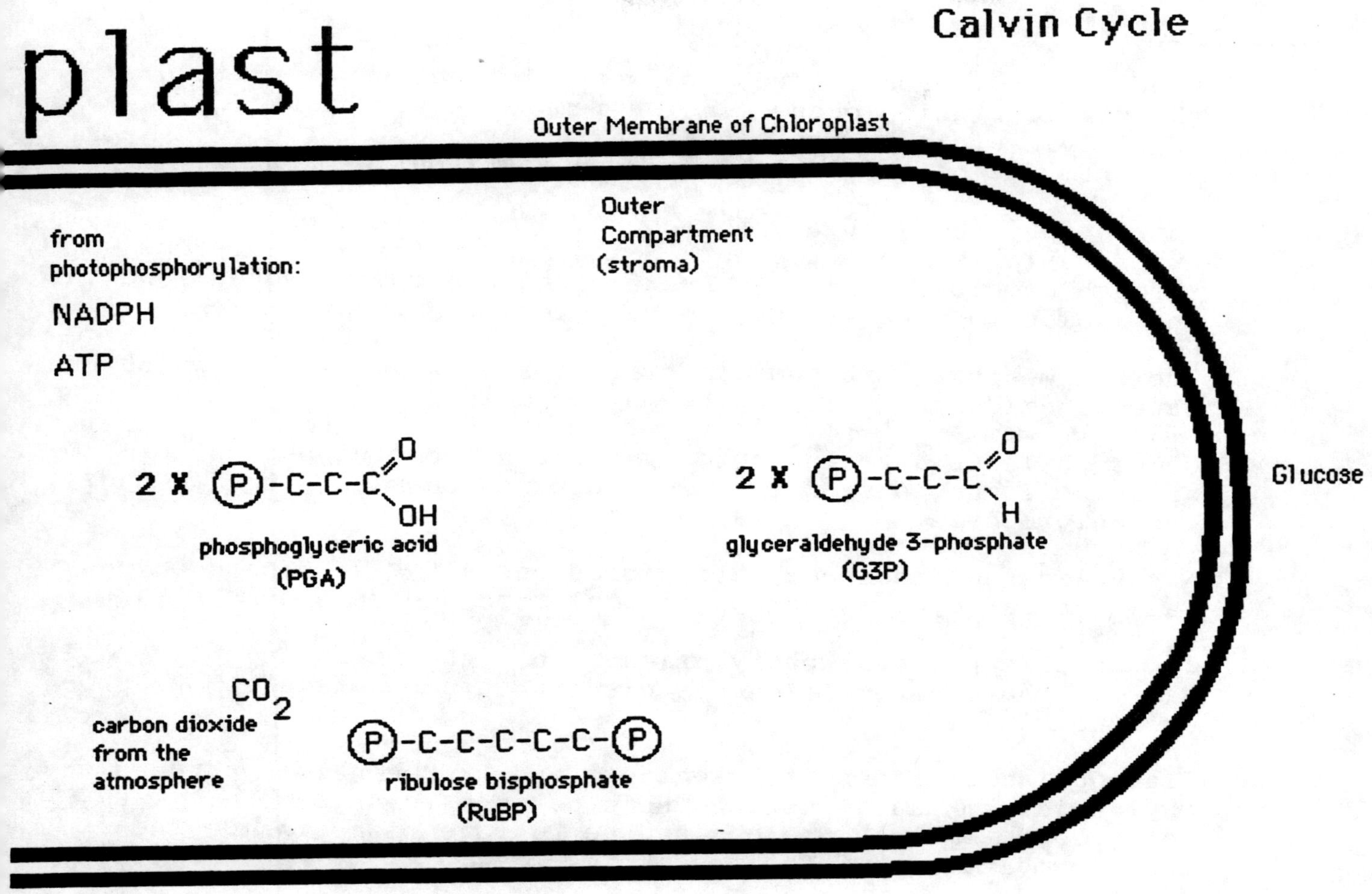

Calvin Cycle

plast

Outer Membrane of Chloroplast

Outer Compartment (stroma)

from photophosphorylation:

NADPH

ATP

2 X (P)-C-C-C(=O)OH

phosphoglyceric acid (PGA)

2 X (P)-C-C-C(=O)H

glyceraldehyde 3-phosphate (G3P)

Glucose

CO_2

carbon dioxide from the atmosphere

(P)-C-C-C-C-C-(P)

ribulose bisphosphate (RuBP)

Notes:

PHOTOSYNTHESIS

Concepts

1. Photosynthesis consists of two sets of reactions: photophosphorylation, which occurs in the membranes of thylakoids, and the Calvin cycle, which occurs in the cytosol of the outer compartments of chloroplasts and photosynthetic bacteria.

2. In photophosphorylation, the energy of red light photons striking chlorophyll is converted into a flow of energized electrons through a membrane protein system, which pumps hydrogen ions into thylakoids to make ATP by membrane-level phosphorylation.

3. Photopigments absorb photons of different wavelengths, which can cause chemical changes in the photopigments.

4. Chlorophyll is a green photopigment that absorbs photons of red and blue light, energizing electrons in the magnesium atoms of the chlorophyll.

5. Noncyclic photophosphorylation produces ATP, NADPH, and oxygen gas, whereas cyclic photophosphorylation produces only ATP.

6. In noncyclic photophosphorylation, red light striking chlorophyll *a* P_{680} in photosystem II causes electrons to be passed to plastoquinone.

7. Plastoquinone transports electrons and hydrogen ions through the thylakoid membrane, passing the electrons to chlorophyll *a* P_{700} in photosystem I and releasing the hydrogen ions inside the inner compartment of the thylakoid.

8. Red light striking chlorophyll *a* P_{700} in photosystem I causes electrons to be passed to $NADP^+$ producing NADPH, which can be used in the Calvin cycle.

9. Electrons removed from water by photosystem II restore the electrons donated by chlorophyll *a* P_{680}, releasing hydrogen ions inside thylakoids and producing oxygen gas as a byproduct.

10. The free energy of hydrogen ions flowing from a high concentration inside thylakoids to a low concentration in the outer compartment is used to produce ATP by membrane-level phosphorylation.

11. In cyclic photophosphorylation, electrons follow a cyclic pathway from chlorophyll *a* P_{700} through an alternative cytochrome system back to chlorophyll *a* P_{700}, building up a hydrogen ion gradient.

12. The Calvin cycle uses carbon dioxide and the outputs of photophosphorylation (ATP and NADPH) to synthesize carbohydrates.

13. In the Calvin cycle, carbon dioxide is added to RuBP to make PGA, which is then converted into PGAL using ATP and NADPH produced by photophosphorylation.

14. The PGAL synthesized in the Calvin cycle can be used to synthesize all of the other biomolecules needed by photosynthetic organisms.

Key Terms

1. Accessory pigments are photopigments found in many plants that absorb different wavelengths of light than chlorophyll does. These accessory pigments channel light energy to chlorophyll in the thylakoid membranes.

2. An antenna complex is an array of chlorophyll and other pigments that can capture light energy and funnel it to the reaction centers of photosystems.

3. The Calvin cycle (also called carbon fixation) is the process of carbohydrate synthesis in autotrophs, using atmospheric carbon dioxide to synthesize carbohydrates, lipids, proteins, and nucleic acids. Carbon fixation takes place in the outer compartment (stroma) of chloroplasts and photosynthetic bacteria.

4. Chlorophyll is a lipid soluble photopigment that absorbs photons of red and blue light, and reflects or transmits green light.

5. Chlorophyll *a* P_{680} is a form of chlorophyll *a* which absorbs light in the reaction centers of photosystem II. Chlorophyll *a* P_{680} gets its name from the fact that it releases electrons most easily when excited by light photons with a wavelength of 680 nm (red light).

6. Chlorophyll *a* P_{700} is a form of chlorophyll *a* which absorbs light in the reaction centers of photosystem I. Chlorophyll *a* P_{700} gets its name from the fact that it releases electrons most easily when excited by light photons with a wavelength of 700 nm (red light).

7. Cyclic photophosphorylation is a form of photosynthesis in which the electrons passed from photosystem I through the cytochrome bf complex eventually return to their starting point in photosystem I. Cyclic photophosphorylation produces only ATP.

8. Cytochromes are protein molecules that can accept electrons, but not hydrogen ions, from the quinones and from other cytochromes. When a quinone carrying both electrons and hydrogen ions passes its electrons to a cytochrome, the hydrogen ions that the quinone is carrying are released into the cytoplasm inside the thylakoid.

9. Magnesium is a metal used as a nutrient by many living organisms. Magnesium does the work in a chlorophyll molecule, by donating electrons to other molecules in response to light.

10. Mesophyll cells are cells of plants specialized for photosynthesis, containing numerous chloroplasts and usually forming two layers inside a plant leaf.

11. Nicotinamide adenine dinucleotide phosphate (abbreviated NADP) is an electron/hydrogen shuttle molecule that can accept two electrons and one hydrogen ion from photosystem I of noncyclic photophosphorylation and donate two electrons and one hydrogen ion to phosophoglycerate (phosphoglyceric acid) in the Calvin cycle of photosynthesis; its oxidized form is $NADP^+$ and its reduced form is NADPH.

12. Noncyclic photophosphorylation is a form of photosynthesis in which the electrons passed from photosystem through cytochromes never return to their starting point in the system. Instead, they are passed through the system to an electron acceptor. Noncyclic photophosphorylation produces both ATP and NADPH.

13. Phosphoglyceraldehyde (abbreviated PGAL) is a three-carbon carbohydrate produced during glycolysis and the Calvin cycle of photosynthesis.

14. Phosphoglycerate (abbreviated PGA) is the ionized form of phosphoglyceric acid, a three-carbon carboxylic acid produced during glycolysis and the Calvin cycle of photosynthesis.

15. Photons are tiny packets of electromagnetic energy, including light; photons have both a particle and wave nature, including a wavelength that is related to the photon's color.

16. Photopigments are pigments (such as chlorophyll), found in plants and other photosynthetic autotrophs, that cause chemical changes when they absorb light.

17. Photosystems are large, protein/photopigment complexes embedded in the membranes of thylakoids. The proteins form a framework to which the photopigment molecules are attached. When light strikes the pigment molecules in a photosystem, energized electrons are donated to quinones in the membrane of a thylakoid.

18. Photosystem I is a photosystem that consists of 13 proteins and approximately 200 light-sensitive chlorophyll molecules and a variable number of other light-sensitive molecules embedded in the proteins. Photosystem I is a functional part of both noncyclic and cyclic photophosphorylation.

19. Photosystem II is a photosystem that consists of 10 proteins and approximately 200 to 250 light-sensitive chlorophyll molecules and a variable number of other light-sensitive molecules embedded in the proteins. Photosystem II is only functional in noncyclic photophosphorylation.

20. A pigment is any material that reflects or transmits photons of some wavelengths of light.

21. Plastocyanin is a molecule in the cytochrome bf complex that holds electrons until they can be passed to photosystem I.

22. Plastoquinone is a quinone molecule that is free to diffuse within the lipid layer of the thylakoid membrane. Plastoquinone carries electrons and hydrogen ions through the thylakoid membrane, donating electrons to a cytochrome and releasing the hydrogen ions inside the thylakoid.

23. A reaction center is the part of a photosystem into which the light energy is passed, and which transforms this energy into a flow of electrons.

24. Ribulose bisphosphate (abbreviated RuBP) is a five-carbon sugar with two phosphates attached. It is an intermediate in the Calvin cycle of photosynthesis.

25. RuBP carboxylase (often called rubisco) is the enzyme that catalyzes the addition of carbon dioxide to RuBP in the Calvin cycle of photosynthesis. Rubisco can also accept oxygen instead of carbon dioxide, thereby leading to photorespiration.

26. The wavelength of any wave-form phenomenon, including a photon of light, is defined as the distance from one wave crest to the next. The wavelengths of light photons are usually measured in nanometers (billionths of a meter = X^{x} 10^{-9} M, abbreviated nm).

Review Questions

1. What are photons? What does *wavelength* mean? How is wavelength related to color? How is wavelength related to energy?

2. What are photopigments? Why do specific photopigments have the colors that they do?

3. What is chlorophyll? How does chlorophyll react to light? What kind of light does chlorophyll react to? What part does magnesium play in this reaction?

4. What are accessory pigments? Name two accessory pigments, their colors, and their functions.

5. What is photophosphorylation? What are the differences between noncyclic and cyclic photophosphorylation? What is the Calvin cycle? How is the Calvin cycle related to noncyclic and cyclic photophosphorylation?

6. What is the overall function of noncyclic photophosphorylation? List in sequential order the steps in the flow of electrons from water through photosystems II and I to $NADP^+$. What are the inputs and outputs of noncyclic photophosphorylation?

7. What are the functions of photosystems I and II? What are the functions of plastoquinone? What are the functions of the cytochrome bf complex? How are all of these related to each other?

8. What is the overall function of cyclic photophosphorylation? List in sequential order the steps in the flow of electrons from chlorophyll *a* P_{700} through the cytochrome systems back to chlorophyll *a* P_{700}. What are the inputs and outputs of cyclic photophosphorylation?

9. What is the overall function of the Calvin cycle? What are the inputs and outputs of the Calvin cycle?

10. List in sequential order the radioactively labeled molecules that would be produced if you provided a C_3 plant with carbon dioxide gas labeled with radioactive carbon ($_{14}C$).

—

NUTRITION, DIGESTION & GAS EXCHANGE

Concepts

1. Animals require five types of macronutrients: water, oxygen, carbohydrates, lipids, and proteins.

2. Animals require two types of micronutrients: vitamins and minerals.

3. Mechanical digestion is the fragmentation of large food materials by mechanical means; chemical digestion is the breakdown of biomolecules using enzymes.

4. Mechanical digestion of all foods and chemical digestion of carbohydrates begin in the mouth.

5. The stomach stores food, continues mechanical digestion, and provides an acid environment for chemical digestion of proteins.

6. The pancreas secretes many of the digestive enzymes, which are conveyed to the small intestine via the pancreatic duct.

7. The liver produces bile, which is stored in the gall bladder and released into the small intestine via the bile duct; bile emulsifies lipids prior to chemical digestion.

8. Most chemical digestion takes place in the small intestine; almost all nutrients are absorbed in the small intestine.

9. Absorption of vitamin K and some water occurs in the large intestine.

10. Gas exchange can occur only through moist membranes.

11. Large organisms require proportionally larger gas exchange surfaces than small animals.

12. Many small invertebrates exchange gases through their body surfaces.

13. Gills are highly folded extensions of the body surface of some aquatic animals through which gases are exchanged.

14. Countercurrent gas exchange is more efficient than is concurrent gas exchange.

15. Some gas exchange occurs through the skin of terrestrial animals, especially amphibians.

16. Insects and some other invertebrates exchange gases through tracheal membranes, whereas most terrestrial vertebrates exchange gases using lungs.

17. Oxygen is exchanged and transported by hemoglobin in vertebrates; the binding of oxygen to hemoglobin can be affected by oxygen concentration and pH (acidity).

18. Carbon dioxide is primarily exchanged and transported in the form of bicarbonate ions in the blood plasma in vertebrates.

Key Terms

1. Alveoli are saclike structures where gas exchange occurs and are at the lower end of each bronchiole of a lung.

2. The anus of an animal is the muscular opening at the end of a tubular digestive system; the anus regulates the expulsion of waste materials from the intestines.

3. Basal metabolism is the energy necessary to maintain anabolic and catabolic cellular processes; this energy is required even if an animal is sleeping.

4. Bile is a soap-like material, synthesized in the liver from a breakdown product of heme and is used to emulsify lipids in the digestive system.

5. Bronchi are the paired tubes that branch from the trachea of the lungs of land vertebrates.

6. Bronchioles are small tubes that branch from the bronchi of a land vertebrate's lung.

7. Carbonic anhydrase is an enzyme carried in the red blood cells (along with hemoglobin) that catalyzes the formation of carbonic acid from carbon dioxide and water in the blood plasma.

8. Chemical digestion is the chemical breakdown of small food particles into individual chemical monomers; chemical digestion is typically carried out by digestive enzymes.

9. In countercurrent gas exchange, gases are exchanged between fluids that move in opposite directions along an exchange surface; countercurrent gas exchange can be nearly twice as efficient as parallel gas exchange because the concentration of oxygen in the external medium is always higher than that in the internal medium.

10. A crop is a sac-like structure located just above the gizzard, which stores food materials and passes them to the gizzard in small quantities at regular intervals.

11. The diaphragm is a muscular sheet of tissue at the anterior end of the abdominal cavity, that contracts and relaxes, forcing air into and out of the lungs.

12. The duodenum is a short, bulblike chamber of the small intestine, located just outside the stomach. In the duodenum, enzymes from the pancreas and bile from the liver are mixed with food particles and water from the stomach.

13. Emulsification is the mixing of one liquid with another; generally, emulsification refers to the mixing of lipids with solutions of water.

14. The epiglottis is a semirigid structure, located at the opening of the trachea of land vertebrates, which is forced over the opening when food slides down the throat, thereby preventing food from entering the trachea and lungs.

15. The esophagus is a muscular tube that connects the mouth and the stomach of vertebrates; the esophagus conducts food from the mouth to the stomach.

16. Essential amino acids cannot be synthesized by an organism and must therefore be eaten regularly. Humans lack the ability to synthesize 8 essential amino acids.

17. Feces are a mixture of undigested food material, water, and bacteria contained within the lower end of the digestive tract of animals.

18. The gall bladder is a thin-walled bag about the size of a golf ball, located on the under surface of the liver, in which bile is stored.

19. Gastric fluid is a mixture of enzymes, hydrochloric acid, and water secreted by the stomach mucosa.

20. Gill arches are small, fanlike structures of fish gills.

21. Gill filaments are tiny fingerlike extensions of the gill arches of fish, which increase the surface area of the gills for gas exchange.

22. Gills are specialized gas exchange structures, generally found in large aquatic animals. Gills are composed of a stiffened framework from which many thin gas exchange surfaces are suspended.

23. A gizzard is a thick-walled, muscular sac that usually contains stones and other hard materials, which grind food like teeth do.

24. A heme group is an iron-containing ring of carbon and nitrogen atoms, most commonly located in hemoglobin molecules and in some cytochromes.

25. One kilocalorie (abbreviated kcal), commonly called a calorie, is the amount of energy needed to raise the temperature of one kilogram of water one degree Celsius.

26. The large intestine (sometimes called the colon) is the last segment of the digestive system of vertebrates and is where some water and vitamin K are absorbed.

27. Lungs are internal moist chambers of land vertebrates, specialized for gas exchange.

28. Macronutrients are nutrients that are needed in large quantities, such as water, oxygen, carbohydrates, lipids, and proteins.

29. Mechanical digestion is the chopping, shredding, and crushing of food materials, yielding smaller food particles; mechanical digestion is typically carried out by teeth and other mouthparts, gizzards, and stomachs.

30. Micronutrients are nutrients that are needed in small quantities, such as nucleic acids, vitamins, and minerals.

31. Minerals are inorganic materials that are needed for metabolism and physiological processes; many minerals are obtained in ionized form.

32. In negative-pressure breathing, the diaphragm, a muscular sheet of tissue at the anterior end of the abdominal cavity, contracts and relaxes, forcing air into and out of the lungs.

33. The pancreas is a glandular organ, generally attached to the first loop of the small intestine of vertebrates, that secretes digestive enzymes and hormones.

34. The pancreatic duct is a pencil-sized tube that conducts enzymes from the pancreas to the small intestine.

35. Partial pressure is the fraction of the total gases in air that is taken up by a particular gas being measured.

36. Pepsin is a digestive enzyme secreted by epithelial cells in pits in the stomach lining; pepsin hydrolyzes large proteins into short polypeptide segments.

37. Peristalsis is the wave-like contraction of muscles lining the digestive system, which forces food through the system from mouth to anus.

38. In positive-pressure breathing, air is gulped into the mouth and then forced into the lungs by contraction of muscles in the lining of the mouth.

39. The rectum is a muscular chamber located at the end of the large intestine, in which feces are stored until they can be eliminated.

40. A rumen is a large, muscular organ, formed from an enlargement of the lower esophagus, in which plant materials can be digested by symbiotic microorganisms.

41. Ruminants are herbivores that have a rumen, in which plants are digested by symbiotic microorganisms.

42. Saliva is a mixture of water, enzymes, and mucous carbohydrates, secreted by the salivary glands into the mouth; saliva lubricates food and begins the digestion of complex carbohydrates.

43. Salivary amylase is an enzyme, contained in saliva, which breaks down complex carbohydrates (starch and glycogen) into disaccharides in the mouth.

44. The small intestine is a tubelike organ the diameter of a small garden hose, coiled in the lower abdomen, in which the majority of chemical digestion of food materials takes place.

45. Spiracles are small openings in the body surface of insects through which atmospheric air can enter the main tracheal tubes of the gas exchange system.

46. The stomach is a muscular, bag-like organ of animals which holds food and generally begins the chemical digestion of most foods.

47. The surface-to-volume ratio is the ratio of the surface area of an organism compared with its total body volume. Large animals have less surface area compared to their body size than small animals do.

48. Teeth are hardened mouthparts of vertebrates, used for biting, shredding, and mashing food materials.

49. Trace elements are required by organisms in very small quantities; typically, less than a milligram. Human trace elements include: iron, fluorine, zinc, copper, selenium, manganese, iodide, molybdenum, and chromium and potentially silicon, vanadium, tin, and nickel.

50. The trachea of a land vertebrate is a large, tubelike structure that conducts air from the nares to the lungs; the trachea is reinforced with rings of semirigid cartilage which prevent it from collapsing.

51. Tracheae are small branched tubes that extend throughout the body of insects, in which gas exchange takes place.

52. Tracheoles are small branches of the tracheae of insects.

53. Villi are small, folded projections of the lining of the small intestine. Villi increase the surface area required for nutrient absorption.

54. Vitamins are small organic monomers that cannot be synthesized by an organism but are necessary in small quantities for metabolism and physiological processes.

Review Questions

1. What are macronutrients? List at least four animal macronutrients.
2. What are micronutrients? List at least two animal micronutrients.
3. What is mechanical digestion? Where and how does it occur?
4. What is the pharynx? What is the esophagus? What is the epiglottis? What are their roles in digestion?
5. What is the stomach? List and describe at least two functions of the stomach.
6. What is the pancreas, and what part does it play in digestion? What is the liver, and what part does it play in digestion? What is bile, and what part does it play in digestion?
7. List the three major segments of the small intestine, and describe the digestive processes that take place in each segment.
8. List and describe at least two processes that take place in the large intestine.
9. What kinds of membranes does gas exchange require? Why?
10. What is the relationship between volume and surface area? What effects does this relationship have on gas exchange in animals?
11. What kinds of animals exchange gases through their outer body surfaces? What are the limits to this process?
12. What are gills? How do gills exchange gases? What process enhances the efficiency of this type of gas exchange?
13. Some land animals exchange gases through their skin; which ones, and what limitations does this type of gas exchange impose?
14. How do insects exchange gases? What are the similarities between this system and the one used by vertebrates?
15. What are lungs? How is the structure of lungs related to their function?
16. What is hemoglobin? What components of its structure allow it to carry out its functions? What factors affect the binding of oxygen to hemoglobin? Describe the effects of these factors.
17. How is carbon dioxide transported inside the bodies of vertebrates
18. How is breathing rate controlled locally and centrally?

FLUID & HEAT REGULATION

Concepts

1. Homeostatic regulating mechanisms maintain the internal environments of cells and multicellular organisms in a relatively steady state.

2. Thermoregulation is the homeostatic regulation of an animal's body temperature.

3. Osmoregulation, the regulation of the fluid and ion concentrations, and excretion of nitrogenous wastes are essential to maintaining homeostasis.

4. Most protozoa and small invertebrates directly regulate their ion and water concentrations and expel wastes by active transport through cell membranes.

5. Insects regulate their ion concentrations and expel wastes via malpighian tubules; they regulate their water concentrations using ion pumping and osmosis in their intestines.

6. The vertebrate liver regulates the chemical composition of the blood and extracellular fluids by removing excess materials and secreting missing materials.

7. The vertebrate kidney is the primary organ of internal fluid osmoregulation and excretion.

8. Freshwater vertebrates maintain fluid and ion balance by excreting water and ammonia, and by actively absorbing ions.

9. Most marine and land vertebrates maintain fluid and ion balance by reabsorbing water from the urine and excreting excess ions and urea.

10. Reptiles, birds, and desert mammals excrete uric acid which is nontoxic and requires less water to excrete.

11. In the kidney, urine is formed by filtration through the glomerulus and reabsorption from the tubules of the nephrons.

12. Water and dissolved ion concentrations are regulated by the proximal and distal convoluted tubules, and by the descending and ascending loops of Henle.

13. Human kidney function is regulated by hormonal and nutritional factors, especially salt intake.

Key Terms

1. Aldosterone is a vertebrate hormone, released by the adrenal cortex, that stimulates the exchange of potassium ions for sodium ions in the distal convoluted tubules. Aldosterone causes the urine to have less water and be more concentrated.

2. Antidiuretic hormone (abbreviated ADH) is a vertebrate hormone that regulates the permeability of cells lining the collecting tubules of the kidneys. When ADH is present, more water is reabsorbed from the urine, resulting in highly concentrated urine.

3. The ascending loop of Henle is the second segment of the loop of Henle of a vertebrate nephron; the ascending loop of Henle is composed of membranes which are impermeable to water, and which actively transport sodium and chloride ions into the surrounding tissue fluids.

4. Bowman's capsules are sacs of epithelial tissue, surrounding the glomeruli of vertebrate nephrons, which contain the liquid (urine) filtered from the blood.

5. Brown fat is a form of animal fat that is capable of very rapid heat production. Brown fat has more mitochondria per unit volume than any other type of tissue, and the electron transport systems of the mitochondria of brown fat cells release more heat than those of other cells.

6. The cloaca is a common opening for the digestive, excretory, and reproductive systems of insects, reptiles, birds, and some other animals.

7. Collecting tubules are branched tubular structures which conduct urine from nephrons to the pelvis of a vertebrate kidney.

8. Concentration of nitrogenous wastes is a process that takes place in the vertebrate kidneys, when water is reabsorbed into the blood from the urine, thereby increasing the amount of nitrogenous waste in the liquid urine prior to its elimination.

9. A contractile vacuole is an organelle of freshwater protozoans that excretes excess water.

10. The descending loop of Henle is the first segment of the loop of Henle of a vertebrate nephron; the descending loop of Henle is composed of membranes which are permeable to water.

11. The distal convoluted tubule is a coiled segment of a vertebrate nephron farthest from the Bowman's capsule and located within the cortex of the kidney. Active transport pumps in the membranes of the cells of the distal convoluted tubule exchange potassium ions in the blood of the vasa recta for sodium ions in the urine of the distal convoluted tubule.

12. Ectotherms are animals that thermoregulate by exchanging heat with their environment.

13. Endotherms are animals that thermoregulate by actively producing heat in their tissues or losing heat by physiological mechanisms.

14. Excretion is the release of waste materials by cells that usually involves the transport of waste materials through the plasma membrane.

15. Filtration is the process by which blood plasma is forced through a membrane permeable to any material smaller than large proteins, forming urine in the nephrons of the vertebrate kidneys.

16. A glomerulus is a spherical ball of capillaries, enclosed within Bowman's capsule of a nephron of a vertebrate kidney, through which the blood is filtered.

17. Heterothermic animals' body temperatures significantly vary over time.

18. Hibernation is a complex physiological and behavioral process in which both activity patterns and body temperature decrease dramatically; hibernation is a state of suspended animation, from which an animal cannot be easily awakened.

19. Homeothermic animals' body temperatures fluctuates over a relatively narrow range over time.

20. Hyperthermia is an abnormal physiological condition in which increased body temperature can cause damage or death.

21. Hypothermia is an abnormal physiological condition in which decreased body temperature can cause damage or death.

22. The kidneys of a vertebrate are a pair of organs, located at the dorsal surface of the body cavity, that regulate the concentrations of water, ions, and nitrogenous wastes in the animal's body.

23. The loop of Henle is an elongated loop of a vertebrate nephron, composed of epithelial tissue, which passes from the cortex of the kidney into the medulla and back to the cortex.

24. Metabolic wastes are wastes produced as a byproduct of the biochemical reactions of metabolism. There are two major types of metabolic wastes produced by animals: carbon dioxide and nitrogenous wastes.

25. Nitrogenous wastes are nitrogen-containing byproducts of the metabolism of proteins and amino acids. The most common nitrogenous wastes are ammonia, urea, and uric acid.

26. Nephrons, the functional units of the vertebrate kidneys, are long, slender tubes composed primarily of epithelial tissue, which filter, regulate, reabsorb, and concentrate materials in the blood and the urine.

27. Osmoregulation is the regulation of the osmotic concentration of the blood and tissue fluids, an essential part of maintaining homeostasis.

28. Panting is rapid, shallow breathing, which helps to evaporate water from the moist surfaces of the respiratory system, thereby absorbing heat energy and lowering an animal's body temperature.

29. The pelvis of the vertebrate kidney consists of a hollow chamber lined with epithelial tissue, in which urine accumulates.

30. The proximal convoluted tubule is a coiled segment of a vertebrate nephron, closest to the Bowman's capsule and located within the cortex of the kidney. In a proximal convoluted tubule, the glucose, amino acids, and some dissolved ions, such as bicarbonate ions, are actively transported out of the nephron and into the blood of the surrounding capillaries.

31. Reabsorption is the process by which glucose, amino acids, some dissolved ions, and other useful materials are transported from the urine back into the blood via the nephrons of the vertebrate kidney.

32. The renal arteries are arteries which branch off the aorta and lead to the kidneys of vertebrates.

33. Secretion is the active transport of non-waste materials out of a cell through the cell membrane. In the vertebrate kidneys, secretion occurs following reabsorption, and involves the transport of detoxified poisons, ions, and other materials from the blood into the urine.

34. Shivering is rhythmic, involuntary contractions of the skeletal muscles, especially those of the arms, shoulders, face, and upper body, which generate heat due to increased electron transport in the mitochondria of the muscle cells.

35. Sweating is the secretion of water, ions, and some waste products onto the skin surface, where it evaporates thereby cooling the skin surface.

36. Thermoregulation is the homeostatic regulation of an animal's body temperature, either physiologically or behaviorally (or both)

37. Urea is a small water-soluble organic molecule composed of one carbonyl with two attached amino groups.

38. The ureter of a vertebrate is a thin walled tube that conducts urine from the kidneys to the urinary bladder.

39. The urethra of a vertebrate is a thin walled tube that conducts urine from the urinary bladder to the outside of the animal.

40. Uric acid is a large water-insoluble organic molecule very similar to the purine nitrogenous bases of nucleic acids.

41. The urinary bladder of a vertebrate is a muscular sac in which urine is stored. In the urinary bladder, the urine from the left and right kidney is mixed and held until it can be released.

42. Urination is the release of urine from the bladder of a vertebrate via the urethra to the external environment.

43. Urine is a solution of liquid wastes composed of water, dissolved nitrogenous waste products, and other excreted materials.

Review Questions

1. Why is homeostatic regulation important to animals?

2. What is thermoregulation? How do ectotherms and endotherms regulate their body temperature? Compare and contrast heterotherms and homeotherms.

3. How do protozoa and small invertebrates regulate their ion and water concentrations?

4. How do insects regulate their ion and water concentrations?

5. What are the regulatory functions of the vertebrate liver?

6. What are the regulatory functions of the vertebrate kidneys?

7. How do freshwater fish regulate their water, ion, and nitrogenous waste concentrations?

8. How do marine fish and land vertebrates regulate their water, ion, and nitrogenous waste concentrations?

9. Describe how the blood is filtered by the glomeruli of the vertebrate kidneys.

10. Describe how nutrients, ions, and water are reabsorbed and nitrogenous wastes are excreted in the nephrons of vertebrate kidneys.

11. How do antidiuretic hormone, aldosterone, and dietary salt regulate blood pressure?

REPRODUCTION

Concepts

1. Animals can reproduce asexually by fission, budding, fragmentation, or parthenogenesis.

2. Fertilization can occur either externally (as in many aquatic animals) or internally (as in most terrestrial animals).

3. The human female reproductive system consists of a vagina, a uterus, two fallopian tubes, and two ovaries.

4. Oogenesis in human females begins during embryonic development and ends following fertilization or prior to menstruation.

5. The human female reproductive cycle is called the menstrual cycle, and includes a follicular phase, ovulation, and a luteal phase.

6. The human male reproductive system consists of two testicles, two vas deferens, and a penis.

7. Spermatogenesis in human males continues throughout adult life, producing millions of sperm cells each day.

8. Human sexual intercourse usually includes four phases: sexual excitation, plateau, orgasm, and resolution.

9. Most forms of birth control involve prevention of fertilization.

Key Terms

1. Abortion is the termination of pregnancy, usually by artificially removing an embryo from the female reproductive tract.

2. The amnion is a membrane that contains the fetus surrounded by amniotic fluid, which cushions the embryo and provides a stable environment.

3. The cervix is a ring of connective tissue with a small central opening, located at the bottom part of the uterus, where it protrudes into the vagina; the cervix regulates the passage of materials to and from the uterus.

4. A condom is a thin, tight-fitting sheath, made of latex rubber or animal skin, which a male human wears over his penis to prevent pregnancy; during ejaculation, the semen is held within the condom and is thereby prevented from entering the female partner's reproductive tract.

5. Copulation is the process of mating during which internal fertilization occurs among animals; during copulation, a male's penis is inserted into the female reproductive tract and semen from the male is expelled through the penis and into the female's reproductive tract.

6. The corpus luteum is a small mass of glandular tissue, produced from the cells of a ruptured follicle of a sexually mature female human; the corpus luteum secretes progesterone, a hormone that stimulates further thickening and vascularization of the endometrium.

7. A diaphragm is a flexible, rubber cup that is inserted into a female human's vagina and placed over the cervix; the diaphragm blocks the opening of the cervix, thereby preventing semen from entering the uterus during sexual intercourse.

8. An egg cell (or ovum) is a haploid gamete, produced by a female animal, that contains large amounts of cytosol and is usually not mobile.

9. Ejaculation is the expulsion of semen from the penis of a male animal; ejaculation of semen into the reproductive tract of a female is part of the process of internal fertilization.

10. The endometrium is the tissue lining the inside surface of the uterus of a woman; the endometrium contains many blood vessels that provide nutrients for a developing embryo.

11. The epididymis is a highly coiled tube, located on the upper surface of the testis of a male mammal, through which sperm cells pass on their way to the vas deferens.

12. External fertilization is fertilization that takes place outside the bodies of mating animals, generally in liquid water and usually involving the synchronized production and release of large numbers of free-swimming gametes.

13. A fallopian tube (or oviduct) is a hollow, curved tube that extends from the upper part of the uterus to the ovary of a female human (a normal woman has two ovaries and two fallopian tubes); egg cells released from the ovaries travel through the fallopian tubes to the uterus.

14. A fertilization membrane is a membrane that forms around a fertilized animal zygote immediately following penetration of the first sperm cell into the egg cell; the fertilization membrane forms a barrier to penetration of the fertilized zygote by additional sperm cells.

15. The follicular phase of the female human menstrual cycle is that period of time, beginning about 5 days after the onset of menstruation and generally lasting 9-11 days, during which follicles and egg cells develop in the ovary. The end of the follicular phase is marked by the release of a mature egg cell (ovulation).

16. Gametogenesis is the process in which animals produce gametes by meiotic cell division.

17. Genitals are the external and internal reproductive organs of animals, including both the gonads and the mating organs.

18. Gonads are the internal sexual organs of female and male animals; gonads produce both sex cells (eggs and sperm) and other materials, including sex hormones.

19. Human Chorionic Gonadotropin (abbreviated HCG), a polypeptide almost identical to GnRH is a hormone released by an embryo during the early stages of pregnancy. HCG stimulates the anterior pituitary gland to release FSH and LH, thereby maintaining the embryo in the uterus.

20. The luteal phase of the female human menstrual cycle is that period of time immediately following ovulation and ending approximately 15 days later, during which a ruptured follicle is transformed into the corpus luteum. The corpus luteum secretes progesterone, a hormone that stimulates further thickening and vascularization of the endometrium.

21. The menstrual cycle is the cyclic changes that occur during one reproductive cycle of a woman; a typical menstrual cycle lasts approximately 28 days. The menstrual cycle consists of three phases: the menstruation phase, the follicular phase, and the luteal phase.

22. Menstruation is the periodic discharge of the menses (blood and other tissue) from the uterus of a sexually mature woman.

23. The menstruation phase of the female human menstrual cycle is that period of time, generally 4 to 7 days long, during which the cells of the outer layers of tissue and of the endometrium loosen and the linings of capillaries disintegrate, causing a loss of blood.

24. Oogenesis is the process by which female animals produce a haploid egg cell (gamete) by meiotic division of a diploid sex cell; this process occurs in the ovaries of the female.

25. Oogonia are stem cells that divide by mitosis to produce stem cells and primary oocytes in female mammals.

26. Oral contraceptives are drugs that prevent pregnancy in female humans by inhibiting the release of egg cells during ovulation, usually by mimiking the hormonal levels of pregnancy.

27. Ovaries are the gonads of female animals; ovaries produce egg cells and secrete female sex hormones.

28. Ovulation is the release of a fertile egg cell from a follicle in the ovary of a female mammal.

29. Parthenogenesis is a form of asexual reproduction in which a female animal produces offspring from unfertilized eggs, without having mated with a male.

30. A penis is the external reproductive organ of a male animal; a penis is a cylindrical structure which has a tubelike duct inside it through which semen can be expelled into the reproductive tract of a female.

31. Polar bodies are haploid cells, produced during the meiotic division of oogenesis, which do not develop into egg cells; in many cases, polar bodies are barely more than haploid nuclei with a surrounding membrane, both of which rapidly degenerate until they disappear.

32. The rhythm method is a form of birth control in which female and male sexual partners abstain from sexual intercourse during the female's fertile period.

33. Semen is a fluid material produced by mammals, containing sperm cells, a sugary food supply, and several hormones, which is ejaculated into the reproductive tract of the female during mating.

34. Seminal vesicles are small sac-like structures, located at the outer ends of the vas deferentia, which produce about 70% of the seminal fluid, the liquid in which the sperm cells are suspended.

35. Seminiferous tubules are tightly packed tubules located inside the testis of a male mammal; in a sexually mature male, sperm cells are produced from stem cells lining the seminiferous tubules.

36. A sperm cell is a haploid gamete, produced by a male animal, that contains little or no cytosol and is usually mobile, having a large undulapodium that it uses to swim toward an egg cell.

37. Spermatogenesis is the process by which male animals produce four haploid sperm cells (gamete) by meiotic division of a diploid sex cell; this process occurs in the testes of the male.

38. Spermatogonia are the stem cells that produce stem cells in the seminiferous tubules of sexually mature males.

39. A spermicide is a chemical that kills sperm cells, thereby preventing pregnancy.

40. Sterilization is a form of birth control in which the reproductive cells (eggs or sperm) are either prevented from reaching the appropriate location for fertilization, or the organs producing those reproductive cells are removed.

41. Testes are the gonads of male animals; testes produce sperm cells and secrete male sex hormones.

42. Tubal ligation is a form of sterilization of female humans, in which the fallopian tubes that conduct egg cells from the ovaries to the uterus are either tied shut or cut, thereby preventing egg cells from reaching the appropriate location for fertilization.

43. The uterus is a muscular reproductive organ of female mammals, inside which offspring develop prior to birth.

44. A vagina is the first segment of the internal reproductive tract of a female animal; a vagina is a muscular tube-like structure into which a male's penis can be inserted during copulation.

45. The vas deferens is a long tube-like duct that extends over the pubic bone from the testis, around and behind the bladder, to the penis of a male mammal; the vas deferens conducts sperm from the testis to the urethra of the penis.

46. A vasectomy is a form of sterilization of male humans, in which the vas deferentia that conduct sperm cells from the testes to the penis are cut, thereby preventing sperm cells from being released during ejaculation.

Review Questions

1. How can some animals reproduce asexually? What are the advantages and disadvantages of such reproduction? List and describe at least three types of asexual animal reproduction.

2. What is external fertilization? Under what kinds of conditions did external fertilization evolve? What is internal fertilization? Under what kinds of conditions did internal fertilization evolve?

3. What are animal reproductive cycles? Why do animal reproductive cycles exist? What kinds of signals influence animal reproductive cycles? How are animal reproductive cycles regulated?

4. Describe and give a brief description of the structures and functions of the female reproductive system.

5. What are the stages of oogenesis in human females? When do they occur? How many egg cells are produced, and when?

6. What are the stages of the human menstrual cycle? What happens during each stage?

7. Describe and give a brief description of the structures and functions of the male reproductive system.

8. What are the stages of spermatogenesis in human males? When do they occur? How many sperm cells are produced, and when?

9. What are the stages of human sexual intercourse? What happens during each stage?

10. List and describe at least five forms of birth control, including a description of how each method prevents conception or birth.

NERVOUS SYSTEMS

Concepts

1. Most animal nervous systems have two components: a peripheral nervous system and a central nervous system.

2. The somatic division of the peripheral nervous system controls skeletal muscles.

3. The autonomic nervous system controls involuntary processes such as breathing, heart rate, and digestion.

4. Simple reflex arcs usually include a sensory neuron, an inter-neuron in the spinal cord, and a motor neuron.

5. The vertebrate brain is the primary site of information processing memory storage, and association.

6. The vertebrate hindbrain - the medulla, cerebellum, pons, and reticular formation - controls autonomic processes.

7. The human midbrain is a switching center for sensory inputs.

8. The vertebrate forebrain functions in motivation, sensory integration, memory, learning, and voluntary behavior.

9. Memory and learning involve modification of synaptic transmission in several locations of the vertebrate central nervous system.

Key Terms

1. The autonomic nervous system is a division of the peripheral nervous system that controls involuntary processes, such as breathing, heart rate, and digestion.

2. The central nervous system (CNS) of an animal includes those neurons that function as interneurons between sensory neurons and motor neurons; the central nervous system performs most of the integration and processing of nervous information.

3. The cerebellum is part of the vertebrate hindbrain, consisting of an enlargement of the dorsal part of the medulla; in cross-section, the cerebellum of humans looks like the branches of a tree. The cerebellum controls balance and coordinates movement.

4. The cerebral cortex is the outer surface of the cerebral hemispheres of the vertebrate forebrain; the cerebral cortex is the principal site of memory storage, behavior, and learning.

5. The cerebral hemispheres of the vertebrate forebrain are hemispherical masses of neurons which have several functions, all related to memory storage, behavior, and learning.

6. The forebrain of a vertebrate consists of the olfactory lobes and the cerebral cortex, located at the front upper surface of the brain; among ancestral vertebrates, the forebrain is almost exclusively devoted to processing chemoreceptive sensations, especially smell, whereas in advanced vertebrates the forebrain is adapted for memory storage and voluntary motor control.

7. A ganglion is an aggregation or bundle of neuron cell bodies; most ganglia lie inside or just outside the central nervous system.

8. Gray matter is a layer of tissue of the brain and spinal cord, composed of the cell bodies of many neurons, especially interneurons.

9. Learning is a process whereby memories of previous sensory inputs and motor outputs are associated with each other and with other memories.

10. Long-term memories are memories that last for very long periods (generally, from the time formed until an animal dies); long-term memories are generally stored in the cerebral cortex of the brain.

11. The medulla oblongata (or medulla) is part of the vertebrate hindbrain, located at the base and rear of the brain, forming the top of the spinal cord. The medulla controls basic vital functions, such as breathing rate and heart rate.

12. Memories are stored representations of sensory inputs and associated motor outputs, usually maintained in neurons and synapses in the central nervous system.

13. The midbrain of a vertebrate is a mass of brain tissue located between the hindbrain and forebrain; in ancestral vertebrates, its functions include learning and memory, whereas in advanced vertebrates, the midbrain is primarily a relay center for sensory and motor information entering and leaving the cerebrum.

14. A nerve is a bundle of axons, generally insulated with myelin sheaths; many nerves contain axons of both sensory and motor neurons.

15. The parasympathetic nervous system is a division of the autonomic nervous system that generally counteracts the effects of the sympathetic nervous system by decreasing breathing and heart rate, decreasing skeletal muscle tone, and increasing digestion.

16. The peripheral nervous system (PNS) of an animal includes all of the neurons that connect sensory receptors and motor effectors with the central nervous system.

17. The pons is part of the vertebrate hindbrain, consisting of an enlargement of the anterior surface of the medulla; neurons in the pons relay information from the forebrain to the cerebellum.

18. A reflex is a rapid, unconscious response to a stimulus, usually performed without direct input from the brain.

19. The reticular activating system is a part of the reticular formation of vertebrates; the function of the reticular activating system is to wake vertebrates by releasing the neurotransmitter acetylcholine, which is stimulatory to most other parts of the brain.

20. Short-term memories are short-lived memories, lasting from a few minutes to a few hours, which are generally stored in the brain and spinal cord.

21. A simple reflex arc is a set of connected sensory receptors, sensory neurons, interneurons, and motor neurons that produces a reflex in response to a specific stimulus; a simple reflex arc does not generally include the brain.

22. The somatic nervous system(sometimes called the voluntary nervous system) is a division of the peripheral nervous system that transmits information to effectors, especially skeletal muscles; it is called *voluntary* because it controls skeletal muscles used in behavior.

23. Spinal nerves are bundles of axons that connect with the spinal cord, generally including (dorsal) sensory nerves and (ventral) motor nerves.

24. The sympathetic nervous system is a division of the autonomic nervous system that generally prepares organ systems for vigorous activity by increasing breathing and heart rate, increasing skeletal muscle tone, and decreasing digestion.

25. White matter is a layer of tissue of the brain and spinal cord, composed of axons and dendrites covered with the lipid myelin.

Review Questions

1. What is the peripheral nervous system of an animal? What is the central nervous system of an animal? How are they similar? How are they different?

2. What is the somatic division of the peripheral nervous system? What kinds of sensory and motor processes does it control?

3. What is the autonomic division of the peripheral nervous system? What kinds of sensory and motor processes does it control? Describe the similarities and differences between the sympathetic and parasympathetic nervous systems.

4. What is a simple reflex arc? What kinds of responses are produced via simple reflex arcs?

5. What are the functions of the vertebrate brain?

6. What are the functions of the vertebrate hindbrain? Describe the structures and functions of at least three parts of the vertebrate hindbrain.

7. What are the functions of the vertebrate midbrain? How have these functions changed during the evolution of vertebrates?

8. What are the functions of the vertebrate forebrain? Describe the structures and functions of at least two parts of the vertebrate forebrain.

9. How do memory and learning occur in the nervous system? Compare and contrast sensory memory, short-term memory, and long-term memory.

SENSORY SYSTEMS

Concepts

1. Sensory receptors convert changes in physical and chemical processes into action potentials in sensory neurons.

2. Sensory receptors of the skin of vertebrates detect seven types of stimuli: heat, cold, touch, tickle, itch, pressure, and pain.

3. Proprioceptors sense the physical state of the body, including position, movement, and equilibrium.

4. Chemoreceptors detect the presence and chemical characteristics of specific molecules.

5. Photoreceptor cells in the eyes detect light.

6. Mechanoreceptors in the ears of animals react to vibrations of the air, water, and solid materials.

7. Hair cells in the organs of Corti of vertebrate ears respond to sounds and other vibrations.

Key Terms

1. Accommodation is the process by which light is focused onto the retina of a vertebrate; accommodation includes focusing of light by the cornea and the lens.

2. Bradykinin is a small polypeptide that causes local vasodilation and the sensation of severe pain.

3. Camera eyes are the large, spherical eyes of cephalopods and vertebrates. A camera eye is composed of a hollow sphere filled with transparent fluid, with a single lens that focuses light and visual images on a single layer of photoreceptors, called a retina.

4. Chemoreceptors are specialized sensory receptor cells that detect molecules of specific materials dissolved in water or suspended in air.

5. The cochlea is a snailshell-shaped structure, filled with fluid, that receives vibrations from the ear ossicles and converts them into action potentials.

6. Compound eyes are large eyes of insects and other arthropods, composed of many individual lens-and-receptor units called ommatidia.

7. Cone cells, or cones, are cone-shaped photoreceptor cells of the vertebrate retina. Cone cells respond only to intense light, and can distinguish different colors of light.

8. The cornea of a vertebrate eye is a thin, transparent layer of modified skin through which light passes before it is focused by the lens.

9. Ear ossicles are small bones, located in the inner ears of mammals, that transmit vibrations of the tympanic membrane to the inner ear.

10. An eye is a sensory organ that can detect visual images; an eye consists of a lens (that focuses light and visual images) and a layer of receptor cells onto which the visual images are focused, separated by a space filled with a transparent fluid.

11. Hair cells are mechanoreceptors, located in vertebrate ears, that can detect movement and vibrations caused by locomotion and sound; movement and vibration of the endolymph of the inner ear causes deformation of the hair cells, which produces action potentials.

12. The iris of a vertebrate eye is a pigmented disk that controls the amount of light entering the eye.

13. A lens is a biconvex transparent disk that can focus light and visual images onto an array of photoreceptor cells.

14. Mechanoreceptors are sensory receptors that react to deformation caused by contact and pressure by generating action potentials.

15. The middle ear of vertebrates is a hollow chamber containing one or more bones, called ear ossicles, that are in contact with the tympanic membrane. Vibrations of the tympanic membrane cause the ossicles to vibrate.

16. The organ of Corti is a thin flexible membrane lined with thousands of tiny hair cells in the basilar membrane of the cochlea. Vibrations of the basilar membrane cause the hair cells to deform, sending action potentials through the neurons of the cochlear nerve.

17. Otoliths are particles of calcium carbonate which gravity can force against the cilia of hair cells in saccules and utricles; the cilia bend, producing action potentials in a pattern that indicates the direction of the force of gravity.

18. The outer ear of a mammal consists of a pinna and an external ear canal. The outer ear gathers vibrations of the air and guides them into the inner ear.

19. The oval window is a thin elastic membrane in the wall of the cochlea of the inner ear of mammals; vibrations of the oval window (caused by vibrations of the ear ossicles) cause vibrations of the fluid filling the cochlea.

20. Pain receptors are dendrites that generate action potentials in response to damage or destruction of nearby cells; such damage causes the production or release of chemicals that bind to receptors in the membranes of pain dendrites and generates action potentials.

21. Photoreceptors are sensory receptor cells that contain photopigments sensitive to specific wavelengths of light.

22. Proprioceptors are sensory receptors that detect internal stimuli in animals.

23. The pupil of a vertebrate eye is a small hole through which light shines. The pupil of the eye dilates (expands) at low light intensities and contracts at high light intensities.

24. The retina of an eye is the curved layer of photoreceptor cells located on the rear surface of the interior of the eyeball.

25. Rod cells, or rods, are elongated, cylindrical photoreceptor cells of the vertebrate retina. Rod cells respond to dim light and moving images, but cannot distinguish different colors of light.

26. The semicircular canals of vertebrates are hollow tubes, located in the ears, that provide sensory information about an animal's spatial position. This information is used to help the animal maintain its balance and equilibrium.

27. Sensory neurons are neurons that transmit information from sensory receptors to the nervous system.

28. Simple eyes are small eyes of insects and other arthropods, composed of a lens, a transparent medium, and a few photoreceptor cells.

29. Smell receptors (also called olfactory receptors) are chemoreceptors that respond to molecules suspended in the air.

30. Taste buds are taste receptors, located in the tongue of a vertebrate, that can react to molecules suspended in food or water.

31. Taste receptors (also called gustatory receptors) are chemoreceptors that respond to molecules suspended or dissolved in water or food.

32. Thermoreceptors are sensory receptors, located in vertebrate skin, that sense heat and cold; thermoreceptors react to changes in temperature by generating action potentials.

33. The tympanic membrane of vertebrates is a thin, elastic membrane (sometimes called the ear drum) that vibrates at the same frequency as vibrations of air or water in contact with it.

34. A vestibular organ of a vertebrate consists of the semicircular canals and the utricle of one ear; vertebrates have two vestibular organs, one in each ear.

Review Questions

1. What are the functions of sensory receptors, and how do they perform such functions? In general, what kinds of things do sensory receptors perceive?

2. What are the various sensory receptors of vertebrate skin, and how do they function? List and describe at least six of these sensory receptors of skin.

3. What are proprioceptors and internal sensors and how do they function? List and describe at least three of these sensory receptors.

4. What are chemoreceptors and how do they function? List and describe at least one of these sensory receptors.

5. What are photoreceptors and how do they function? How do photoreceptors differ from the sensory receptor cells discussed so far?

6. Describe in detail the structures and functions of the vertebrate eye, including a discussion of the rod and cone cells and how they produce action potentials in sensory neurons.

7. Describe what sound is and how tympanic membranes and ears detect it.

8. Describe in detail the structures and functions of the mammalian ear, including a discussion of the hair cells of the organs of Corti and how they produce action potentials in sensory neurons.

GREEK AND LATIN ROOTS

PREFIX/SUFFIX	SOURCE/WORD	MEANING
a-	Greek/a- = not	not, without
acet-	Latin/acetum = vinegar	pertaining to a 2-carbon carbohydrate, vinegar
an-	Greek/an- = not	not, without
aer-	Greek/aer = air	air
allo-	Greek/allos = other	different
amyl-	Latin/amylum = starch	carbohydrate
ante-	Latin/ante- = before	before, front
-ase		enzyme, especially that breaks down substrates
atrial, atrium	Latin/atrium = entrance	entrance
aur-	Latin/auris = ear	pertaining to the ear
auto-	Greek/autos = self	self
bathy-	Greek/bathus = deep	deep sea
bi-, bis-	Latin/bis = two	two
bio-, biol, bios-	Greek/bios = life	biology, life, living
carbo-	Latin/carbo = charcoal	carbon
cent-	Latin/centum = hundred	one hundred
centro-	Greek/kentron = center	center
ceph-	Greek/kephale = head	head
cerv-	Latin/cervix = neck	neck
chem-	Greek/khemeia = chemical	chemical
chloro-	Greek/khloros = green	green
chrom-	Greek/khroma = color	colored
chron-	Greek/khronos = time	time
cil-	Latin/cilium = eyelash	pertaining to cilia
circ-	Latin/circum = around	around
co-, com-, con-	Latin/com- = together	with
coel-	Greek/koilos = hollow	cavity, space
counter-	Latin/contra = against	against
cyc-	Greek/kuklos = circle	circular
cyto-	Greek/kutos = hollow vessel	cell
cyst-	Greek/kustis = bladder	hollow ball
de-	Latin/de- = from	not, remove
dec-	Latin/decem = ten	ten
dendr-	Greek/dendron = tree	branch
derm-, -dermis	Greek/derma = skin	skin
deutero-	Greek/deuteros = second	second
di-	Greek/di- = two	two
dia-	Greek/dia = apart	to pass through
dorsal	Latin/dorsum = back	back, upper surface
dyn-	Greek/dunamis = power	active
eco-	Greek/oikos = household	environment
ecto-	Greek/ektos = outside	outside, outside of, external
embry-	Greek/embruon = to grow	embryo, early stage of development

PREFIX/SUFFIX	SOURCE/WORD	MEANING
en-	Latin/en- = inside	in
endo-	Greek/endon = within	within, inside of, into
epi-	Greek/epi = upon	on, upon
erg-	Greek/ergon = work	energy
erythr-	Greek/eruthros = red	red
eth-	Greek/ethos = character	behavior
eu-	Greek/eus = good, true	true, well
ex-, exo-, extra-	Greek/ex = out of	outside, out of
fibr-	Latin/fibra = fiber	fiber, thread
flagell-	Latin/flagellum = little whip	whip
flor-	Latin/flos = flower	of flowers
gastr-	Greek/gaster = belly	stomach
gen-, gene, -gen	Greek/genes = born	life, heredity, origin
geo-	Greek/ge = earth	gravity, rock, Earth
germ-	Latin/germen = bud	seed
gluc-, gly-	Greek/gleukos = sweet wine	pertaining to glucose or sugar
glycer-	Greek/glukus = sweet	pertaining to a 3-carbon carbohydrate
haplo-	Greek/haplous = single	single, one set
hemi-	Latin/hemi- = half	half
hemo-	Greek/haima = blood	blood
hepat-	Greek/hepar = liver	liver
herb-	Latin/herba = herb	plant
hetero-	Greek/heteros = other	different
homeo-, homo-	Greek/homos = same	same
homin-	Latin/homo = man	human
hydr-, hydro-	Greek/hudor = water	water
hyper-	Greek/huper = over	more, above
hypno-	Greek/hupnos = sleep	pertaining to sleep
hypo-	Greek/hupo = under	below, less
in-	Latin/in- = not	not
inter-	Latin/inter = between	between, among
intra-	Latin/intra- = within	within
iso-	Greek/isos = same	same
karyo-	Greek/karuon = kernel	pertaining to the nucleus
kilo-	Greek/khilioi = thousand	one thousand
lac-	Latin/lac = milk	milk
leuc-, leuk-	Greek/leukos = white	white
lig-	Latin/ligare = bind	tie together
limn-	Greek/limne = lake	lake
lip-, lipo-	Greek/lipos = fat	fat, fatty
logi-, -logy	Greek/logos = reason	knowledge
lys-, lyso-, -lysis	Greek/luein = unbind	breakdown, cut
macro-	Greek/makros = large	big
mal-	Latin/malus = bad	bad
mega-	Greek/megas = great	big, million
mel-	Greek/melas = black	dark
mer-, mero-	Greek/meros = unit	unit, part

PREFIX/SUFFIX	SOURCE/WORD	MEANING
meso-	Greek/mesos = middle	middle
meta-	Greek/meta = change	middle, change, beyond
micro-	Greek/mikros = small	small, microscopic, millionth
mid-	Old English/mid = middle	middle
milli-	Latin/mille = thousand	one thousandth
mono-	Greek/monos = one	one
morph-	Greek/morphe = shape	shape, form, appearance
mort-	Latin/mors = death	dead, death
moto-	Latin/movere = move	move
muco-	Latin/mucus = mucus	pertaining to mucus
multi-	Latin/multus = much	many
myc-, myco-	Greek/mukes = fungus	fungus
myo-	Greek/mus = muscle	muscle
neg-	Latin/negare = deny	not
neo-	Greek/neos = new	new
nephr-	Greek/nephros = kidney	kidney
neuro-	Greek/neuron = nerve	nerves, nervous system
neutro-	Latin/neuter = neither	neutral
nitro-	Semitic/nitron = nitrogen	pertaining to nitrogen
non-	Latin/non = not	not, cannot
nucl-	Latin/nux = kernel	center, pertaining to nucleus
omni-	Latin/omnis = all	all, everything
onco-	Greek/onkos = mass	pertaining to cancer
oo-	Greek/oion = egg	egg
oral	Latin/os = mouth	pertaining to mouth
-ose		sugar
osmo-	Greek/osmos = thrust	pertaining to the movenent of water
osteo-	Greek/osteon = bone	pertaining to bones
ovi-	Latin/ovum = egg	egg, of eggs
oxi-, oxy-	Greek/oxus = acid	pertaining to oxygen
paleo-	Greek/palai = long ago	old
para-	Greek/para = beside	near, alongside
patho-	Greek/pathos = suffering	bad
pep-, pept-	Greek/peptein = digest	stomach, protein
peri-	Greek/peri = around	surrounding
perme-	Latin/permeare = penetrate	to go through
phag-	Greek/phagein = eat	to eat
pheno-	Greek/phainein = to show	appearance
phospho-	Greek/phosphoros = bringing light	pertaining to phosphorous
photo-	Greek/phos = light	light
phylo-	Greek/phulon = race	to classify
phyt-	Greek/phuton = plant	plant
plasm-	Greek/plassein = to shape	inside of cell
poly-	Greek/polus = many	many
por-	Greek/poros= pore	opening
post-	Latin/post = after	after, behind

PREFIX/SUFFIX	SOURCE/WORD	MEANING
pre-	Latin/prae = before	before
prim-	Latin/primus = first	first
pro-, proto-	Greek/pro = before	first
pseudo-	Greek/pseudein - to lie	false
pulmo-	Latin/pulmo = lung	lungs
quadr-, quatr-	Latin/quadri = four	four
radia-	Latin/radius = ray	moving away
re-	Latin/re- = again	again
ren-, renal	Latin/renes = kidneys	kidney
rhizo-	Greek/rhiza = root	pertaining to roots
ribo-	German/ribonsäure = current sugar	related to 5-carbon sugar and/or RNA
sarco-	Greek/sarx = flesh	muscle
sclero-	Greek/skleros = hard	hard
sin-, sinu-	Latin/sinus = curve	curving
soma-	Greek/soma = body	body
sperm-, -sperm	Greek/sperma = seed	seed
spiro-	Latin/spira = coil	spiral
sporo-, -spore	Greek/spora = seed	pertaining to spores
stoma-	Greek/stoma = mouth	mouth, hole
stroma-	Greek/stroma = covering	inside, matrix
sub-	Latin/sub = under	below, under
sulf-	Latin/sulfur = sulfur	pertaining to sulfur
sym-, syn-	Greek/sun = together	together
teleo-, telo-	Greek/telos = end	end, last
term-	Latin/terminus = end	end, last
tetra-	Greek/tetra = four	four
thermo-	Greek/therme = heat	heat
thromb-	Greek/thrombos = clot	clot
trach-	Greek/trakhus = rough	pertaining to the trachea, tubular
trans-	Latin/trans = beyond	across, on the other side of, beyond
tri-	Greek/treis = three	three
uni-	Latin/unus = one	one
ura-, uri-	Latin/urina = urine	pertaining to urine
vascu-	Latin/vasculum = small vessel	tubular
vege-	Latin/vegetare = to enliven	pertaining to vegetables, non-moving
ventr-	Latin/venter = belly	front, belly
vert-	Latin/vertere = to turn	backbone, upright
ves-	Latin/vesica = bladder	container
vir-	Latin/virus = poison	pertaining to virus, poisonous
vita-, viva-	Latin/vita = life	life, living
vitr-	Latin/vitrum = glass	glassy, hard
voc-	Latin/vox = voice	pertaining to the voice, auditory
xero-	Greek/xeros = dry	dry
zoo-	Greek/zoion = living thing	animal
zygo-	Greek/zugon = yoke	pertaining to a fertilized egg

UNITY & DIVERSITY AMONG LIVING THINGS

OBJECTIVES

The student should be able to:

- Define life in terms of the functions performed by living organisms.
- Describe some of the schemes by which organisms are classified.
- Recognize the role of the cell as the basic unit of structure and function of most living things.
- Identify major biochemical compounds and some of the metabolic reactions in which these compounds are involved.
- Identify the appropriate tools and/or techniques used for cell study.
- Recognize that a unity of pattern underlies the diversity of living things.

I. Concept of Life

A. Definition
Scientists have been unable to agree upon a single definition of life. This syllabus characterizes life by the functions that living organisms perform.

B. Life Functions

1. Nutrition
Nutrition includes the activities of an organism by which it obtains materials from its environment and processes them for its use.

2. Transport
Transport involves the absorption and distribution of materials within an organism.

3. Respiration
Respiration includes those processes which provide the energy necessary for the maintenance of life functions.

4. Excretion
Excretion involves the removal of cellular waste products.

5. Synthesis
Synthesis involves those chemical activities by which large molecules are built from smaller ones.

6. Regulation
Regulation involves the control and coordination of the various activities of an organism.

7. Growth
   Growth involves an increase in cell size and/or cell numbers. This process utilizes the products of synthesis.

8. Reproduction
   Reproduction involves the production of new individuals. Species survival is dependent upon reproduction.

C. Metabolism
Metabolism is the total of all the life activities required to sustain life.

D. Homeostasis
Life functions are carried out by an organism in an integrated manner that results in the maintenance of a stable internal environment. This maintenance is known as homeostasis.

II. Diversity of Life

A. Necessity for Classification
In order to study the unity and diversity of living organisms in an organized manner, biologists classify organisms.

B. A Scheme of Classification
There is some disagreement as to the best classification system. In one modern system, organisms are grouped into five kingdoms. Each kingdom is divided into phyla. Phyla are categories which indicate major differences in structure among organisms.

The classification system used in this syllabus utilizes five kingdoms: Monera, Protista, Fungi, Plant, and Animal. This five kingdom system is based on the following criteria:

1. The presence or absence of a nuclear membrane within the cell.

2. Unicellularity versus multicellularity.

3. Type of nutrition.

KINGDOMS	CHARACTERISTICS	EXAMPLES
MONERA	Primitive cell structure lacking a nuclear membrane. The cells of monerans are prokaryotic.	
Bacteria Blue-Green Algae		
PROTISTA	Predominately unicellular organisms with plant-like and/or animal-like characteristics.	
Protozoa	Animal-like in their mode of nutrition.	Paramecium, ameba
Algae	Plant-like in their mode of nutrition.	Spirogyra
FUNGI	Cells are usually organized into branched, multinucleated filaments which absorb digested food from their environment. The term multinucleated is used in place of multicellular since well-defined cell partitions are lacking.	Yeast, bread mold, mushroom
PLANT	Multicellular, photosynthetic organisms.	
Bryophytes	Lack vascular tissue, therefore no true roots, stems, or leaves.	Moss
Tracheophytes	Possess vascular tissue, true roots, stems, and leaves.	Geranium, fern, bean, pine tree, maple tree, corn
ANIMAL	Multicellular organisms that ingest their food.	
Coelenterates	Two cell layers, hollow body cavity.	Hydra, jellyfish
Annelids	Segmented body walls.	Earthworm sandworm
Arthropods	Jointed appendages, exoskeleton	Grasshopper lobster, spider
Chordates	Dorsal nerve cord.	Shark, frog, human

This five-kingdom system of classification is predicated on the idea that monerans are the most primitive.

Most classification systems suggest relationships among organisms which may indicate common ancestry.

C. Nomenclature
The modern system of naming organisms is based upon binomial nomenclature devised by Linnaeus. In this system, the first part of the organism's name, in Latin, is its genus, and the second part of the name, in Latin, indicates its species. A species is a group of organisms that are similar in structure and can mate and produce fertile offspring.

III. Unity of Life

A. Structure of Living Organisms

1. Cell Theory
Cells are the basic units of structure and function of living things. Cells come from pre-existing cells.

a. Historical Background
The improvement of the microscope and microscopic techniques throughout the last four centuries has allowed scientists to observe cells better and to develop the cell theory. Scientists such as Leeuwenhoek, Hooke, Brown, Schleiden, Schwann, and Virchow contributed to the establishment of the cell theory.

b. Methods of Cell Study
Continuing advances in techniques and instrumentation have enabled biologists to increase their understanding of cell structures and functions.

1) Instrumentation

INSTRUMENTS	UNDERSTANDINGS
Compound light microscope	Parts, uses
Electron microscope	Advantages, limitations
Dissecting microscope	Examination of opaque objects
Ultracentrifuge	Separation of cell part according to density
Microdissection instruments	Removal, addition, and/or transfer of individual cell organelles

2) Measurement
The minute size of most cells requires the use of a small unit for measurement. This unit is known as the micrometer (um). One thousand micrometers is equal to one millimeter. Micrometer is a term currently used to replace the term micron.

3) Techniques
The development of staining techniques using such solutions as iodine and methylene blue has made possible a more detailed study of cell structures.

c. Cell Organelles
In cells, various specialized functions occur in subcellular structures known as organelles. Some major organelles and their functions are:

ORGANELLE	FUNCTION
Plasma membrane (cell membrane)	Regulates the transport of certain materials into and out of the cell.
Cytoplasm	A fluid-like environment between the nucleus and the plasma membrane in which other organelles are suspended and within which many biochemical processes occur.
Nucleus	Surrounded by the nuclear membrane; genetic information contained within chromosomes directs the activities of the cell.
Nucleolus	Involved with the synthesis of ribosomes.
Endoplasmic reticulum	A series of interconnecting channels associated with storage, synthesis, and transport of substances within the cell.
Ribosome	Site of protein synthesis. May be free in the cytoplasm or attached to membranes
Mitochondrion	Site of cellular respiration
Golgi complex	Synthesizes, packages, and secretes cellular products

ORGANELLE	FUNCTION
Lysosome	Contains digestive enzymes
Vacuole	A space in a cell surrounded by a membrane which may contain water or other materials is a vacuole. Specialized vacuoles are present in unicellular organisms. Food vacuoles are digestive organelles and contractile vacuoles help maintain water balance.
Centriole	A cylindrical structure found in the cytoplasm which appears to function during the division of certain cells. Centrioles are common to animal cells and rare in plants.
Chloroplast	Pigment-containing structure which serves as a site for photosynthesis.
Cell wall	A nonliving structure which surrounds and supports a cell.

2. Exceptions to the Cell Theory
There are several exceptions to the cell theory:
- The first cell could not have arisen from a previously existing cell.
- Viruses are not composed of cells but do contain genetic material and can reproduce in the presence of a host cell.
- Although considered organelles, mitochondria and chloroplasts contain genetic material and can reproduce in the presence of a cell.

B. Chemistry of Living Organisms

*1. Chemical Elements in Living Matter
The cell is a complex *chemical factory* composed of some of the same elements found in the nonliving environment. Of all the elements present in living matter, carbon, hydrogen, oxygen, and nitrogen are present in the greatest percentages. Some examples of elements found in smaller quantities are sulfur, phosphorus, magnesium, iodine, iron, calcium, sodium, chlorine, and potassium.

*2. Chemical Compounds in Living Matter
Organisms consist of inorganic and organic compounds.

a. Inorganic Compounds
Inorganic compounds are compounds that lack the combination of the elements carbon and hydrogen. The principal inorganic compounds in living things include water, salts, inorganic acids, and bases. Students should be able to differentiate between ionic and covalent bonding.

b. Organic Compounds
Organic compounds are compounds which contain both the elements carbon and hydrogen.

The major categories of organic compounds found in living things are carbohydrates, lipids, proteins, and nucleic acids.

1) Carbohydrates

a) Composition
Carbohydrates consist of the elements carbon, hydrogen, and oxygen. Hydrogen and oxygen atoms are most often present in a 2:1 ratio. The basic unit of the carbohydrate is the monosaccharide. Glucose, $C_6H_{12}O_6$, is an example.

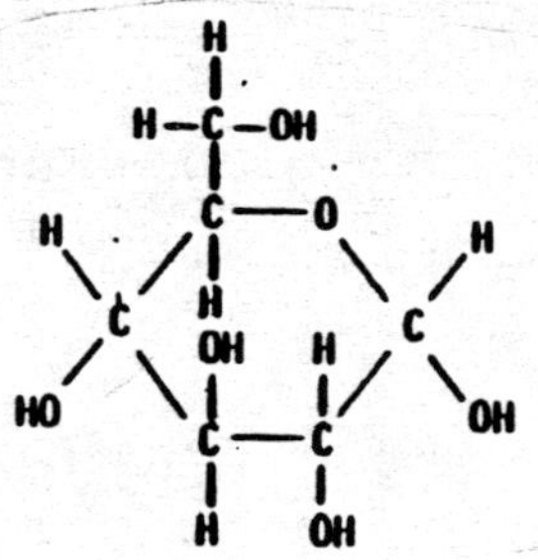

Two monosaccharides chemically combine as a result of dehydration synthesis and form a disaccharide. Maltose, $C_{12}H_{22}O_{11}$, is an example.

$C_6H_{12}O_6 + C_6H_{12}O_6 \rightarrow C_{12}H_{22}O_{11} + H_2O$
Glucose + Glucose → Maltose + water

Formation of Maltose

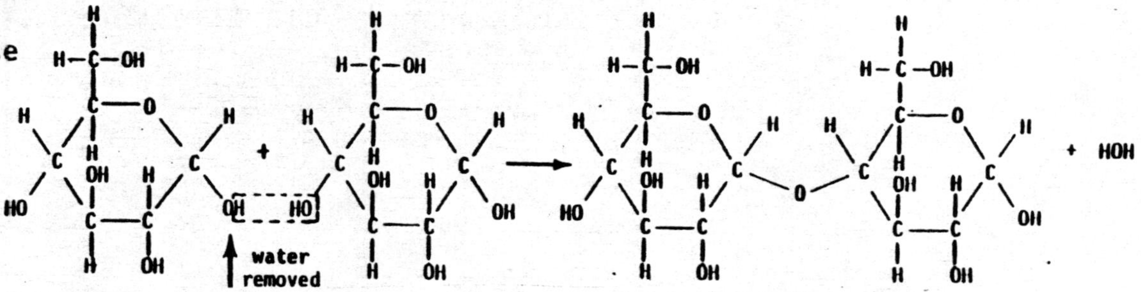

water removed

Many monosaccharides chemically combine by dehydration synthesis and form a polysaccharide such as starch.

Formation of a polysaccharide

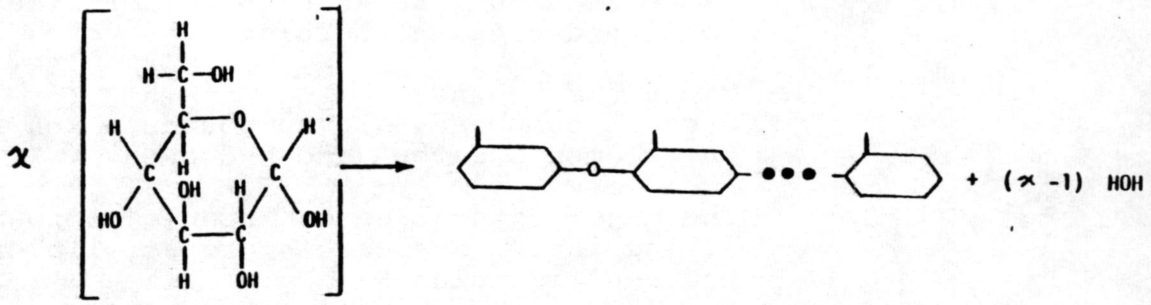

b) Examples
Carbohydrates include all sugars and starches Examples of simple sugars include glucose, fructose, and ribose. Examples of disaccharides include maltose and sucrose. The names of sugars end in <u>ose</u>. Examples of polysaccharides include starches, cellulose, and glycogen.

c) Functions
In organisms, carbohydrates are used primaril as sources of energy, and also as components of cell structures such as the cell wall.

2) Lipids

a) Composition
Lipids, like carbohydrates, contain carbon, hydrogen, and oxygen. However, the ratio of hydrogen to oxygen is much greater than 2:1, and is not constant from one lipid to another.

Some lipids are the product of the dehydratio synthesis of three molecules of fatty acids and one molecule of glycerol.
3 fatty acids + glycerol → lipid + 3 water

Formation of a Lipid

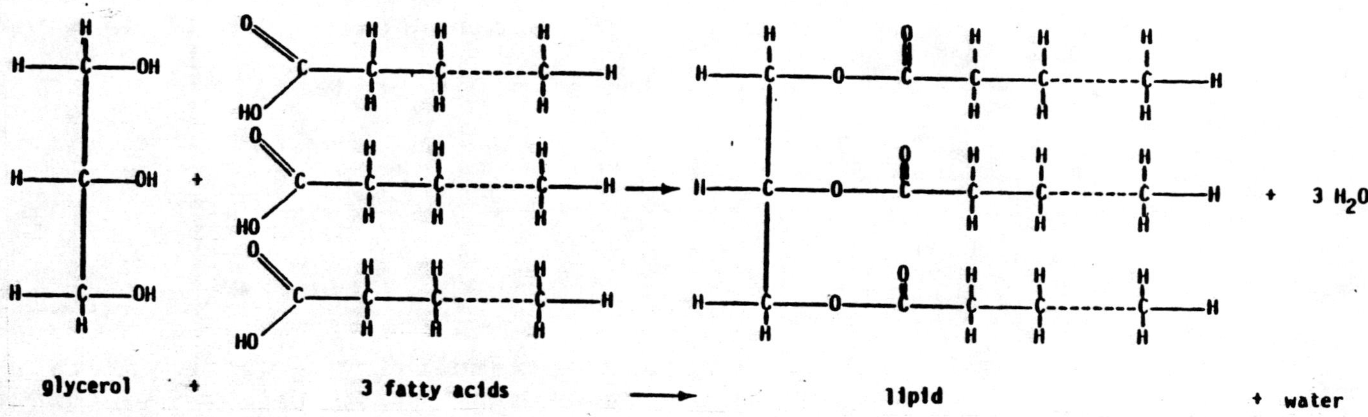

b) Examples
Lipids include fats and oils.

c) Functions
Lipids are used primarily as sources of stored energy and also as components of cell structures such as cell membranes.

3) Proteins

a) Composition
Proteins contain carbon, hydrogen, oxygen, nitrogen, and, in many instances, sulfur. A protein is composed of building blocks known as amino acids.

Twenty amino acids are usually found in living systems. Some proteins contain special amino acids that supplement the basic set of 20 amino acids. All the special amino acids are formed by modification of a common amino acid.

Generalized Structure of an Amino Acid

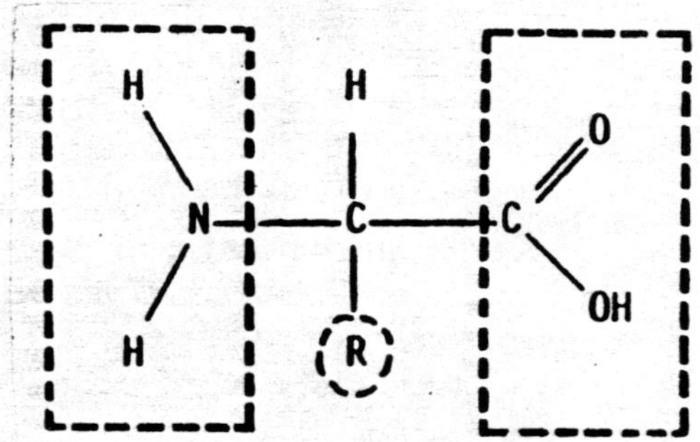

Amino group   carboxyl (acid) group

Ⓡ represents a variable group and is the basis for the variety of amino acids.

Two amino acid units can be chemically combined by dehydration synthesis and form a dipeptide.

Amino acid + amino acid → dipeptide + water

Formation of a Dipeptide

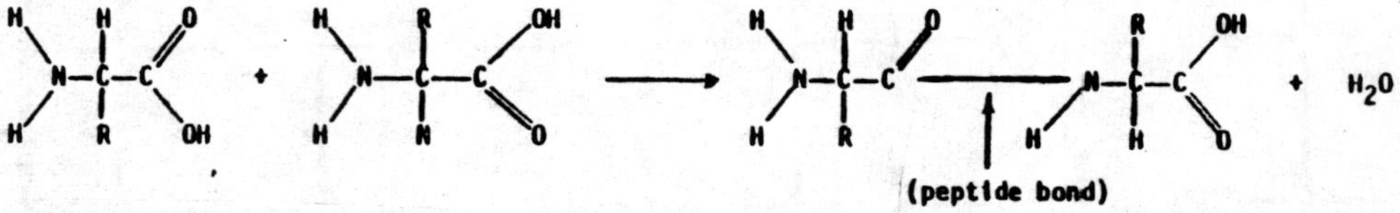

+ → + H_2O

(peptide bond)

Polypeptides result from the dehydration synthesis of many amino acids. A protein is usually composed of one or more polypeptide chains.

There is an extremely large number of different proteins. The bases for variability include differences in the number, kinds, and sequence of amino acids present.

b) Examples
Proteins include insulin, hemoglobin, and enzymes.

c) Functions
Proteins are components of cell structures and enzymes.

3. Chemical Control
Living matter is in a state of dynamic chemical activity. Perhaps the most significant distinction between living and nonliving matter is the continuous and controlled chemical activity present in living systems.

a) The Role of Enzymes
Enzymes are organic catalysts that are the principal regulators of most chemical activity in living systems.
- Each chemical reaction occurring in an organism requires a specific enzyme.
- Enzymes modify the rate of reactions.

1) Structure
Enzymes are large complex proteins consisting of one or more polypeptide chains whose names end in <u>ase</u>.

a) Protein Nature
All enzymes are either exclusively proteins or are proteins with non-protein parts known as coenzymes. Often, vitamins function as coenzymes.

b) Active Site
Usually enzyme molecules are much larger than the molecules with which they interact. The specific way in which these chains fold results in the formation of pockets into which reacting molecules fit. This specific area of the enzyme is the active site.

2) Function
Evidence has accumulated to permit biochemists to develop a model of enzyme action which is useful in visualizing the nature of its function and which is consistent with the available evidence.

a) Enzyme-Substrate Complex
It is thought that, for an enzyme to affect the rate of a reaction, the following events take place.
- The enzyme must form a temporary association with the substance or substances whose reaction rate it affects. These substances are known as substrates.
- This association between enzyme and substrate is thought to involve a close physical association between the molecules and is called the enzyme-substrate complex.
- While the enzyme-substrate complex is formed, the enzyme action takes place.
- Upon completion of the reaction, the enzyme and product(s) separate. The enzyme molecule is now available to form additional complexes.

Although enzymes may be reused in cells, they eventually are destroyed and new ones must be synthesized.

b) *Lock and Key* Model
The inference that a particular enzyme molecule will only interact with a single type of substrate has given rise to the *lock and key* model of enzyme specificity. Like a key that will open only a particular lock, a particular enzyme will usually only form a complex with one particular type of substrate.

b. Factors Influencing Action of Enzymes
The rate of enzyme action is not fixed, but varies according to the environmental conditions of the reacting substances.

Such factors as pH, temperature, and relative amounts of enzyme and substrate can determine the rate of enzyme action.

1) Temperature
In general, as temperature increases, the rate of enzyme action increases. The temperature at whic an enzyme is most effficient is the optimum temperature.

At relatively high temperatures, however, the shape of enzyme molecules tends to be altered, thus rendering the enzyme ineffective. This distortion of enzyme molecules at high temperatures is enzyme denaturation. For many enzymes in the human body, denaturation begins to occur at around 40°C .

The response to changing temperature for many enzymes of humans is illustrated in the graph below:

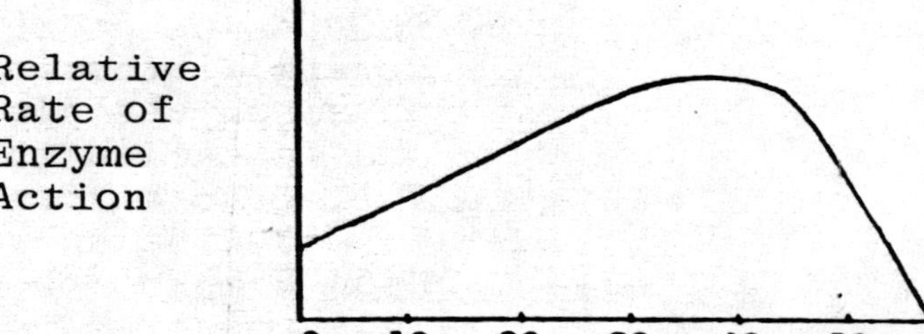

2) Relative Amounts of Enzyme and Substrate
The rate of enzyme action also varies according to the amount of available substrate molecules. When an excess of substrate is added to a system with a fixed concentration of enzymes, the rate of enzyme action tends to increase to a point and then remain fixed as long as the enzyme concentration remains constant.

The graphs below illustrate the pattern of enzyme action rates when an excess of substrate is added to a system with a fixed enzyme concentration:

Relative
Rate of
Enzyme
Action

Increasing Substrate Concentration
(Enzyme Concentration Constant)

3) pH

The rate at which enzyme-regulated reactions occur varies according to the pH of the environment.

- The pH scale indicates the hydrogen ion (H^+) concentration.
- The pH scale extends from 0-14. A pH of 7 indicates a neutral condition. Acids have a pH of less than 7 and bases have a pH greater than 7.

For many enzyme-controlled reactions, a pH of 7 provides the optimum environment.

Other enzymes work best within different pH ranges. Specific pH ranges of enzymes are illustrated below:

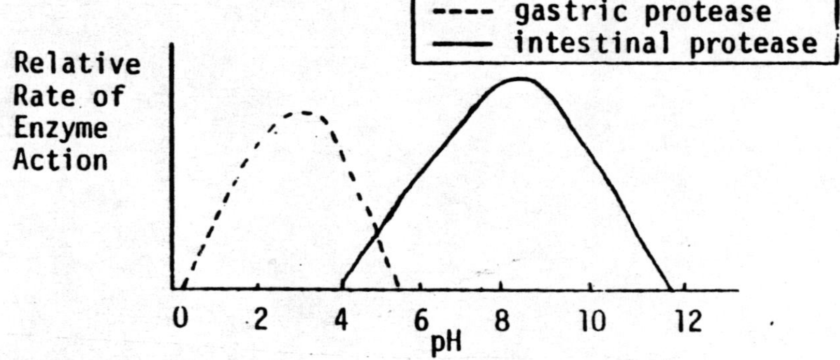

MAINTENANCE IN LIVING THINGS

Among living organisms, there is a universality of the functions which maintain life. These include the obtaining, processing, and distribution of essential materials, the removal of metabolic wastes, and the regulation of all metabolic processes.

While these functions are universal, organisms possess various structures and behavioral patterns which enable them to perform these functions efficiently in their environment. These structures and/or patterns are known as adaptations.

OBJECTIVES

The student should be able to:

- Identify and describe the basic functions necessary to maintain homeostasis.
- Identify and compare the adaptations of selected organisms for carrying out these life functions.
- Recognize that a unity of pattern underlies the diversity of living things.
- Correlate biochemical reactions with physiological functions.
- Observe and recognize that structure and function complement each other and culminate in an organism's successful adaptation to its environment.

I. Nutrition

Nutrition includes those activities by which organisms obtain and process materials needed for energy, growth, repair, and regulation.

Two types of nutrition are autotrophic and heterotrophic.

A. Autotrophic Nutrition

The ability of most plants and certain monerans and protists to manufacture organic compounds from inorganic raw materials is autotrophic nutrition. A second mode of autotrophic nutrition is chemosynthesis. An awareness of this process may facilitate understanding of the nitrogen cycle.

1. Process of Photosynthesis

Photosynthesis, the process during which light energy is converted into the chemical energy of organic molecules, is one type of autotrophic nutrition.

a. Significance

Most of the chemical energy available to organisms results from photosynthetic activity.

Photosynthesis is the source of most of the oxygen in the air.

b. Process

Most cells which carry on photosynthesis contain chloroplasts. These chloroplasts contain pigments which include chlorophylls. The variety of pigments contained within the chloroplasts can be separated by a technique called chromatography.

In the chloroplasts, CO_2 and H_2O are used in the formation of simple sugar molecules and oxygen.

Light energy is trapped by chlorophyll and converted into the chemical energy of simple sugar molecules. Red and blue wavelengths of light are most effective for this energy conversion because of their relativel high degree of absorption by chlorophyll molecules. Wavelengths of green light are less effective than red or blue.

Simplified summary statements for photosynthesis are:

$$\text{Carbon dioxide} + \text{water} \xrightarrow[\text{Chlorophyll Enzymes}]{\text{Light Energy}} \text{glucose} + \text{water} + \text{oxyge}$$

$$6CO_2 + 12H_2O \xrightarrow[\text{Chlorophyll Enzymes}]{\text{Light Energy}} C_6H_{12}O_6 + 6H_2O + 6O_2$$

In photosynthesis, two major sets of reactions occur: light and dark reactions. The use of various isotope has led to a greater understanding of these reactions

Photochemical (light) reactions - These reactions occur within layered membranes inside the chloroplast Stacks of these membranes, the grana, contain the enzymes and the pigments necessary for the light reactions. Some of the energy absorbed by the chlorc phyll pigments is used to *split* water molecules, producing hydrogen atoms and oxygen gas. This process is photolysis. The use of the isotope-oxygen 18 has shown that all of the oxygen liberated during photosynthesis is from water molecules. An energy transfer compound, ATP, is produced within the chlorc plasts during the light reactions. Details of this phase are still under investigation.

Carbon-Fixation (dark) reactions - These reactions occur within the chloroplasts in the stroma. The stroma is the dense solution outside the grana. Enzymes necessary for the dark reactions are found ir the stroma. Hydrogen atoms from the light reaction and the carbon dioxide molecules participate in a series of chemical changes which produce a three-carbon sugar (PGAL) from which other molecules, including glucose, are synthesized. The isotope carbon-14 has been used to trace the pathways of carbon fixation.

c. Results

The glucose which is formed may be:

1. Used as an energy source in cellular respiration.
2. Synthesized into other metabolic compounds.
3. Converted into storage products by dehydration synthesis and other reactions.

Before these storage products can be used, they are converted into simpler molecules by digestion within the cells (intracellular digestion), rather than in a specialized digestive system.

Once digestion is completed, the end products can be used in the cell or they can be transported to other tissues.

2. Adaptations for Photosynthesis

Algae and green plants are autotrophic organisms which carry on photosynthesis.

A large percentage of photosynthesis is carried on by unicellular algae present in the oceans. In these organisms, raw materials necessary for photosynthesis are absorbed directly into the individual cells.

Most terrestrial plants have specialized organs adapted for photosynthesis. Although photosynthesis may occur in the stems of some plants, the organs which are most highly adapted for this process are the leaves.

- Most leaves provide a large surface area for the absorption of light energy.
- The chief functions of the outer cell layers of the leaf (epidermis) and the waxy covering of the epidermis (cuticle) are: the protection of the internal tissues of the leaf from excessive water loss, resistance to invasion by fungi, and protection from mechanical injury.
- Openings in the cuticle and epidermis are called stomates. Their size is regulated by guard cells. Stomates allow the exchange of O_2, CO_2, and H_2O between the external environment and internal air spaces.
- Most photosynthesis occurring in leaves takes place in the palisade layer which is located under the upper epidermis.
- The spongy layer contains many interconnected air spaces which are surrounded by moist surfaces. The exchange and circulation of gases occur here. The spongy layer also carries on photosynthesis.

- In most leaves, chloroplasts are present in the palisade and spongy layers and in the guard cells.
- Conducting tissue, located in the veins of the leaves, carries water to the photosynthesizing cells and distributes food to other plant organs.

B. Heterotrophic Nutrition
Organisms unable to make organic molecules from inorganic raw materials are heterotrophs. Examples of groups of heterotrophic organisms include bacteria, fungi, protozoans, and animals.

1. Processes for Heterotrophic Nutrition
Heterotrophic organisms obtain preformed organic molecules from their environment.

a. Ingestion
Ingestion is the process of taking in food.

b. Digestion
Digestion is the conversion of large, insoluble molecules to smaller soluble molecules.

Digestion can be intracellular or it can be extracellular followed by the absorption of end-products.

1) Mechanical Breakdown
Food is mechanically broken down by physical means, such as cutting, grinding, and tearing which increases the surface area of the foods prior to chemical digestion.

2) Chemical Digestion
Large organic molecules are changed chemically to smaller organic molecules by enzymatic hydrolysis.

Complete digestion of large molecules produces end products as indicated:

Large Molecules	End Products
Carbohydrates	Simple sugars
Lipids	Fatty acids and glycerol
Proteins	Amino acids

The end products of chemical digestion are the same in all organisms.

c. Egestion
Egestion is the removal (elimination) of undigested or indigestible material by the heterotrophic organism.

Heterotrophs may not be able to digest all food components either because they may lack specific enzymes, or because the time that food is exposed to available enzymes may be too short.

2. Adaptations for Heterotrophic Nutrition

a. Fungi
Fungi live on or in their food supply. The filamentous body of a fungus, such as bread mold, contains special filaments called rhizoids which penetrate the food source and secrete digestive enzymes. This results in extracellular digestion and the subsequent absorption of digested nutrients.

b. Protozoans
In the ameba, food is ingested by means of pseudopods. This engulfing process is phagocytosis.

In the paramecium, as a result of the action of cilia, food is ingested through a fixed opening located in the oral groove.

Intracellular digestion of this food occurs within a food vacuole after it merges with a lysosome. The end products of the digestion are then absorbed into the cytoplasm.

In the paramecium, undigested materials are egested through a fixed opening called the anal pore.

c. Animals

1) Hydra
The hydra has a sac-like digestive cavity with a single opening. Food is ingested through this opening with the aid of tentacles and passes into the digestive cavity.

In the digestive cavity, extracellular digestion occurs as a result of enzymes which are secreted by specialized cells located in the lining of the cavity. Partially digested food is then engulfed by phagocytic cells lining the cavity and digestion is completed intracellularly.

Undigested material is egested through the same opening through which ingestion occurred.

2) Earthworm
A tube-like digestive system with two openings is present. This one-way digestive tract allows food to be processed in an efficient manner as it passes through specialized organs.

Food is ingested through the mouth, passes through the esophagus into the crop, where it is temporarily stored, and then into the gizzard where mechanical breakdown occurs. From the gizzard, the food passes into the intestine where most chemical digestion takes place and where end products are absorbed into the circulatory system

Undigested material is egested through the anus.

3) Grasshopper
In the grasshopper, the structure and function of the digestive system are essentially similar to that of the earthworm. Food moves in one direction from mouth to anus.

The grasshopper possesses highly specialized mouth parts for mechanical breakdown. Salivary glands and gastric caeca secrete hydrolytic enzymes into the digestive tract for chemical digestion.

4) Human
The digestive system is essentially similar to that of the grasshopper and earthworm in that it contains:
- A tube-like system with two openings
- Specialized organs and glands for mechanical breakdown and chemical digestion.

II. Transport
The process of transport involves the absorption and circulation of materials throughout an organism.

A. Process

1. Absorption
Absorption is the process whereby the end products of digestion, as well as other dissolved solids and gases, enter the fluids and the cells of an organism.

a. Structure of the Cell Membrane
The cell membrane selectively regulates the entry and exit of materials. This aids cells in maintaining homeostasis.

A currently accepted model of the cell membrane is the <u>fluid-mosaic</u> model. This model suggests that the membrane is a double lipid layer in which large proteins float. Many small particles, such as molecules, diffuse through the membrane. Most larger molecules such as proteins and starches cannot diffuse into or out of cells unless they are chemically digested. The size of the molecule does not seem to be the sole determining factor in all cases.

In 1972, S.J. Singer proposed a model for the cell membrane that has become widely accepted. This model shows a double phospholipid layer positioned with the hydrophobic tails away from the membrane surface and the hydrophilic heads toward the outer and inner membrane surfaces. This is similar to the Danielli model. However, in Singer's Fluid-Mosaic Model, the proteins are not limited to the surfaces of the membrane but rather are embedded in the lipid layers like *floating icebergs in a fatty sea*.

b. Function of the Cell Membrane
The cell membrane has both passive and active roles in transporting materials into and out of cells.

1) Passive Transport
In passive transport, the movement of the materials through the cell membrane is the result of the kinetic energy of the particles in motion.

Diffusion, a form of passive transport, is a process in which the net movement of ions or soluble molecules is from a region of higher concentration to a region of lower concentration. The diffusion of water through a membrane is osmosis.

2) Active Transport
Active transport is a process in which cellular energy is used to move particles through a membrane. This movement is from a region of low concentration toward a region of high concentration. Carrier proteins embedded in the cell membrane aid the transport of materials.

3) Pinocytosis
Pinocytosis is a process whereby vacuoles formed at the cell surface bring in large dissolved molecules.

4) Phagocytosis
Phagocytosis is a process in which a cell engulfs undissolved large particles by flowing around them and enclosing them in a vacuole.

2. Circulation
The transport of materials within cells and/or throughout multicellular organisms is circulation.

Intracellular circulation is accomplished by diffusion, cyclosis, and possibly, by movement throughout the endoplasmic reticulum.

Intercellular circulation may be by diffusion or by transport through vascular tissue.

B. Adaptations

Intracellular circulation occurs within all living cells.

Intercellular circulation varies with the complexity of the organism.

1. Plants

Simple multicellular plants, bryophytes, lack vascular tissue. Intercellular transport is accomplished by diffusion.

Higher plants, tracheophytes, possess vascular tissue for intercellular transport.

a. Roots

Roots are structures specialized for anchorage, nutrient storage, absorption of water and soluble salts, and for the conduction of materials to the stem.

1) Root Hairs

Root hairs are elongated epidermal cells which increase the surface area of the root for the absorption of water and minerals.

The movement of materials through the semi-permeable membrane of root hairs involves both diffusion, including osmosis, and active transport.

2) Xylem

The xylem is specialized transport tissue extending from the roots to the leaves. The principal function of the xylem tissue is the conduction of water and minerals upward in the plant.

The mechanism by which water is transported through the xylem is best explained by the hypothesis of transpirational pull. Transpirational pull involves the transpiration of water vapor through the stomates. This exerts a pulling force on the column of water in the xylem. Because of the cohesive and adhesive properties of water, the water column does not break and is drawn up from the roots.

Under conditions of high humidity, root pressure may play a role in pushing water up through the xylem of small plants.

3) Phloem

Phloem conducts organic food materials both upwar[d] and downward to plant tissues for immediate use or storage.

b. Stems
Although the structure of the stem is different from that of the roots, the vascular tissues are continuous.

c. Leaves
Leaves contain veins which are extensions of the conducting tissues in the stem.

2. Animals

a. Hydra
Since most of its cells are in direct contact with a watery environment, the hydra is able to survive without a special transport system.

Flagellated cells aid in the circulation of materials throughout the gastrovascular cavity. Intercellular circulation is by diffusion.

b. Earthworm
Many cells of the earthworm are not in direct contact with the external environment. An internal, closed circulatory system where blood is contained within vessels transports materials throughout the organism. The hemoglobin dissolved in the blood distributes respiratory gases between the external environment and the cells. Water and dissolved materials, including the end products of digestion, are transported from the digestive system to the cells of the organism. Aortic arches pump the blood within the blood vessels.

An infolding of the earthworm's digestive tube is an adaptation which increases the absorptive surface through which digestive end products enter the blood.

c. Grasshopper
The grasshopper has an internal, open, circulatory system which brings materials in contact with all cells. In contrast to a closed circulatory system, in an open system blood is distributed into sinuses by means of a pulsating blood vessel.

As in the earthworm, the grasshopper has an infolded digestive tube which increases the absorption area.

d. Human
The human circulatory system is a closed system with hemoglobin for oxygen transport. There is a pumping structure called the heart. Infoldings of the digestive tube increase the absorption area for nutrients.

III. Respiration

Respiration is a process that occurs continuously in the cells of all organisms.

It involves the transfer of the stored chemical energy in food molecules to a form readily usable by organisms. It usually also involves an exchange of gases between the organism and its environment.

A. Process

1. Cellular

Cellular respiration refers to those enzyme-controlled reactions in which the potential energy of organic molecules, such as glucose, is transferred to a more available form of energy. This available form of energy is stored in adenosine triphosphate molecules. When ATP is hydrolyzed, energy is released and ADP is formed. This reaction is reversible. This energy can be used for metabolic activities which require energy.

$$H_2O + ATP \underset{\longleftarrow}{\overset{\longrightarrow}{\text{ATP-ase}}} ADP + P + \text{Energy}$$

If the energy transfer reactions involve the use of molecular oxygen, the process is aerobic respiration. The majority of organisms carry on aerobic respiration. If free oxygen is not used, the process is anaerobic respiration.

a. Anaerobic Respiration (Fermentation)

Some cells lack the enzymes necessary for aerobic respiration and other cells revert to anaerobic respiration when oxygen is lacking. The enzymes for anaerobic respiration are located in the cytoplasm of cells.

1) Description

During most types of anaerobic respiration, glucose is gradually broken down in a series of enzyme-controlled reactions to either lactic acid or alcohol and CO_2. The end products vary depending on the type of organism. Lactic acid is produced in animals and is associated with muscle fatigue. Lactic acid is also produced by some bacteria and is important in the production of cheeses, buttermilk, and yogurt. Alcohol and CO_2 are usually produced by yeast and bacteria. These end products are useful in the baking and brewing industries.

As a result of anaerobic respiration, there is a net gain of 2 ATP.

$$\text{Glucose} \xrightarrow{\text{enzymes}} \text{2 lactic acid} + \text{2 ATP}$$

$$\text{Glucose} \xrightarrow{\text{enzymes}} \text{2 alcohol} + 2CO_2 + \text{2 ATP}$$

The end products, lactic acid and/or alcohol, still contain a great deal of potential energy.

2) Chemical Aspects
The first series of reactions in anaerobic respiration involves the conversion of glucose to pyruvic acid.

The conversion of pyruvic acid to either lactic acid or alcohol and CO_2 occurs without any further yield of energy.

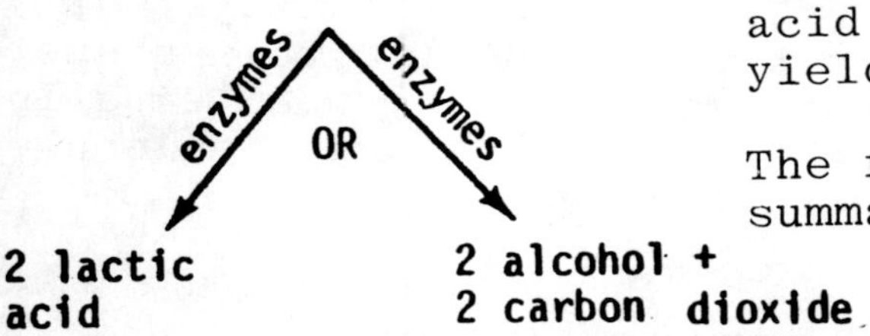

The reactions of anaerobic respiration may be summarized as follows:

$$\text{Glucose} + \text{2 ATP} \xrightarrow{\text{enzymes}} \text{2 pyruvic acid} + \text{4 ATP}$$

enzymes OR enzymes

2 lactic acid | **2 alcohol + 2 carbon dioxide**

b. Aerobic Respiration
Many of the enzymes involved in aerobic cellular respiration are located in the mitochondria.

1) Description
During this process, and due to the presence of oxygen, the chemical energy of glucose is released gradually in a series of enzyme-controlled reactions.

The summary equation for aerobic respiration of glucose is:

$$\text{Glucose} + \text{oxygen} \xrightarrow{\text{enzymes}} \text{water} + \text{carbon dioxide} + \text{ATP}$$

$$C_6H_{12}O_6 + 6\ O_2 \xrightarrow{\text{enzymes}} 6H_2O + 6CO_2 + 36^*\ \text{ATPs}$$

Aerobic respiration is more efficient than anaerobic.

*Authorities now believe that 38 ATPs are produced per molecule of glucose in all prokaryotic organisms but that 36 ATPs are produced by respiration in eukaryotic organisms.

2) Chemical Aspects
Investigations of the chemical reactions occurring during glucose oxidation indicate that, although there are many enzyme-catalyzed steps, there are two basic phases: the anaerobic and the aerobic.

Anaerobic phase: Glucose is oxidized to two molecules of pyruvic acid and the energy released is used to synthesize four molecules of ATP. Since the energy of two ATP molecules is required to activate this phase, there is a net gain of two ATPs.

Aerobic phase: The pyruvic acid molecules are oxidized and the energy released. Thirty-four ATP molecules are synthesized during this phase. Oxygen acts as a hydrogen acceptor, resulting in the formation of water. Carbon dioxide molecules are produced as a result of some intermediate reactions.

The net gain in the complete breakdown of one glucose molecule in aerobic respiration is therefore 36* ATPs. (*See previous note)

The relationship between the anaerobic and aerobic phases of cellular respiration are summarized below:

$$\text{glucose} + 2\text{ ATP} \xrightarrow{\text{enzymes}} 2\text{ pyruvic acid} + 4\text{ ATP}$$

anaerobic phase

$$2\text{ pyruvic acid} + \text{oxygen} \xrightarrow{\text{enzymes}} \text{carbon dioxide} + \text{water} + 34\text{ ATP}$$

aerobic phase

AEROBIC CELLULAR RESPIRATION

2. Gas Exchange
Gas exchange involves the diffusion of gases between the organism and its environment.

B. Adaptations
While the chemical processes of respiration are similar in most organisms, various adaptations for the exchange of respiratory gases are present in living things.

1. Monera, Protista, and Fungi
In these organisms, gas exchange occurs by diffusion through thin, moist membranes. This gas exchange surface is an external surface.

2. Plants
Plants have various methods for gas exchange.

a. Leaves
The outer covering is dry and impermeable and not a gas exchange surface. Gas exchange occurs across the membranes of internal cells. These cells are bounded by moist intercellular spaces. Access to these spaces is through the stomates.

b. Stems
Stems of woody plants contain lenticels which permit the exchange of gases. Lenticels are small areas of loosely exposed cells.

c. Roots
Gas exchange occurs across the moist membranes of root hairs and other epidermal cells.

3. Animals

a. Hydra
Each cell of the hydra is in contact with the watery environment and gas exchange occurs by diffusion.

b. Earthworm
As a terrestrial organism, the problem of the retention of a moist gas exchange surface is solved by the secretion of mucus by the skin. This maintains a moist surface which facilitates the diffusion of gases into and out of the blood. Hemoglobin aids in the transport of oxygen to the body cells.

c. Grasshopper
Since the grasshopper possesses an open circulatory system lacking hemoglobin, gas transport and gas exchange are accomplished by tracheal tubes. The tracheal tubes terminate internally in moist membranes where gases are exchanged. The external body surface is dry and impermeable. Access to the tracheal tubes is through spiracles.

d. Human
Human skin is impermeable to respiratory gases. The lungs are a thin, moist, internal gas exchange surface. Hemoglobin aids in the transport of oxygen.

IV. Excretion

A. Process
The removal of cellular waste products of an organism is excretion.

1. Products
The metabolic activities of living organisms result in the production of waste materials.

Metabolic Activity	Wastes
Respiration	Carbon dioxide + water
Dehydration synthesis	Water
Certain metabolic processes	Mineral salts
Protein metabolism	Nitrogenous wastes

Nitrogenous wastes are produced when excess amino acids are utilized in cellular respiration.

Nitrogenous wastes vary from the extremely toxic ammonia to the less toxic urea and the nontoxic uric acid.

2. Results
Wastes may be either toxic or nontoxic. When toxic wastes are produced, they are normally released, as in animals, or sealed off and stored, as in plants. Non-toxic wastes may either be retained, released, or recycled in other metabolic activities.

B. Adaptations
Organisms display various adaptations for excretion. Adaptations vary depending on the metabolic activities of the organism and the environment in which it lives.

1. Protista
Special excretory structures are absent in many unicellular organisms. Excretion is accomplished by diffusion through cell membranes.

a. Freshwater Protozoans
In the ameba and paramecium, carbon dioxide, ammonia and mineral salts diffuse through the cell membrane directly into the watery environment. The contractile vacuole functions in osmoregulation in freshwater protozoans.

b. Algae
The waste product of respiration, carbon dioxide, can be recycled in the photosynthetic process.

Some of the oxygen produced during photosynthesis is recycled for respiration.

2. Plants
Plants recycle the photosynthetic and respiratory gases.

Excess gases leave the plant through the stomates, lenticels, and epidermal cells of the root.

Some waste products, such as organic acids which might be toxic, are stored in vacuoles where they cause no injury to the plant.

3. Animals

a. Hydra
Excretion in the hydra is essentially similar to that of the protozoans.

b. Earthworm
Carbon dioxide is excreted by diffusion through the moist skin of the earthworm.

Pairs of excretory organs called nephridia located in most body segments of the earthworm excrete water, mineral salts, and urea into the terrestrial environment.

c. Grasshopper
Carbon dioxide diffuses from the grasshopper's body fluids into tracheal tubes and is expelled through spiracles.

Water, mineral salts, and insoluble uric acid crystals accumulate in the malpighian tubules and are transported to the digestive tube where most of the water is reabsorbed. Minerals and uric acid are expelled with the fecal material.

The excretion of uric acid is a water-conserving mechanism of particular advantage to an egg-laying terrestrial organism. Uric acid is insoluble and can be stored in the egg without exerting harmful toxic or osmotic effects.

d. Human
CO_2 and H_2O are excreted through the respiratory system.

Humans possess nephrons, excretory structures similar to the nephridia of earthworms, for the excretion of water, salt, and urea.

V. Regulation
Regulation is the coordination and control of the life activities. Coordination of all life functions depends on special control mechanisms. These mechanisms include nerve control (found in multicellular animals) and chemical control (common to all organisms).

A. Nerve Control
Nerve control depends mainly on the functioning of the neurons (nerve cells).

1. Functional Definitions

a. Stimulus
A change in the external or internal environment which initiates an impulse.

b. Receptors
Structures specialized to detect certain stimuli.

c. Impulse
An electro-chemical charge generated along a neuron.

d. Response
A reaction to a stimulus.

e. Effectors
Organs of response such as muscles or glands.

f. Neuron
The nerve cell is a cell specially adapted for the transmission of impulses. It is composed of:

1) Dendrites
Fibers which detect the stimulus and generate impulses toward the cyton.

2) Cyton
Cell body containing the nucleus.

3) Axon
A fiber that transmits the impulse away from the cyton toward the terminal branches, and

4) Terminal Branches
Ends of the axons which secrete neurotransmitters

g. Synapse
Junction between adjacent neurons or between neuron and effector.

h. Neurotransmitters
Chemicals, such as acetylcholine, which, when secreted, aid in the transmission across the synapse.

2. Adaptations in Animals

a. Hydra
The hydro possesses a nerve net composed of modified neurons. There is no central nervous system and impulses may travel in either direction over the neuron.

b. Earthworm
The nervous system of the earthworm consists of a primitive brain composed of fused ganglia, a ventral nerve cord, and peripheral nerves.

The presence of this central nervous system permits impulses to travel over definite pathways from receptors to effectors.

c. Grasshopper
The grasshopper's nervous system is similar to that of the earthworm. The grasshopper possesses sensory organs which include eyes, tympana, and antennae.

d. Human
The human central nervous system consists of a highly developed brain and dorsal nerve cord which permit impulses to travel over definite pathways. There are also many highly developed receptors.

B. Chemical Control
Similar to nerve control, chemical control coordinates body processes by transmitting messages from one part of the organism to another.

Unlike nerve control, chemical control is achieved through hormonal action in both plants and animals.

1. Chemical Control in Plants

a. Characteristics of Plant Hormones
Plant hormones are chemicals produced by cells which affect the growth and development of other cells.

Plant hormones function in the coordination of processes such as growth, tropisms, and reproduction.

There are no plant organs specialized exclusively for hormone production.

Plant hormone production is most abundant in actively growing areas such as the cells at the tips of roots and stems, buds, and seeds.

b. Role of Plant Hormones
Auxins are one type of plant hormone.

Auxins influence division, elongation, and differentiation of plant cells.

Unequal distribution of auxins causes unequal growth responses called tropisms.

Unequal auxin distribution can be caused by external stimuli such as light and gravity.

Tropisms are usually adaptive growth responses that enhance the survival of the plant.

Hormones promote other developmental changes, including flowering, fruit formation, and seed development.

Hormone responses depend upon the hormones involved, their concentrations, and the tissues affected.

2. Chemical Control in Animals
Chemical control in animals differs from that in plants since animals possess cells specialized solely for hormone production.

a. Endocrine Control
Endocrine glands synthesize and secrete hormones which control the activities of animals.

Hormones are chemicals secreted in one area of the body which affect responses in other areas.

The circulatory system aids in the distribution of these hormones since the endocrine glands are ductless.

b. Role of Animal Hormones
Current research indicates that hormones exist in a wide variety of organisms and that the hormones themselves have wide distribution among animals.

Hormones interact and exert control on metabolic activities such as metamorphosis and reproduction.

VI. Locomotion
Locomotion is the ability to move from place to place.

A. Advantages
Locomotion increases the probability of survival among animals and many protista. Some of the advantages of locomotion are increased opportunities to obtain food, seek shelter, avoid predators, move away from toxic wastes, and mate.

B. Adaptations

1. Protista

a. Algae
Some algae move by means of flagella.

b. Protozoans
The locomotive structures utilized by paramecia are cilia. Locomotion in ameba is by pseudopods.

2. Animals

a. Hydra
The hydra is essentially a sessile organism. The presence of contractile fibers permits some motion, including a type of somersaulting.

b. Earthworm
Locomotion is accomplished through the interactions of muscles and setae. The setae permit temporary anchorage in the soil and the muscles produce extensions and contractions of the animal's body.

c. Grasshopper
The grasshopper has an exoskeleton made of chitin. Locomotion is accomplished by interactions of muscles with jointed, chitinous appendages.

d. Human
Humans have an endoskeleton. Locomotion is accomplished by the interaction of muscles and jointed appendages.

—

HUMAN PHYSIOLOGY

OBJECTIVES

The student should be able to:

- Recognize that humans are not unique in their performance of the functions necessary to maintain life.
- Apply scientific information to food choice decisions.
- Identify the major structures and functions of the human body and their role in the maintenance of homeostasis.
- Describe the interrelationships among the systems of the human body.
- Describe the structure and function of the major organs of the human body.

I. Nutrition

Nutrition includes those activities by which organisms obtain and process nutrients needed for energy, growth, repair, and regulation. Humans are heterotrophic and, therefore, must ingest food. Food includes nutrients and roughage. Nutrients include usable carbohydrates, protein, lipids, vitamins, minerals, and water. Vitamins, minerals, and water are small molecules and can be absorbed without digestion. Carbohydrates, lipids, and proteins require digestion. Nutritional requirements vary with an individual's age, sex, and activities.

A. Functional Organization

The human digestive system consists of a continuous one-way gastrointestinal tract and the accessory organs which function in conjunction with the tract. Food is moved through the GI tract by slow, rhythmic muscular contractions called peristalsis.

1. Oral Cavity

Ingestion of food occurs through the mouth. The oral cavity contains the teeth, tongue, and the openings from the salivary glands.

The teeth function in the mechanical breakdown of food which serves to increase the surface area of the food for enzyme action.

The chemical digestion of carbohydrates begins here. The salivary glands secrete saliva which contains the enzyme amylase which digests starch.

Carbohydrates, which should constitute 50 percent of the diet, are a source of energy for the body.

In addition to serving as energy sources, complex carbohydrates provide nondigestible materials which increase the amount of roughage. Complex carbohydrates are found in fresh fruits and vegetables, as well as whole grains.

2. Esophagus
As a result of swallowing, food moves into the esophagus. Peristaltic action of the esophagus moves the food to the stomach.

3. Stomach
The stomach is a muscular organ. Its lining contains gastric glands which secrete enzymes and hydrochloric acid. Hydrochloric acid provides an optimum pH for the hydrolytic activity of gastric protease. Under the influence of this enzyme, protein digestion begins.

4. Small Intestine
Partially digested food enters the small intestine. The small intestine is a long, convoluted tube in which the major portion of food is digested.

Accessory structures, the gall bladder and pancreas, empty their secretions into the small intestine.

The secretion from the gall bladder is bile. Bile is produced in the liver and stored in the gall bladder. Bile emulsifies fats in the small intestine. Emulsification serves to increase the surface area of fats for subsequent chemical action.

a. Chemical Digestion
The pancreas secretes several enzymes, including intestinal protease, lipase, and amylase.

Intestinal glands that line the intestinal wall secrete protease, lipase, and disaccharides, such as maltase.

Chemical digestion of proteins, lipids, and carbohydrates is completed here.

b. Absorption
The lining of the small intestine contains numerous villi which increase the surface area to facilitate absorption. Capillaries and small lymphatic vessels, lacteals, extend into the villi.

Fatty acids and glycerol are absorbed through the villi into the lacteals and are transported in the lymph.

Monosaccharides and amino acids are absorbed through the villi and enter the capillaries to be transported to the liver where they are temporarily stored. From there, they are available for distribution by the blood.

Glucose is stored as the polysaccharide glycogen. Breakdown of glycogen releases glucose for transport.

Amino acids are temporarily stored and distributed to the cells as needed for protein synthesis.

Twenty amino acids are necessary for body cells to synthesize the required proteins needed to maintain and repair body tissues.

Although humans can convert one amino acid into another, eight cannot be synthesized and must be consumed as part of the diet. These are called essential amino acids.

In order to synthesize new proteins, all the necessary amino acids must be present at the same time. If there is an insufficient supply of any one amino acid, protein synthesis will be limited, and the amino acids will be deaminated and used for energy production.

Complete protein foods provide all the essential amino acids.

Incomplete proteins lack one or more of the essential amino acids. A balanced diet may be attained by making incomplete protein foods complement each other. Incomplete protein foods (wheat and beans) complement each other more effectively if they are eaten at the same time.

5. Large Intestine
Undigested food and water enter the large intestine where water is absorbed. Strong peristaltic action forces feces out through the anus.

B. Mechanism for Chemical Digestion
Hydrolysis is the splitting of large, insoluble molecules into small, soluble molecules with the addition of water. In organisms, this process is regulated by hydrolytic enzymes and is illustrated by the following:

$$\text{maltose + water} \xrightarrow{\text{maltase}} \text{glucose + glucose}$$

$$\text{proteins + water} \xrightarrow{\text{protease}} \text{amino acids}$$

$$\text{lipids and water} \xrightarrow{\text{lipase}} \text{3 fatty acids and 1 glycerol}$$

In a similar fashion, polysaccharides such as starch are completely hydrolyzed to simple sugars.

The process of hydrolysis is illustrated by the following equations representing the breakdown of the disaccharide, maltose, into two glucose molecules.

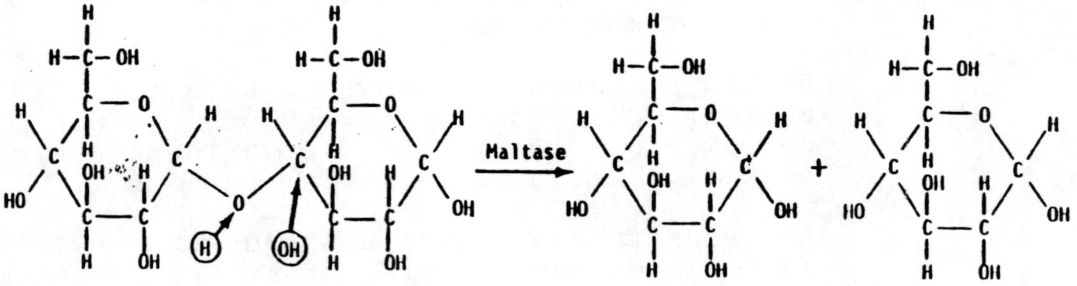

Maltase

$$\text{maltose} + \text{water} \xrightarrow{\text{maltase}} \text{glucose} + \text{glucose}$$

During hydrolysis, in the presence of water and proteases, the peptide bonds are broken resulting in the production of amino acids.

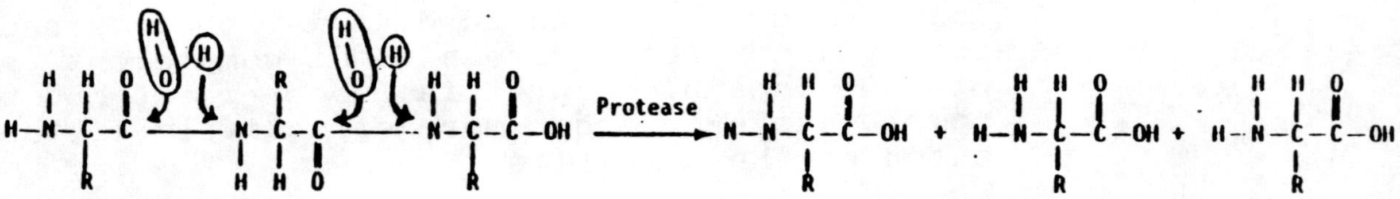

Protease

$$\text{polypeptide} + \text{water} \xrightarrow{\text{protease}} \text{amino acids}$$

In the presence of water molecules and lipase, lipids are hydrolyzed to one glycerol and three fatty acid molecules.

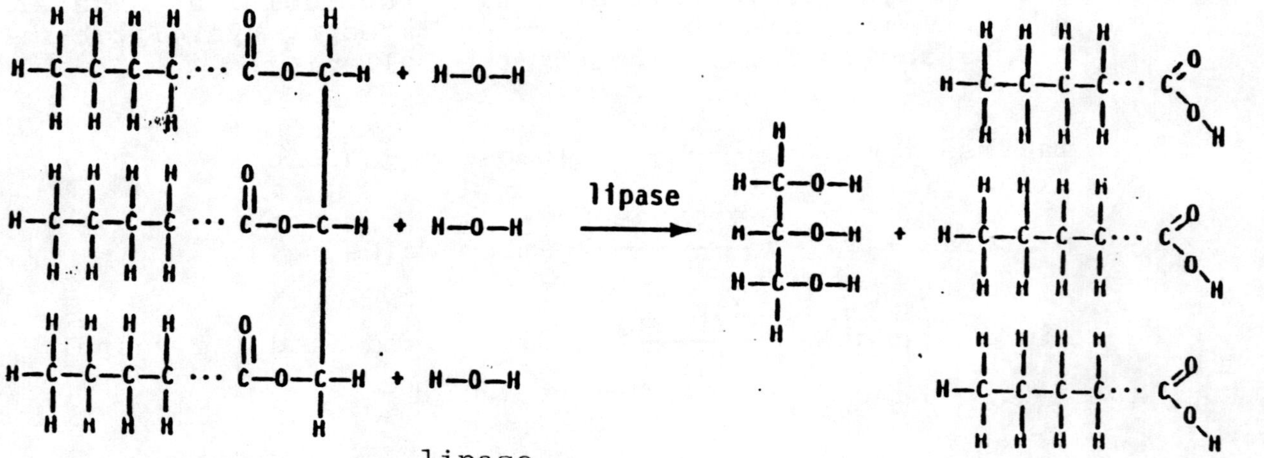

lipase

$$\text{fat} + \text{water} \xrightarrow{\text{lipase}} \text{glycerol} + \text{fatty acids}$$

Fats contain a high quantity of potential energy and are necessary for the synthesis of cell membranes. However, increased fat consumption represents a potentially dangerous change in an individual's dietary pattern. It is important to be aware of not only how much but also what kind of fat is eaten. Fats are described as saturated or unsaturated.

Saturated fats are solid at room temperature. There is evidence that increased intake is one of many factors that predisposes humans to cardiovascular disease.

Polyunsaturated fats (oils) are liquid at room temperature and do not appear to be linked to cardiovascular disease.

C. Some Malfunctions of the Digestive System

1. Ulcers
An erosion of the surface of the alimentary canal generally associated with some kind of irritant.

2. Constipation
A condition in which the large intestine is emptied with difficulty. Too much water is absorbed and the solid waste hardens.

3. Diarrhea
A gastrointestinal disturbance characterized by decreased water absorption and increased peristaltic activity of the large intestine. This results in increased, multiple, watery feces. This condition may result in severe dehydration.

4. Appendicitis
An inflammation of the appendix.

5. Gallstones
An accumulation of hardened cholesterol deposits in the gall bladder.

II. Transport
The process of transport involves the absorption and circulation of materials throughout an organism.

A. Functional Organization
A function of the human circulatory system is the transport of dissolved and suspended materials throughout the body.

1. Transport Media

a. Blood
Blood is a fluid tissue composed of plasma in which red blood cells, white blood cells, and platelets are suspended.

Blood, serving as a transport medium, helps to maintain homeostasis for all cells of the body.

1) Plasma
The plasma, which is made up mostly of water, contains dissolved inorganic ions, wastes, hormones, nutrients, and a variety of proteins including antibodies, clotting factors, and enzymes.

2) Red Blood Cells
Red blood cells, which lack nuclei when mature, contain hemoglobin which combines with and distributes oxygen.

3) Platelets
Platelets are smaller than either red or white blood cells and play a key role in blood clot formation.

Blood clotting involves a series of enzyme-controlled reactions resulting in the formation of protein fibers that trap blood cells and form a clot. Although all reactants are present in the blood, the rupturing of the platelets and the release of an enzyme appear to initiate the process.

4) White Blood Cells
Several types of white blood cells exist.

a) Phagocytic White Blood Cells
Phagocytic white blood cells engulf and destroy bacteria at the site of infection by the process of phagocytosis. This is a normal defense against infection.

b) Lymphocytes
Lymphocytes are another type of white blood cell that is associated with the immune response. These white blood cells produce specific antibodies which act against foreign molecules known as antigens.

(1) Immunity
Immunity involves the accumulation of specific antibodies in the plasma of the blood enabling the individual to resist specific diseases.

Immunity can be acquired in the following ways:

(a) Active Immunity
The antigen-antibody reaction occurs within the body in response to either contact with the disease-causing organisms or their products, or by receiving a vaccination.

(b) Passive Immunity
A temporary form of immunity can be produced by the introduction of antibodies into the body.

(2) Allergies
Many people are allergic to various substances -- dust, pollen, insect bites, foods, drugs, and others. The body responds to these substances as if they were antigens and produces antibodies.

These antibodies may cause inflammations and/or result in the release of a chemical substance called histamine. The histamine causes the allergic response.

(3) Applications
Knowledge of immunity has resulted in the ability to type blood and transplant organs.

(a) Blood Typing
Blood typing in the ABO blood group is based on the presence or absence of antigens on the surface of red blood cells. Two types of antigens are known: *A* and *B*.

In addition, plasma may contain the antibodies, anti-A and/or anti-B.

Antigens in red cells	Antibodies in plasma	Blood Type
A	Anti-B	A
B	Anti-A	B
A & B	Neither Anti-A nor Anti-B	AB
Neither A nor B	Anti-A & Anti-B	O

(b) Organ Transplants
Rejection of organ transplants occurs when the recipient's body produces antibodies in response to the antigens present in the donor's organ.

b. ICF and Lymph
Intercellular fluid (ICF) derived from blood plasma surrounds all living cells of the body. When ICF passes into the lymph vessels, it is called lymph.

2. Transport Vessels

a. Arteries
Arteries are relatively thick-walled, muscular blood vessels which transport blood from the heart to all parts of the body. Their contraction (pulse) aids in the flow of blood.

b. Capillaries
Capillaries are tiny blood vessels with walls only one cell thick. They readily exchange materials between the blood and the intercellular fluid.

c. Veins
Veins are relatively thin-walled blood vessels possessing valves which prevent the backflow of blood. The veins return blood to the heart.

d. Lymph Vessels
Lymph vessels include extremely small tubes with walls only one cell thick. These vessels branch through all the body tissues. Major lymph vessels have lymph nodes which contain phagocytic cells which filter bacteria and dead cells from the lymph. Valves, present in some lymph vessels, aid in the movement of the lymph.

3. Transport Mechanisms

a. Structure and Function
The muscular heart is a four-chambered pump composed of two atria and two ventricles. The ventricles have thicker walls than the atria. The heart pumps blood through the arteries creating a blood pressure.

1) Circulation Through the Heart
The right atrium receives deoxygenated blood from the body through the vena cavae. The left atrium receives oxygenated blood from the lungs through the pulmonary vein. Blood passes through valves from the atria to the ventricles. Valves prevent the backflow of blood into the atria. The right ventricle pumps deoxygenated blood to the lungs through the pulmonary artery; the left ventricle pumps oxygenated blood to the rest of the body through the aorta. Valves between these arteries and the ventricles prevent the backflow of blood into the ventricles.

Blood pressure refers to the pressure exerted on the walls of the arteries during the pumping acti of the heart. During the contraction of the ventricles (systole), a great pressure is exerted on the arterial walls; during the relaxation of the ventricles (diastole), less pressure is normally exerted on the arterial walls.

2) Pulmonary and Systematic Circulation
Circulation to and from the lungs is pulmonary circulation. Circulation to and from the rest of the body is systemic circulation.

3) Coronary Circulation
The muscle tissue of the heart is supplied with blood through a system of coronary blood vessels.

4) Lymphatic Circulation
Tissue fluid may be drained through lymph vessels. These lymph vessels join larger vessels which ultimately form two main trunks that empty lymph into certain veins of the circulatory system.

B. Some Malfunctions of the Transport System

1. Cardiovascular Diseases
Cardiovascular diseases are malfunctions involving the heart and blood vessels.

a. High Blood Pressure
High blood pressure is the most common form of cardiovascular disease characterized by increased arterial pressure. This can be caused by a number of variables, including stress, dietary factors, heredity, cigarette smoking, and aging.

High blood pressure can lead to damage to the lining of arteries and a weakening of the heart muscle.

b. *Heart Attack*
Heart attacks, as they are called, include:

1) Coronary Thrombosis
Coronary thrombosis is a blockage in the coronary artery or its branches resulting in O_2 deprivation in the heart muscle. The deprived muscle usually becomes damaged.

2) Angina Pectoris
Angina pectoris is a narrowing of the coronary arteries causing an inadequate supply of oxygen to the heart muscle. Often, an intense pain radiating from chest to shoulder and arms is felt.

2. Blood Conditions
Blood conditions are abnormalities in the circulatory fluid.

a. Anemia
Anemia is the impaired ability of the blood to transport sufficient amounts of oxygen. This can be due to reduced amounts of hemoglobin and/or red blood cells.

b. Leukemia
Leukemia is a disease of the bone marrow characterized by uncontrolled production of nonfunctional white blood cells.

III. Respiration
Respiration involves the processes of cellular respiration and gas exchange.

A. Cellular
In humans the process of cellular respiration is essentially the same as that of other aerobic organisms.

Under conditions of oxygen deprivation, muscle cells respire anaerobically, and lactic acid is produced.

B. Gas Exchange
The function of the human respiratory system is to transport gases between the external environment and the internal gas exchange surfaces.

1. Functional Organization of the Respiratory System
The respiratory system is composed of a network of passageways which permit air to flow from the external environment to the lungs.

a. Nasal Cavity
The nasal cavity is exposed to the air through nostrils. This cavity is lined with a ciliated mucous membrane which filters, warms, and moistens the air.

b. Pharynx
The pharynx is the area in which the oral cavity and nasal cavity meet. Food is prevented from entering the trachea by the epiglottis.

c. Trachea
The trachea is kept open by rings of cartilage. The ciliated mucous membrane which lines the trachea traps microscopic particles and sweeps them toward the pharynx. Deposits from cigarette smoke and other atmospheric pollutants may interfere with the action of cilia.

d. Bronchi
The two major subdivisions of the trachea are the bronchi. The bronchi are lined with mucous membrane and ringed with cartilage. Each bronchus extends into a lung where it subdivides many times forming progressively smaller bronchioles.

e. Bronchioles
Bronchioles are lined with mucous membrane but lack cartilage rings. Tiny bronchioles terminate with the alveoli.

f. Alveoli
Alveoli are the functional units for gas exchange. They are thin, moist, and surrounded by capillaries.

g. Lung
Each bronchus with its bronchioles and alveoli is called a lung.

2. Mechanisms for Gas Exchange

a. Breathing
The lungs are highly elastic and respond passively to the actions of the diaphragm and rib cage.

Movements of the diaphragm and rib cage cause pressure changes in the chest cavity which move air into or out of the lungs. This process is known as breathing.

The breathing rate is regulated by the concentration of CO_2 in the blood and its effect on the medulla of the brain. This is an example of a feedback mechanism which aids in the maintenance of homeostasis.

b. Gas Exchange
The capillaries which surround the alveoli are involved in gas exchange between the blood and the alveoli. In the blood, oxygen is carried by the red blood cell as oxyhemoglobin. Oxygen, which is loosely bound to the hemoglobin, diffuses into the cells where it is used during aerobic cellular respiration.

The end products of aerobic cellular respiration, CO_2 and H_2O, diffuse into the blood. Carbon dioxide is carried primarily in the plasma in the form of the bicarbonate ion. CO_2 and H_2O are released from the lungs.

C. Some Malfunctions of the Respiratory System

1. Bronchitis
Bronchitis is the inflammation of the membrane of the bronchial tubes.

2. Asthma
Asthma is an allergic response characterized by constriction of the bronchial tubes.

3. Emphysema
Emphysema is a change in the structure of the lung characterized by enlargement and degeneration of the alveoli resulting in decreased lung capacity.

IV. Excretion

Many organs are involved in the removal of metabolic wastes in humans.

A. Functional Organization

1. Lungs

Carbon dioxide and water, waste products of respiration, diffuse from the blood into the alveoli. These gases are removed from the body during exhalation.

2. Liver

The liver is a large, multi-purpose organ whose excretory functions include the breakdown of red blood cells and the production of urea following amino acid deamination.

3. Sweat Glands of the Skin

Water, salts, and some urea diffuse from the blood into the sweat glands and are subsequently excreted as perspiration.

Perspiration is only incidentally excretory, its primary function being temperature regulation. Evaporation of the sweat (98% water and 2% salts and urea) occurs when heat is absorbed from skin cells. This absorption of heat lowers body temperature. Temperature regulation is an example of homeostasis.

4. Urinary System

a. Kidneys

The kidneys perform two major functions:
- They excrete most of the urea.
- They control the concentration of most of the constituents of the body fluids.

Arteries bring blood to the kidneys where microscopic nephrons are involved in filtration and reabsorption. Water, salts, urea, amino acids, and glucose are filtered from the glomerulus into the cuplike Bowman' capsule. As these materials move through the tubule of the nephron, water, minerals, and digestive end products are reabsorbed by active transport into capillaries associated with the tubule. Veins carry blood away from the kidneys. Blood pressure plays a vital role in filtration.

After reabsorption, the fluid that remains in the tubule is urine.

b. Ureter

Urine flows from the kidneys through the ureters to the urinary bladder.

c. Urinary Bladder
The urinary bladder stores the urine.

d. Urethra
Periodically, urine is excreted from the bladder through the urethra.

B. Malfunctions

1. Kidney Diseases
Diseases associated with the malfunctioning of the kidney or the nephron.

2. Gout
A disease associated with uric acid production and its deposition in the joints resulting in arthritic-like attacks.

V. Regulation
Regulation is achieved by the integration of the nervous system and the endocrine system.

The nervous and endocrine systems of humans show certain similarities and certain differences.

Similarities include:
- Both secrete chemicals.
- Both play a major role in homeostasis.

Differences include:
- Nerve responses are more rapid than endocrine responses.
- Nerve responses are of shorter duration than endocrine responses.

A. Nervous System

1. Functional Organization

a. Neurons
The neuron is the basic cellular unit of the nervous system. The nervous system is composed of three structurally different types of neurons: sensory neurons, interneurons, and motor neurons.

1) Sensory Neurons
Sensory neurons transmit impulses from receptors to the brain and spinal cord.

Sense organs are structures where sensory neurons are concentrated. These include the eyes, ears, tongue, nose, and skin.

2) Motor Neurons
Motor neurons transmit impulses from the central nervous system to effectors.

3) Interneurons
Interneurons relay nerve impulses between sensory and motor neurons. Interneuron is the new term for associative neuron.

b. Nerves
Nerves are bundles of neurons or parts of neurons. They can be sensory nerves, motor nerves, or mixed nerves.

Nerves are specialized for the transmission of impulses over long distances.

c. Central Nervous System

1) Brain
The brain is a large mass of neurons located in the cranial cavity. The cerebrum, the cerebellum and the medulla are the three major divisions of the brain, each having specialized functions.

a) Cerebrum
The cerebrum is the center for voluntary activity. In specific areas, sensory impulse are interpreted, motor activities may be initiated, and memory, thinking, and reasoning occur.

Habits, which are acquired by repetition, are examples of conditioned behavior. The repetition establishes pathways for nerve impulse transmission which permit rapid automatic responses to various stimuli.

b) Cerebellum
The cerebellum coordinates motor activities and aids in maintaining balance.

c) Medulla
The medulla controls involuntary activities such as breathing, heartbeat, blood pressure, and peristalsis.

2) Spinal Cord
The spinal cord lies within, and is protected by, the vertebrae of the spinal column. The spinal cord is continuous with the brain.

The spinal cord coordinates activities between the brain and other body structures. It is a center for reflex actions.

Reflex actions are inborn, involuntary patterns of behavior.

Reflex behavior involves a pathway (reflex arc) over which impulses travel. In a spinal reflex there is a pathway from receptors to a sensory neuron to interneurons in the spinal cord to a motor neuron to an effector.

d. Peripheral Nervous System
The peripheral nervous system is located outside the central nervous system and consists of nerves extending throughout the body.

The peripheral nervous system is separated into the somatic and autonomic nervous systems.

1) Somatic Nervous System
It consists of nerves that control the voluntary muscles of the skeleton.

2) Autonomic Nervous System
The autonomic nervous system consists of the nerves that control cardiac muscle, glands, and smooth muscle. It is generally considered to be an involuntary system. The distinction between *voluntary* and *involuntary* is not clear-cut.

2. Some Malfunctions of the Nervous System

a. Cerebral Palsy
A group of congenital diseases characterized by a disturbance of the motor functions.

b. Meningitis
Inflammation of the membranes surrounding the brain and spinal cord.

c. Stroke
A disease resulting from a cerebral hemorrhage or a blood clot in the cerebral vessel which may result in brain damage.

d. Polio
A viral disease of the central nervous system which may result in paralysis and is preventable through immunization.

B. Endocrine System
The endocrine glands, located in various parts of the body, and their hormones, make up the endocrine system.

Hormones are transported by the circulatory system and affect various tissues or organs.

1. Functional Organization

a. Hypothalamus
The hypothalamus is a small region of the brain. Although part of the central nervous system, it has an endocrine function. It produces hormones which influence the pituitary gland.

b. Pituitary Gland
The pituitary gland, located at the base of the brain secretes numerous hormones. One of these hormones, a growth-stimulating hormone, has widespread effect on the body. The growth-stimulating hormone stimulates the elongation of long bones.

Other pituitary hormones control specific endocrine glands. Examples of these include:
- Thyroid Stimulating Hormone (TSH) - stimulates the thyroid gland to produce its hormone, thyroxin.
- Follicle Stimulating Hormone (FSH) - stimulates activity in the ovaries and testes.

c. Thyroid Gland
The thyroid gland, which is located in the neck, produces thyroxin, which contains iodine. Thyroxin regulates the rate of metabolism in the body and is essential for normal physical and mental development.

d. Parathyroid Glands
The parathyroid glands, patches of tissue embedded in the thyroid gland, produce and secrete the hormone parathormone. Parathormone controls the metabolism of calcium which is necessary for nerve function, blood clotting, and proper growth of teeth and bones.

e. Adrenal Glands
The adrenal glands are two small glands located on top of the kidneys. Each gland consists of two distinct regions. The outer portion is the adrenal cortex, and the inner mass is the adrenal medulla.

The adrenal cortex secretes two types of steroid hormones. One type promotes the conversion of body fat and protein into glucose. The other type promotes the reabsorption into the bloodstream of sodium and chloride ions by the kidney tubules. This affect the water balance and helps maintain blood pressure.

The adrenal medulla secretes adrenalin in times of emergency. Adrenalin increases the blood sugar level and accelerates the heart and breathing rates.

f. Islets of Langerhans
The islets of Langerhans are small groups of cells located in the pancreas. They secrete the hormones insulin and glucagon.

Insulin facilitates the entrance of glucose into the cells. It lowers blood sugar levels by promoting the movement of sugar from the blood into the liver and muscles where it is stored as glycogen. Glucagon stimulates the release of sugar from the liver into the blood.

g. Gonads
Testes, the male sex glands, secrete testosterone which influences the development of the male secondary sex characteristics. In the female, ovaries are responsible for the secretion of several hormones. One of these ovarian hormones is estrogen which influences the development of the female secondary sex characteristics.

2. Mechanisms
A type of self-regulation, known as negative feedback, is associated with endocrine regulation. The negative feedback mechanism operates on the principle that the level of one hormone in the blood stimulates or inhibits the production of another hormone. The relationship between TSH and thyroxin is an illustration of the homeostatic feedback mechanism in the body.

3. Malfunctions

a. Goiter
Enlargement of the thyroid gland usually resulting from the gland's inability to manufacture thyroxin. This is often associated with an iodine deficiency in the diet.

b. Diabetes
A disorder characterized by an insulin deficiency which results in an elevated blood sugar level.

VI. Locomotion
Human locomotion involves the interaction of bones, cartilage, muscles, tendons, and ligaments.

A. Functional Organization

1. Bones
The human endoskeleton consists of bones of various shapes and sizes.

The functions of the bones include: support and protection of body structures, anchorage sites for muscle action, leverage for body movement, and production of blood cells in the marrow.

2. Cartilage
Although the human skeleton consists primarily of bone, another type of connective tissue, cartilage, is also present. Cartilage is flexible, fibrous, and elastic.

The functions of cartilage include: pliable support, flexibility of joints, and cushioning effects in joints.

Cartilage is found in both the embryo and the adult.

Embryo - Cartilage makes up most of the embryo's skeleton By adulthood, most of this cartilage is replaced by bone.
Adult - Cartilage is found at the end of ribs between vertebrae, at the ends of bones, and in the nose, ears, and trachea.

3. Muscles
There are three major types of muscles in the human body: visceral muscles which are involuntary in action and smooth in appearance; cardiac muscles which are involuntary in action and striated in appearance; and skeletal muscles which are voluntary in action and striated in appearance.

Skeletal muscles are controlled by the nervous system. They serve to move the bones in a coordinated manner. Muscles usually operate in pairs which include: extensors which extend limbs, and flexors which return the limbs.

Vigorous activity of skeletal muscles may lead to an oxygen deficiency which can result in anaerobic respiration and a buildup of lactic acid. Lactic acid production is associated with fatigue.

4. Tendons
Tendons are composed of connective tissue. They are tough, inelastic, fibrous cords which attach muscles to bones.

5. Ligaments
Ligaments are composed of tough elastic connective tissue Ligaments connect the ends of bones at movable joints such as the elbow, fingers, knee, and vertebral column.

B. Some Malfunctions Associated with Locomotion

1. Arthritis
An inflammation of the joints.

2. Tendonitis
An inflammation of the tendon usually at the bone juncture. This condition is common to athletes.

REPRODUCTION AND DEVELOPMENT

OBJECTIVES

The student should be able to:

- Describe the processes of mitosis, meiosis, and fertilization.
- Recognize the role of mitosis, meiosis, and fertilization in reproductive cycles.
- Compare the processes of asexual and sexual reproduction in terms of methods and results.
- Compare the adaptations for sexual reproduction and development in both plants and animals.
- Explain the relationships among numbers of eggs, methods of fertilization, and sites of embryonic development, as they relate to species survival.
- Describe the development of plant and animal embryos.
- Describe hormonal interactions in the human male and female.

I. Asexual Reproduction

Asexual reproduction is the production of new organisms without the fusion of nuclei. The new organisms develop from a cell or cells of the parent.

*A. Mitotic Cell Division

All cells arise from other cells by cell division. This process involves both nuclear duplication and cytoplasmic division.

<u>Mitosis</u> - an orderly series of complex changes in the nucleus, normally involving an exact duplication of the complete set of chromosomes and the separation of these chromosomes into two identical sets.

<u>Cytoplasmic Division</u> - the division of cytoplasm which occurs either during or after mitosis resulting in the formation of two daughter cells, each containing an identical set of chromosomes.

1. Processes

a. Mitosis

The process of mitosis involves:

- Replication of each single-stranded chromosome during the nondividing period, resulting in double-stranded chromosomes. Individual strands of a double-stranded chromosome are known as chromatids and are joined by a centromere.
- Disintegration of the nuclear membrane during the early stages of division.
- Synthesis of a spindle apparatus.

- Attachment of double-stranded chromosomes to the spindle apparatus at the centromere region of the chromosomes.
- Replication of each centromere which results in the formation of two single-stranded chromosomes, which are moved along the spindle apparatus to opposite ends of the cell.
- Nuclear membrane formation around each set of chromosomes, forming two nuclei.

The major result of mitosis is the formation of two daughter nuclei which are identical to each other and to the original nucleus, in the number and types of chromosomes.

b. Cytoplasmic Division
Division of the cytoplasm usually, but not always, accompanies mitosis.

The methods of cytoplasmic division differ in plant and animal cells.

2. Comparison Between Plant and Animal Mitotic Cell Division
Mitosis is similar in plant and animal cells. However, in animal cells, centrioles aid in the formation and orientation of the spindle apparatus.

Cytoplasmic division is accomplished in animal cells by a *pinching in* of the cell membrane, thus separating the two nuclei; while in plant cells, a cell plate is synthesized.

3. Uncontrolled Cell Division
Cancer is a group of diseases often characterized by uncontrolled cell division of certain abnormal cells.

B. Types of Asexual Reproduction

1. Binary Fission
Binary fission involves the equal division of the nuclear materials and cytoplasm of an organism resulting in two new organisms.

2. Budding
In unicellular organisms, such as yeast, budding is similar to fission except that the cytoplasmic division is unequal. The new cells may detach from each other or may remain together and form a colony.

In multicellular organisms, such as hydra, budding refers to the production of a multicellular outgrowth from the parent organism. The bud and the parent may detach from each other or may remain together and form a colony.

3. Sporulation
In many organisms, spores, which are single, specialized cells, are released from the parent and can develop into new individuals. (Example: bread mold)

4. Regeneration
Regeneration is the development of an entire new organism from a part of the original organism. An example is the starfish which may develop from a single ray and part of the central disc.

Regeneration also refers to the replacement of lost structures. A lobster may regenerate a lost claw.

Generally, invertebrate animals possess more undifferentiated cells than do vertebrate animals. As a result, invertebrates exhibit a higher degree of regenerative ability than most vertebrates.

5. Vegetative Propagation
Some multicellular plants reproduce asexually by vegetative propagation. In this process new plants develop from roots, stems, or leaves of the parent plant. Some examples of vegetative propagation include:

Examples:	Organisms
cuttings	coleus, geranium
bulbs	onion
tubers	potato
runners	strawberry
grafting	seedless orange

II. Sexual Reproduction
Sexual reproduction involves the production of specialized sex cells (gametes) and the fusion of their nuclei (fertilization) producing a fertilized egg (zygote).

A. Reproduction and Development in Animals

1. Gametogenesis
Each body cell of an organism contains the diploid (2n) number of chromosomes characteristic of that species. These chromosomes are present in the homologous pairs. Homologous chromosomes contain genes for the same traits.

Gametogenesis is the process in which gametes are produced. It involves meiotic cell division and cell maturation. This process occurs in specialized organs called gonads. Some organisms have only male or female gonads while others have both and are called hermaphrodites.

a. Meiosis
Meiosis is a process which involves reduction division. During this process, the chromosome number is reduced by one-half and monoploid nuclei which contain one chromosome of each homologous pair are formed.

1) Process

a) First Meiotic Division
The process of meiosis involves two division

The first meiotic division is the reduction division and involves:
- Replication of each single-stranded chromo some during the nondividing period, result ing in double-stranded chromosomes.
- Synapsis - the intimate pairing of homolog chromosomes, resulting in the formation of tetrads.
- Alignment of homologous pairs and their subsequent movement along the spindle apparatus toward opposite ends of the cell
- Cytoplasmic division.

b) Second Meiotic Division
The second meiotic division involves:
- Alignment of double-stranded chromosomes in the middle of the spindle apparatus.
- Replication of centromeres.
- Migration of single-stranded chromosomes along the spindle apparatus toward opposit ends of the cell.
- Cytoplasmic division.

As a result of meiosis, diploid (2n) primary sex cells divide and form monoploid (n) cell which mature into specialized reproductive cells.

The distribution of the homologous chromosomes between the resultant nuclei is random resulting in variation.

2) Comparison with Mitotic Cell Division
Mitosis is associated with growth and asexual reproduction; meiosis, with sexual reproduction.

As a result of mitotic cell division, the daughte cells are identical to the original cell.

As a result of meiotic cell division, daughter cells have one-half the number of chromosomes of the original cell.

b. Spermatogenesis
The male gonads, testes, produce male gametes, sperm. The primary sex cell undergoes meiosis and produces four monoploid cells. Each of these cells usually matures into a motile sperm cell.

c. Oogenesis
The female gonad is the ovary, and the gamete is the ovum (egg). The ovum is larger than the sperm and contains stored nutrients in the form of yolk. Only one monoploid egg cell is usually formed from each primary sex cell that undergoes meiosis and maturation. The other cells produced are polar bodies. These result from unequal cytoplasmic divisions and degenerate.

2. Fertilization
Fertilization is the union of a monoploid sperm nucleus (n) with a monoploid egg nucleus (n). In the resulting diploid zygote, the species number of homologous chromosomes (2n) is restored.

a. External Fertilization
Reproduction in many aquatic vertebrate animals such as fish and amphibians is characterized by external fertilization. The gametes fuse outside the body of the female. Usually, large numbers of eggs are required to insure species survival.

b. Internal Fertilization
Reproduction in most terrestrial vertebrate animals is characterized by internal fertilization. The gametes fuse in the moist reproductive tract of the female.

3. Embryonic Development

a. Process
The zygote, or fertilized egg, undergoes a series of mitotic cell divisions called cleavage. Once cleavage begins, the zygote becomes a developing embryo.

1) Cleavage
Cleavage is a series of mitotic cell divisions that leads to the formation of the blastula, a single layer of cells which is a hollow ball-type structure.

During cleavage, there is no increase in individual cell size.

2) Gastrulation
In certain animals, one side of the blastula becomes indented (gastrulation) forming the gastrula, which has an inner layer, the endoderm, and an outer layer, the ectoderm. A third layer, the mesoderm, forms between the ectoderm and the endoderm.

3) Differentiation
These three embryonic layers differentiate and give rise to the various tissues, organs, and systems of the multicellular animal.

- The nervous system and the skin originate from the ectoderm layer.
- The muscles, circulatory system, skeleton, excretory system, and gonads originate from the mesoderm layer.
- The lining of the digestive and respiratory tracts, and portions of the liver and pancreas, originate from the endoderm.

4) Growth
Growth is an increase in cell number as well as in cell size. Early development consists chiefly of the differentiation and growth of cells and tissues.

b. Site

1) External Development
External development occurs outside of the female's body.

a) In Water
The eggs of many fish and amphibians are fertilized externally and develop externally in an aquatic environment.

The developing embryo's source of food is the yolk stored in the egg.

b) On Land
Eggs of birds, many reptiles, and a few mamma develop externally on a land environment afte internal fertilization.

The developing embryo's source of food is the yolk.

Some adaptations for animals which develop externally on land are a shell which provides protection and membranes which help provide a favorable environment for embryonic development. These embryonic membranes include:
- The amnion which contains the amniotic fluid. This fluid provides a watery enviro ment, protects the embryo from shock, and prevents adhesion of embryonic tissues to the shell.
- The yolk sac which surrounds the yolk. Blo vessels which penetrate the yolk sac transport food to the developing embryo.

- The allantois which functions as a respiratory membrane and a storage site for the nitrogenous waste, uric acid.
- The chorion which is an outer membrane surrounding the other embryonic membranes.

2) Internal Development
Internal development involves the growth of the embryo within the body of the parent.

a) Placental Mammals
Mammals have internal fertilization. The embryo(s) develops internally within a structure called the uterus.

The eggs of mammals have relatively little yolk and, therefore, are very small.

Within the uterus, a specialized organ, the placenta, is formed from embryonic and maternal tissues. It is through this structure that the exchange of nutrients, wastes, and respiratory gases between the mother and the embryo occurs.

There is no direct connection between maternal and embryonic bloodstreams. Transport is accomplished by diffusion and active transport.

An umbilical cord, containing blood vessels, attaches the embryo to the placenta. Humans are placental mammals. In a few mammals, such as the marsupials, there is no placenta.

b) Marsupials
In marsupials, internal fertilization and internal embryonic development occur without direct nourishment from the parent.

The source of food is the yolk stored in the egg. The embryo is born at a relatively premature stage compared to placental mammals, and completes its development externally in a pouch which contains mammary glands.

4. Reproduction and Development in Humans

a. Gametogenesis

1) Male Reproductive System
The male reproductive system performs two major functions: the production of sperm cells and the deposition of these cells within the female reproductive tract.

Sperm production occurs in the testes. The teste are located in the scrotum where the temperature is 1-2 degrees Celsius cooler than normal body temperature. This provides an optimum temperatu for sperm production and storage.

From the testes, sperm move through several tube including the urethra. The urethra is a tube contained within the penis. The penis is a structural adaptation for internal fertilization

Glands secrete a liquid into these tubes. The liquid serves as a transport medium for the sper - an adaptation for life on land. This liquid a the sperm cells constitute semen.

In addition to producing sperm, the testes also produce the male sex hormone, testosterone. Thi regulates the maturation of sperm and the develo ment of secondary sex characteristics, such as beard development and voice pitch.

2) Female Reproductive System
Ovaries are paired structures located within the lower portion of the body cavity. Ovaries produce eggs in tiny cavities called follicles. Following ovulation, the egg cell is transported through an oviduct (Fallopian tube) to the uterus. At the lower end of the uterus, known as the cervix, is a muscular tube, the vagina.

At birth, all of the potential eggs that a femal will ovulate are present in immature form. Usually only one egg is released at the time of each ovulation.

In addition to eggs, the ovaries also produce th female sex hormones estrogen and progesterone. These regulate the development of secondary sex characteristics such as the development of the mammary glands and the broadening of the pelvis. The hormones also have a coordinating role in th menstrual cycle.

a) Menstrual Cycle
The menstrual cycle begins at puberty and ceases at menopause. Menopause is the permanent cessation of the menstrual cycle. The duration of this cycle is approximately 28 days but may vary considerably and may be interrupted by pregnancy, illness, and other factors.

The menstrual cycle consists of four stages:

- Follicle stage - this stage involves the maturation of an egg within the follicle and the secretion of the hormone estrogen. Estrogen initiates vascularization of the uterine lining.
- Ovulation - the release of an egg from the follicle.
- Corpus luteum stage - the corpus luteum forms from the follicle following ovulation. It secretes progesterone which enhances the vascularization of the uterine lining.
- Menstruation - the periodic shedding of the thickened uterine lining. It occurs when fertilization does not take place.

b) Role of Hormones
The reproductive cycle of the human female involves the interaction of the hormones from the hypothalamus, pituitary gland, and ovaries.

During the menstrual cycle, under the influence of the hormones from the hypothalamus, the pituitary gland releases hormones (FSH and LH) which influence the functioning of the ovaries. The ovaries, in turn, secrete hormones (estrogen and progesterone) which produce changes in the uterus.

In addition, the hormones from the ovaries regulate the secretion of hormones by the pituitary gland and the hypothalamus. This is an example of a negative feedback mechanism.

b. Fertilization
Fertilization usually occurs in the upper portion of the oviduct.

If the egg is not fertilized within approximately 24 hours after ovulation, it deteriorates.

Cleavage of the fertilized egg begins in the oviduct, and six to ten days later, the resulting embryo may become implanted in the uterine lining.

If more than one egg is released and fertilized, multiple births may result. Identical twins develop from one zygote which separates during cleavage. Fraternal twins develop from two eggs, each fertilized by separate sperm cells.

The technique of *in vitro* fertilization and subsequent implantation that has been perfected in animals has now been applied to humans with some degree of success.

c. Development

1) Prenatal Development
Prenatal development includes the following processes:
- Cleavage occurs in the oviduct.
- Gastrulation usually occurs after the embryo is implanted in the uterus.
- Differentiation and growth result in the formation of specialized tissues and organs from the embryonic layers of the gastrula.

The processes involved in prenatal development are dependent upon the supplying of a proper balance of nutrients to the developing embryo.

Some structures associated with prenatal development are: the placenta, amnion, and umbilical cord.

2) Birth
Birth usually occurs after a gestation period of approximately nine months.

3) Postnatal Development
Development continues with various parts of the body growing at different rates.

Although the development of the organism is often assumed to conclude with the mature adult, it actually continues throughout the life of the organism and terminates with death.

The term aging is applied to the complex developmental changes that occur naturally with the passage of time.

The cause or causes of the aging process are still not fully understood. It appears that the aging process results from the interplay of hereditary and environmental factors. One recent definition of death is the irreversible cessation of all brain functions.

B. Reproduction and Development in Flowering Plants
The process of meiosis and fertilization occur in the flower, a plant structure specialized for reproduction.

1. Flower Structure
The flower may contain both the male reproductive organ, the stamen, and the female reproductive organ, the pistil. In some species, certain flowers contain only stamens, while others contain only pistils. Petals and sepals may also be present in flowers.

The stamen is composed of an anther and filament. As a result of meiosis, the diploid cells of the anther produce pollen grains which contain monoploid nuclei.

The pistil is composed of the stigma, style, and the ovary. As a result of meiosis, ovule(s) developing within the ovary contain the monoploid egg nucleus.

2. Pollination
Pollination is the transfer of pollen grains from the anther to the stigma.

Self-pollination is the transfer of pollen from the anther to the stigma of the same flower or to the stigma of another flower on the same plant. Cross-pollination is the transfer of pollen from an anther of one flower to a stigma of a flower on another plant. Cross-pollination is an adaptation which enhances variations.

Pollination may be accomplished by wind, insects, and birds. In some instances, the colored petals act as a visual attractant for insects while nectar acts as a chemical attractant.

In flowering plants, the problem of reproduction in a dry, external environment is partially solved by the presence of the thick wall of the pollen grain. This prevents dehydration of its contents during its transfer to the female reproductive organ.

Following pollination, the pollen grain germinates on the stigma and forms a pollen tube which extends into the ovule. Sperm nuclei are formed at this time in the pollen tube from the monoploid nucleus in the pollen grain. The pollen tube is an adaptation for internal fertilization.

3. Fertilization and Embryo Development
The union of male and female nuclei in the ovule results in a zygote.

The zygote undergoes development resulting in the formation of the embryo. The ripened ovule develops into the seed. A seed consists of a seed coat, which develops from the outer coverings of the ovule, and an embryo. The ripened ovary develops into the fruit.

The plant embryo consists of the hypocotyl, epicotyl, and the cotyledon(s). The hypocotyl develops into the root and, in some species, the lower portion of the stem; the epicotyl develops into the leaves and upper portions of the stem; and the cotyledon(s), which contain stored food, provide the nutrients for the germinating plant.

4. Germination
In flowering plants, seeds develop inside a fruit. Fruits are specialized structures which aid in seed dispersal.

Under suitable environmental conditions, seeds germinate For most seeds, these conditions include: sufficient moisture, proper temperature, and sufficient oxygen.

The development of a seed into a mature plant capable of reproduction involves cell division, differentiation, and growth.

5. Growth
Growth in higher plants is restricted largely to specifi regions known as meristems.

Apical meristems are found in the tips of roots and stems and are responsible for growth in length. Some plants also contain an active lateral meristem region, the cambium, located between the xylem and phloem. This is responsible for the growth in diameter of roots and stems

The growth regions contain undifferentiated cells which undergo active mitotic cell division and elongation. As a result of differentiation, the various tissues and organs are developed.

TRANSMISSION OF TRAITS FROM GENERATION TO GENERATION

OBJECTIVES

The student should be able to:

- Explain the transmission of genetic traits using the gene-chromosome theory.
- Predict the probable results of genetic crosses.
- Identify some patterns of inheritance by interpreting pedigree charts.
- List various mutations and describe their consequences.
- List several practical applications of the principles of genetics.
- Recognize the role of heredity and environment in gene expression.
- Describe some techniques used in genetic research.
- Describe some genetically-related disorders in humans.
- Describe the basic structure of the DNA molecule and its assumed role in heredity.
- Explain changes in a population on the basis of the Hardy-Weinberg Principle.

I. Foundations of Genetics

A. Mendelian Principles

Mendel developed some basic principles of heredity without any knowledge of genes or chromosomes. His principles of dominance, segregation, and independent assortment were established through the mathematical analysis of large numbers of offspring produced by crossing pea plants.

As a result of analyzing specific mathematical ratios associated with certain characteristics in the offspring, Mendel proposed that characteristics were inherited as a result of the transmission of hereditary factors.

B. Gene-Chromosome Theory

The significance of Mendel's work was not immediately recognized. After his work was rediscovered, evidence from the microscopic study of dividing cells and breeding experiments with *Drosophila* enabled scientists to link the presence of chromosomes and their migration during meiosis with the hereditary factors which Mendel proposed in his principles.

Mendel's hereditary factors, now called genes, exist at definite loci in a linear fashion on chromosomes. Two genes associated with a specific characteristic are known as alleles and are located on homologous chromosomes. The gene-chromosome theory provides the mechanism to account for the hereditary patterns which Mendel observed.

II. Some Major Genetic Concepts

A. Dominance

In some patterns of heredity, if only one of the genes in an allelic pair is expressed, it is called a dominant allele; the gene which is present but not expressed is called the recessive allele.

By convention, a capital letter symbolizes a dominant allele. The lower case form of the same letter symbolizes the recessive allele. For example, in certain pea plants, the allele for tallness (T) is dominant and the allele for shortness (t) is recessive.

If two genes of an allelic pair are the same, the genetic makeup, genotype, is said to be homozygous (TT or tt).

If two genes of an allelic pair are different, the genetic makeup is said to be heterozygous or hybrid (Tt).

When an individual homozygous for the dominant trait is crossed with an individual homozygous for the recessive trait, the appearance (phenotype) of the offspring, known as the F_1 generation, is like that of the dominant parent. The genotype of these offspring is heterozygous.

Offspring resulting from the cross between members of the F_1 generation comprise the F_2 generation.

B. Segregation and Recombination

When gametes are formed during meiosis, there is a random segregation of homologous chromosomes.

As a result of fertilization, alleles recombine. As a consequence, new allelic gene combinations are likely to be produced.

Segregation and recombination is illustrated by the following diagram which represents the cross between two individuals heterozygous for tallness.

Segregation into gametes

Probable recombination of alleles during zygote formation

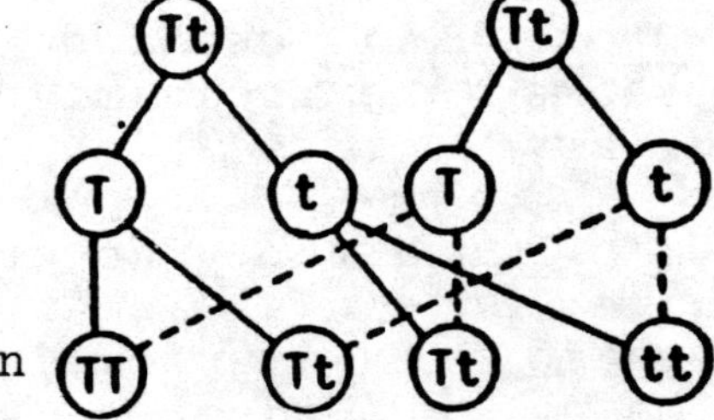

Diploid cells

Monoploid cells

Diploid cells

Assuming large numbers of such crosses, the phenotypic ratio of tall offspring to short offspring is 3:1 and the genotypic ratio of homozygous tall offspring to heterozygous tall offspring to homozygous recessive offspring is 1:2:1.

To determine the genotype of an individual showing the dominant phenotype, it is crossed with a homozygous-recessive individual. Recessive phenotypes among the offspring indicate a heterozygous parent. This procedure is known as a test cross.

C. Intermediate Inheritance
Sometimes traits are not clearly dominant or recessive due to the complex nature of gene action. In intermediate inheritance, the heterozygous offspring are phenotypically different than their homozygous parents. There are different degrees of intermediate inheritance. One is codominance. As molecular genetics and classical genetics begin to merge, long-held concepts of classical genetics become less definitive. The actual interactions of gene products shed new light on our concepts of dominance and recessiveness. Dominance and recessiveness may, in fact, be relative terms.

Codominance involves the expression of two dominant alleles. This results in the simultaneous expression of both alleles in the phenotype of the heterozygous individual. For example, in the inheritance of coat color in roan cattle, the following symbols can be used: C^RC^R represents the genotype of the homozygous red coat. C^WC^W represents the genotype of the homozygous white coat. C^RC^W represents the genotype of the heterozygous roan coat. The coat of the roan animal is composed of a mixture of red and white hairs.

Examples of codominance in humans are sickle-cell anemia and blood groups. Incomplete or partial dominance as exhibited by pink snapdragons and four o'clocks is another type of intermediate inheritance in which the heterozygous individuals exhibit a phenotype intermediate between either homozygous parent.

In all instances of intermediate inheritance, the F_2 offspring of heterozygous parents exhibit a 1:2:1 phenotypic ratio.

D. Independent Assortment
If the genes for two different traits are located on different chromosome pairs (nonhomologous chromosomes), they segregate randomly during meiosis and, therefore, may be inherited independently of each other.

E. Gene Linkage
If the genes for two different traits (nonallelic genes) are located on the same chromosome pair (homologous chromosomes), they are said to be linked and, therefore, are usually inherited together.

F. Crossing Over

During synapsis in the first meiotic division, the chromatids in a homologous pair of chromosomes often twist around each other, break, exchange segments, and rejoin. This results in a rearrangement of linked genes and increases the variability of offspring.

G. Multiple Alleles

In some instances, an observed pattern of heredity can not be explained on the basis of a single pair of alleles. Experimental evidence indicates that in such patterns multiple alleles are involved. In this pattern no more than two of these alleles for the given trait may be present within each cell.

In a population of humans, the inheritance of the ABO blood group may be explained using a model that employs three alleles (I^A, I^B, and i). In this model, alleles I^A and I^B are codominant with each other and i is recessive to both I^A and I^B.

Genotypes associated with each blood type in the ABO group are:

Blood Type	Genotype
A	I^AI^A or I^Ai
B	I^BI^B or I^Bi
AB	I^AI^B
O	ii

H. Sex Determination

Diploid cells of many organisms contain two types of chromosomes: autosomes and sex chromosomes.

In each human cell, there are 22 pairs of autosomes and one pair of sex chromosomes. The sex chromosomes are designated as X and Y. The XX condition produces females, and the XY condition produces males.

The sex of a human is genetically determined at fertilization when a sperm cell containing either an X or Y chromosome unites with an egg cell containing an X chromosome.

I. Sex Linkage

Morgan's work with Drosophila demonstrated that genes for certain traits are located on the X chromosomes. These genes are said to be sex-linked and do not appear to have corresponding alleles on the Y chromosome.

Since many sex-linked genes are recessive, they are expressed more frequently in males than in females. Hemophilia and color-blindness are examples of sex-linked traits in humans.

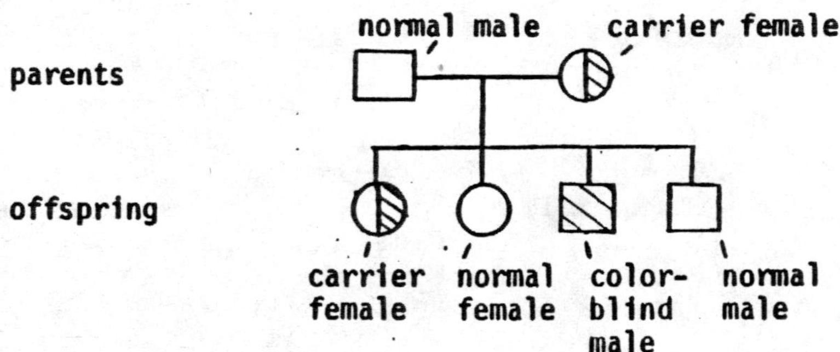

III. Mutations

Changes in the genetic material are called mutations. If these mutations occur in sex cells, they may be transmitted to the next generation.

Mutations occurring only in the body cells may be perpetuated in the individual but will not be passed on to the offspring by sexual reproduction.

A. Types

Mutations may be classified as chromosomal alterations or gene mutations.

1. Chromosomal Alterations

A chromosomal alteration is a change in the number of chromosomes or in the structure of the chromosomes.

The effects of chromosomal alterations are often visible in the phenotype of an organism because many genes are usually involved.

a. Change in Chromosome Number

During meiosis, homologous chromosomes separate from each other. This separation is known as disjunction. Sometimes a pair of homologous chromosomes fails to separate from each other (nondisjunction). This results in gametes with more (or less) than their normal (n) chromosome number. If these gametes are involved in fertilization, the resulting zygote may have more (or less) than the normal (2n) chromosome number.

For example, in humans, Down's syndrome usually results from the possession of an extra chromosome. This is due to the nondisjunction of chromosome number 21 in one of the parents.

Occasionally, the disjunction of a complete set of chromosomes (2n) fails to occur during gamete formation. The resulting 2n gamete sometimes fuses with a normal n gamete, producing a 3n zygote. If two 2n gametes fuse, a 4n zygote results. The possession of extra sets of chromosomes is known as a polyploid condition. This is rather common in plants but rare in animals.

In plants, some polyploid individuals are usually larger or more vigorous than diploid varieties. Some polyploid individuals are sterile (seedless). Examples include strains of cotton, wheat, potatoes, alfalfa, apples, tobacco, and zinnias. Polyploid watermelons are nearly seedless.

b. Change in Chromosome Structure
Alterations in chromosome composition may result from random breakage and recombination of chromosome parts.

Some examples of changes in chromosome structure are:
- Translocation - the transfer of a section of one chromosome to a nonhomologous chromosome.
- Additions and deletions - the loss or gain of a portion of a chromosome.

2. Gene Mutations
A gene mutation involves a random change in the chemical nature of the genetic material (DNA).

While the effects of some gene mutations, such as albinism are obvious, the effects of other gene mutations may not be as readily noticed.

The adaptive value of a gene mutation is dependent upon the nature of the mutation and the type of environment with which the organism interacts.

*B. Mutagenic Agents
Although mutations may occur spontaneously, their incidence may be increased by such agents as:
- Radiation - x-rays, ultraviolet, radioactive substances, and cosmic rays.
- Chemicals - formaldehyde, benzene, and asbestos fibers.

IV. Genetic Applications to Animal and Plant Breeding
Artificial selection, including inbreeding and hybridization, and the maintenance of desirable mutations by vegetative means are methods used by scientists to improve, produce, and maintain new varieties of animals and plants. Illustrative genetic applications are seedless oranges, hybrid roses, apple varieties, breeds of dogs, cattle, and horses.

V. Interaction of Heredity and Environment
The environment interacts with genes in the development and expression of inherited traits.

The relationship between gene action and environmental influence has been studied in many organisms. Examples include:
- Effect of light on chlorophyll production
- The effect of temperature on hair color in the Himalayan rabbit
- Identical twin studies

VI. Human Heredity

The principles of genetics appears to hold for all organisms including humans. The acquisition of knowledge of human genetics has been limited because humans are not suitable subjects for experimentation. An increased knowledge of human genetics has resulted from the expansion of the field of genetic counseling.

Human genetic disorders are often detected through genetic counseling and the use of the following techniques.

A. Techniques for Detection

The presence of many genetic disorders can be detected either before or after birth. In some instances, carriers of genetically-related disorders may also be identified.

Some of these techniques include:
- Screening - chemical analysis of body fluids such as blood and urine
- Karyotyping - the preparation of an enlarged photograph showing paired homologous chromosomes from a cell
- Amniocentesis - the removal of amniotic fluid for chemical and/or cellular analysis

B. Genetically Related Disorders

Some genetically related disorders in humans include phenylketonuria, sickle-cell anemia, and Tay-Sachs.

1. Phenylketonuria (PKU)

PKU is a condition characterized by the development of mental retardation and has been shown to occur when an individual is homozygous with respect to a recessive mutant gene.

The symptoms of the disorder apparently result from the inability of a gene to synthesize a single enzyme necessary for the normal metabolism of phenylalanine.

Urine analysis of newborns allows for proper dietary treatment to prevent the mental retardation associated with this disorder.

2. Sickle-Cell Anemia

Sickle-cell anemia is a homozygous condition resulting in the formation of abnormal hemoglobin and sickled red blood cells. It is characterized by severe pain due to obstructed blood vessels and anemia caused by the fragility of red blood cells. This disorder is more likely to occur among individuals of African descent. Heterozygous and homozygous individuals may be detected by blood screening. An afflicted fetus may be detected by amniocentesis.

3. Tay-Sachs
Tay-Sachs is a recessive genetic disorder characterized by the malfunctioning of the nervous system, caused by the deterioration of nervous tissue. This deterioration is due to the accumulation of fatty material as a result of the inability to synthesize a specific enzyme. This fatal disorder is more likely to occur among Jewish people of Central European descent.

Carriers may be detected through blood screening. Chemical analysis of amnionic fluid can detect an afflicted fetus.

VII. Modern Genetics

A. DNA as the Hereditary Material
In recent years, biochemists have found that deoxyribonucleic acid is the genetic material which replicates and is passed from generation to generation. DNA controls cellular activit by influencing the production of enzymes.

In order to understand the chemical nature of the gene, the chemical structure of nucleic acids must be understood.

1. DNA Structure
DNA, found in the nucleus of cells, is a polymer. It is a very large molecule consisting of thousands of smaller, repeating units known as nucleotides.

a. DNA Nucleotide
A DNA nucleotide is composed of three parts:
- A phosphate group
- A deoxyribose (5-carbon sugar) molecule
- A nitrogenous base of either adenine, thymine, guanine, or cytosine.

A nucleotide may be represented as follows:

b. Watson-Crick Model
Watson and Crick developed a model of the DNA molecul In this model the DNA molecule consists of two comple mentary chains of nucleotides.

- The DNA molecule has a *ladder* type organization. The uprights of the *ladder* are composed of alternating phosphate and deoxyribose molecules. Each rung of the *ladder* is composed of bases held together by relatively weak hydrogen bonds. Base pair combinations are restricted to: adenine (A)-thymine (T), and guanine (G)-cytosine (C).
- This *ladder* is thought to be twisted in the form of a double helix.

The Watson-Crick model can be used to explain the principal actions of genes:
- Maintaining genetic continuity by means of replication.
- Controlling cellular activity by controlling production of specific enzymes.

2. DNA Replication
DNA is believed to replicate in the following manner during the processes of mitosis and meiosis.
- Double-stranded DNA unwinds and *unzips* along weak hydrogen bonds between the base pairs.
- Free nucleotides in the nucleus are incorporated, in sequence, forming two double strands of DNA which are identical to each other and to the original DNA molecule.

3. Gene Control of Cellular Activities
The control of cellular activities involves both DNA and RNA.

a. RNA
RNA, like DNA, is composed of nucleotide building blocks. However, there are three major differences between the structure of DNA and RNA molecules. In RNA:
- ribose is substituted for deoxyribose.
- uracil is substituted for thymine.
- there is a single chain of nucleotides.
There are three types of RNA: messenger RNA, transfer RNA, and ribosomal RNA.

b. Genetic Code
Evidence strongly suggests that a genetic code exists. This code contains the information for the sequence of amino acids in a particular protein. The code is present in messenger RNA molecules which are complementary to DNA molecules.

The RNA code is a triplet code (codon) based on various sequences of three bases in the messenger RNA molecule.

c. Protein Synthesis
DNA serves as a template for the synthesis of messenger RNA from free RNA nucleotides.

The messenger RNA molecules, carrying a specific code determined by the base sequence of the original DNA molecules, move from the nucleus to the cytoplasm where they become associated with ribosomes composed in part of ribosomal RNA. It is thought that ribosomal RNA temporarily binds messenger RNA to the ribosomes.

Specific transfer RNA molecules pick up and transfer to the ribosomes specific amino acid molecules found in the cytoplasm. At the ribosomes, each specific transfer RNA molecule bonds to a particular codon. Particular polypeptide chains are formed as the amino acids associated with the transfer RNA molecules are bonded in a sequence determined by the base sequence of the messenger RNA.

d. The *One Gene-One Polypeptide Hypothesis*
A hypothesis called the *one gene-one enzyme hypothesi* proposed that the synthesis of each enzyme in a cell was governed by the action of a single gene (a specific sequence of DNA nucleotides). However, the name of this hypothesis has been changed to the one gene-one polypeptide hypothesis since it is now known that a single enzyme may be composed of several polypeptides and a synthesis of each polypeptide is governed by a different gene.

A modern definition of the gene is the sequence of nucleotides in a DNA necessary to synthesize a polypeptide.

e. Individuality of Organisms as Related to Their DNA
Since the sequence of nucleotides in DNA determines the sequence of nucleotides in messenger RNA, DNA ultimately determines the sequence of the amino acids in specific proteins. The specificity of enzymes is dependent on their protein makeup, and, since the individuality of a cell is largely a function of the enzymes it possesses, it is evident that DNA determines the individuality of an organism.

f. Gene Mutations

1) Description
Gene mutations may be interpreted biochemically as any change in the base sequence of an organism DNA.

2) Types
Gene mutations include the addition and/or deletion of bases in the DNA sequence, as well as the substitution of one base for another base in the DNA sequence.

B. Genetic Research

1. Cloning
Cloning is the process of producing a group of genetically identical offspring from the cells of an organism. This technique shows great promise in agriculture. Plants with desirable qualities can be rapidly produced from the cells of a single plant. The cloning of animals is still in the early stages of research.

2. Genetic Engineering
Genetic information may be transferred from one organism to another, resulting in the formation of recombinant DNA. New genes can be introduced into an organism as a result of this transfer. The cell can then synthesize the chemical coded for by these new genes. Examples of these chemicals include: insulin, interferon, and human growth hormone.

Such genetic engineering has potential for the correction of genetic defects and the development of agriculturally desirable plants and animals.

C. Population Genetics
The study of factors which affect gene frequencies in populations of sexually reproducing organisms is known as population genetics.

1. Population
A population includes all members of a species inhabiting a given location.

2. Gene Pool
The gene pool of a population consists of the sum total of all the heritable genes for the traits in a given population.

3. Gene Frequency
The gene frequency is the percentage of each allele for a particular trait in a population.

4. The Hardy-Weinberg Principle
Hardy and Weinberg studied populations of sexually reproducing individuals. Their studies resulted in the formulation of the Hardy-Weinberg Principle. This principle states that the gene pool of a population tends to remain stable (i.e., gene frequencies remain constant) if certain conditions are met. These conditions for gene pool stability include:

- Large populations
- Random mating
- No migration
- No mutation

The stability of a population suggested by the Hardy-Weinberg Principle rarely occurs since some or all of the conditions for gene pool stability may not be met. The unstable gene pool that results tends to produce change in the population.

—

EVOLUTION

OBJECTIVES

The student should be able to:

- Understand that evolution is a process of change.
- Recognize that evolutionary theory is supported by observations and inferences from many branches of science.
- Describe some of the supporting data for evolutionary theory.
- Discuss the historical development of evolutionary theory.
- Describe a hypothesis which attempts to explain how primitive environmental conditions may have contributed to the formation of initial life forms.

I. Evolution

Evolution is a process of change through time.

II. Evolution Theory

Evolution theory is a unifying principle for the biological sciences. It provides an explanation for the differences in structure, function, and behavior among life forms.

Evolution includes the change in characteristics of populations through generations. Thus, existing life forms have evolved from earlier life forms.

A. Supporting Observations

Observations supporting the theory of organic evolution can be made through the study of the geologic record and comparative studies in the fields of cytology, biochemistry, anatomy, and embryology.

1. Geologic Record

Geologists have dated the earth to be between four and one-half and five billion years old. This age was determined by radioactive dating of rocks. It is assumed that the earth is at least as old as the oldest rocks and minerals composing its crust.

Fossils are the direct or indirect remains of organisms preserved in media such as sedimentary rock, amber, ice, or tar.

Fossils have been found which indicate that organisms existed over three billion years ago. Fossils of prokaryotic life forms indicate an age of 3.4 billion years or greater. (Fig-tree chert of South Africa.)

Upper, undisturbed strata generally contain fossils of more complex organisms, whereas the lower strata contain fossils of simpler life forms.

When comparing fossils in undisturbed strata, fossils can be found in upper strata which, although different from fossils in lower strata, resemble those fossils. This suggests links between modern forms and older forms, as well as divergent pathways from common ancestors.

2. Comparative Cytology
The cell is the unifying structure for living things. Organelles such as the plasma membrane, ribosomes, and mitochondria, are structurally and functionally similar in most divergent organisms.

3. Comparative Biochemistry
Nucleic acids, their structure and function, are similar in living organisms.

Many different organisms have similar proteins and enzyme

The closer the relationship among organisms, the greater their biochemical similarity, thus suggesting evolutionary relationships.

4. Comparative Anatomy
A comparative study of certain organisms indicates similarities in anatomical features.

Homologous structures are anatomical parts that are similar in structure and origin although they may function differently.

Homologous bones exist in the forelimbs of many different vertebrates such as frogs, birds, bats, horses, whales, and humans.

5. Comparative Embryology
Comparison of early embryonic development among groups of organisms reveals similarities which suggest common ancestry. Early vertebrate embryos closely resemble one another. As development proceeds, the distinctive traits of each species become apparent.

B. Theories of Evolution
Theories of evolution are attempts to explain the diversities among species. Adaptations are a major component of these theories. Adaptations are features (structure, function, or behavior) which make a species better suited to live and reproduce in its environment.

1. Lamarck
Lamarck's theory encompassed two main ideas:
- Use and Disuse - New organs arise according to the needs of an organism and the size of organs is determined by the degree to which they are used.

- Transmission of Acquired Characteristics - Useful characteristics acquired by an individual during its lifetime can be transmitted to its offspring. These acquired characteristics result in species better adapted to their environment.

Weismann's experiments involving the removal of the tails of mice over several generations helped to disprove Lamarck's theory of the inheritance of acquired characteristics.

2. Darwin

Darwin's theory of evolution was based on variation and natural selection. It encompassed the following ideas:

- Overproduction - Within a population, more offspring are born than can possibly survive.
- Competition - Since the number of individuals in a population tends to remain constant from generation to generation, a struggle for survival is suggested.
- Survival of the Fittest - The individuals who survive are the ones best adapted to exist in their environment due to the possession of variations that maximize their fitness.
- Reproduction - Individuals that survive and then reproduce transmit these variations to their offspring.
- Speciation - As time and generations continue, adaptations are perpetuated in individuals and new species evolve from a common ancestral species.

Darwin's theory of natural selection did not explain the genetic basis for variations.

3. Modern Evolutionary Theory

The modern theory of evolution supports Darwin's concepts of variation and natural selection and incorporates the genetic basis of variation in individual organisms and populations.

a. Producing Variation

The genetic basis for variation within a species is provided by mutations and sexual reproduction.

Mutations are spontaneous and provide the raw material for evolution.

Sexual reproduction involves the sorting out and recombination of genes, thus producing and maintaining variations.

b. Natural Selection

Natural selection involves the struggle of organisms to survive and reproduce in a given environment.

Traits which are beneficial to the survival of an organism in a particular environment tend to be retained and passed on and, therefore, increase in frequency within a population.

Traits which have low survival value to organisms tend to diminish in frequency from generation to generation.

If environmental conditions change, traits that were formerly associated with a low survival value may, in a changed environment, have greater survival value and increase accordingly.

Examples include:
- Roaches, mosquitoes, and houseflies resistant to insecticides. (Resistance is not in response to the insecticide. The insecticide acts as a selecting agent.)
- Penicillin-resistant strains of microorganisms.

1) Geographic Isolation
Geographic isolation favors speciation by segregating a small group from the main population. Changes in gene frequencies are more likely in small populations than in large populations.

In time, this isolated population may evolve into separate species due to the following factor(s):
- It may have possessed different initial gene frequencies than the main population.
- Different mutations occur within the main population and the isolated population.
- Different environmental factors and, thus, different selection pressures may be acting on each population.

It is probable that initially the isolated population had a different gene frequency than the original population. This is the Founder Effect.

Examples include Darwin's finches on the Galapagos Islands, and marsupials in Australia.

2) Reproductive Isolation
These separated groups may become so divergent that if geographic barriers were removed, interbreeding could not take place. Thus, the two populations have become reproductively isolated and have become two distinct species.

c. Time Frame for Evolution
While the essentials of Darwin's theory of evolution, variation, and natural selection are generally accepted within the scientific community, considerable discussion exists within this community as to the time frame in which evolution occurs.

Gradualism and Punctuated Equilibrium are attempts by scientists to address the question of the rate of evolution.

1) Gradualism
Gradualism proposes that evolutionary change is slow, gradual, and continuous.

2) Punctuated Equilibrium
Punctuated Equilibrium proposes that species have long periods of stability (typically several million years) interrupted by geologically brief periods of significant change during which new species may evolve.

According to some scientists, geologically brief periods represent approximately one percent of the duration of a species.

The fossil record indicates that most invertebrate species have an average duration of 5-10 million years.

III. Heterotroph Hypothesis
Some scientists have proposed the heterotroph hypothesis as an explanation for how early life forms may have developed on the primitive earth.

According to this hypothesis, the first life forms were not able to synthesize their own organic nutrients from inorganic compounds. Like many scientific explanations of incompletely understood phenomena, the heterotroph hypothesis is based upon logical extensions of certain basic assumptions.

A. Primitive Life Forms

1. Raw Materials
It is assumed that the primitive earth was an exceptionally hot body consisting of inorganic substances in solid, liquid, and gaseous states, with a rich supply of energy in the environment.

a. Matter
Water, condensing and falling as rain, carried dissolved atmospheric gases (ammonia, methane, and hydrogen) and minerals into the seas, forming a *hot, thin soup*.

b. Energy Sources
In addition to heat, energy in the form of lightning, solar radiation (including x-rays and ultraviolet rays), and radioactive materials in the rocks, provided an energy rich environment.

2. Synthesis
Energy from the environment contributed to the formation of chemical bonds among the dissolved particles in the *hot, thin soup* of the seas. This type of synthesis led to the formation of organic molecules such as simple sugars and amino acids.

Experiments by Miller have simulated the primitive environment in the laboratory and have resulted in the production of organic compounds.

In time, these organic molecules interacted and formed more complex organic molecules.

Experiments by Fox have demonstrated interactions among these organic molecules.

3. Nutrition
Some of the large, complex molecules formed aggregates. These aggregates probably incorporated molecules from the seas as *food*, thus carrying on heterotrophic nutrition.

4. Reproduction
In time, as these aggregates became increasingly complex and highly organized, the ability to reproduce evolved. These aggregates are considered to have been alive when they developed the ability to reproduce.

B. Heterotroph to Autotroph
It is thought that these heterotrophs evolved a pattern of respiration similar to the anaerobic process of fermentation. Extended periods of fermentative activity by these organisms added quantities of carbon dioxide to the environment.

Some heterotrophs evolved a means of using the carbon dioxide to synthesize organic compounds. These were the pioneer autotrophs.

C. Anaerobe to Aerobe
Autotrophic activity added free oxygen to the environment.

Some autotrophs and heterotrophs evolved mechanisms by which they used this oxygen to derive energy.

Present day organisms may be heterotrophic or autotrophic; aerobic or anaerobic.

ECOLOGY

OBJECTIVES

The student should be able to:

- Describe the interdependency of organisms on each other and on their environment.
- Identify and define the ecological levels of organization of the living world.
- Identify and describe the components that form and maintain an ecosystem.
- Explain how interactions of living organisms with each other and their environment result in succession.
- Assess human influence on the balance of nature.

I. Ecology

Ecology is the study of the interactions among organisms and their interrelationships with the physical environment. No organism exists as an entity, separate and distinct from its environment.

II. Ecological Organization

A. Population

A population is all the members of a species inhabiting a given location.

B. Community

All the interacting populations in a given area represent a community.

C. Ecosystem

An ecosystem is the living community and the physical environment functioning together as an interdependent and relatively stable system.

D. Biosphere

The biosphere is the portion of the earth in which life exists. It is composed of numerous complex ecosystems.

III. Ecosystems

The ecosystem is the structural and functional unit studied in ecology.

A. Ecosystem Structure and Function

An ecosystem involves interactions between abiotic and biotic factors. An ecosystem is a self-sustaining unit if the following requirements are met:

- A constant source of energy and a living system capable of incorporating this energy into organic compounds
- A cycling of materials between organisms and their environment

1. Components
Components of the ecosystem involve interacting abiotic and biotic factors.

a. Abiotic Factors
The abiotic environment includes physical and chemica factors which affect the ability of organisms to live and reproduce.

The abiotic factors include:
- Intensity of light
- Range of temperatures
- Amount of moisture
- Type of substratum
- Availability of inorganic substances such as minerals
- Supply of gases such as O_2, CO_2, N_2
- pH

Each of these factors varies in the environment and, as such, may act as a limiting factor, determining the types of organisms which may exist in that environment.

Examples include:
- A low annual temperature common to the northern latitudes determines in part what species of plants can exist in that area.
- The amount of oxygen dissolved in a body of water will help determine which species of fish will exist there.
- The salt-laden air and water of coastal areas limit what species can exist in those regions.

b. Biotic Factors
Biotic factors are all the living things that directl or indirectly, affect the environment. Thus, the organisms, their presence, parts, interaction, and wastes, all act as biotic factors.

Biotic factors interact in many ways such as in nutritional relationships and symbiotic relationships

1) Nutritional Relationships
Nutritional relationships involve the transfer of nutrients from one organism to another within an ecosystem.

a) Autotrophs
These organisms can synthesize their own food from inorganic compounds and a usable energy source.

b) Heterotrophs
These organisms cannot synthesize their own food and are dependent upon other organisms for food. On the basis of this dependency, organisms are classified as either saprophytes, herbivores, carnivores, or omnivores.

(1) Saprophytes
Saprophytes include those heterotrophic plants, fungi, and bacteria which live on dead matter.

(2) Herbivores
Herbivores are those animals which consume plants.

(3) Carnivores
Carnivores are those animals which consume other animals. These include:
- Predators - Animals which kill and consume their prey.
- Scavengers - Animals which feed on other animals they have not killed.

(4) Omnivores
Omnivores are those animals that consume both plants and animals.

2) Symbiotic Relationships
Different organisms may live together in a close association. This living together in close association is known as symbiosis. Symbiotic relationships may or may not be beneficial to the organisms involved. Symbiotic relationships may include: nutritional, reproductive, and protective relationships.

Types of symbiosis include:

a) Commensalism
In this relationship, one organism is benefited and the other is not adversely affected. (+, O). Examples include: barnacles on whales, and orchids on large tropical trees.

b) Mutualism
In this relationship, both organisms benefit from the association (+,+). Examples include: nitrogen-fixing bacteria within the nodules of legumes, and certain protozoa within termites.

c) Parasitism
In this relationship, the parasite benefits at the expense of the host (+, -). Examples include: athlete's foot fungus on humans, and tapeworm and heartworm in dogs. Recent experimental research indicates that lichens may represent a controlled parasitic relationship of the fungus on an algal host.

2. Energy Flow Relationships
If an ecosystem is to be self-sustaining, it must contain a flow of energy.

a. Energy Flow
Those life activities which are characteristic of living organisms require the expenditure of energy.

The pathways of energy through the living components of an ecosystem are represented by food chains and food webs.

b. Food Chain
Green plants convert radiant energy from the sun into chemical energy (food). A food chain involves the transfer of energy from green plants through a series of organisms with repeated stages of eating and being eaten.

c. Food Web
In a natural community, the flow of energy and materials is much more complicated than is illustrated by any one food chain. Since practically all organisms may be consumed by more than one species, many interactions occur among the food chains of any community. These interactions are described as a food web.

Interactions in a food web involve:

1) Producers
The energy for a community is derived from the organic compounds synthesized by green plants. Autotrophs are therefore considered the producers.

2) Consumers
Organisms that feed directly upon green plants are primary consumers or herbivores. Secondary consumers, or carnivores, feed upon other consumers. Omnivores may be either primary or secondary consumers.

3) Decomposers
Organic wastes and dead organisms are eventually broken down to simpler substances by decomposers, such as the bacteria of decay. Through this

action, chemical substances are returned to the environment where they can be used by other living organisms.

d. Pyramid of Energy
There is much more energy at the producer level in a food web than at the consumer levels, and there is more energy at the primary consumer level than at the secondary consumer level. A pyramid of energy can be used to illustrate the loss of usable energy at each feeding level.

Each consumer level of the food pyramid utilizes approximately 10 percent of its ingested nutrients to build new tissue. This new tissue represents the food for the next feeding level. The remaining energy is lost in the form of heat and unavailable chemical energy. Eventually, the energy in an ecosystem is lost and is radiated from the earth's system. Thus, an ecosystem cannot sustain itself without the constant input of energy from the sun.

e. Biomass Pyramid
In general, the decrease of energy at each successive feeding level means that less biomass (amount of organic matter) can be supported at each level. Thus, the total mass of carnivores in a particular ecosystem is less than the total mass of the producers.

The decrease of biomass at each feeding level is illustrated by a pyramid of biomass.

3. Material Cycles
In a self-sustaining ecosystem, material must be cycled among the organisms and the abiotic environment. Thus, the same materials can be reused.

a. Carbon-Hydrogen-Oxygen Cycle
The carbon-hydrogen-oxygen cycle involves the processes of respiration and photosynthesis.

b. Water Cycle
The water cycle involves the processes of photosynthesis, transpiration, evaporation and condensation, respiration, and excretion.

c. Nitrogen Cycle
The nitrogen cycle is an example of a material cycle involving decomposers and other soil bacteria which, in part, break down and convert nitrogenous wastes and the remains of dead organisms into materials usable by autotrophs.

- Atmospheric nitrogen is converted into nitrates by nitrogen-fixing bacteria.
- Plants use nitrates for protein synthesis.
- Animals which eat plants convert the plant protein into animal protein.
- Nitrogenous wastes and the bodies of dead plants and animals are broken down by decomposers and ammonia is released.
- Ammonia may be converted into nitrates by nitrifying bacteria.
- Nitrogen containing compounds may also be broken down by denitrifying bacteria, resulting in the release of nitrogen into the atmosphere.

A summary of the nitrogen cycle could be represented by:

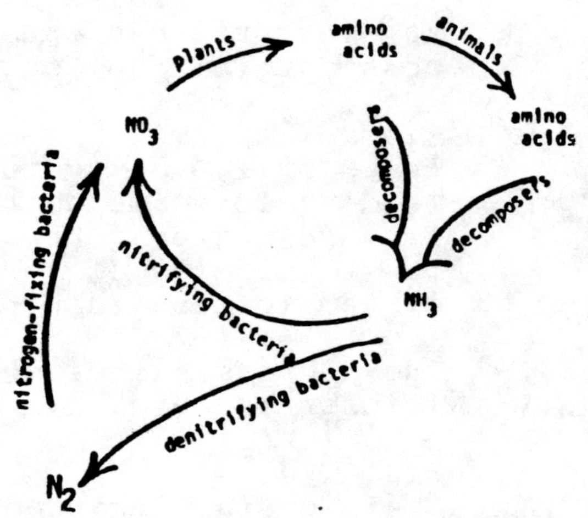

B. Ecosystem Formation
Ecosystems tend to change with time until a stable system is formed. The type of ecosystem that is formed depends on the climatic limitations of a particular geographical area.

*1. Succession
The replacement of one community by another until a stabl stage (climax) is reached is called ecological successior

a. Pioneer Organisms
Succession may be said to begin with pioneer organism since these are the first plants to populate a given location. Lichens, for example, are the pioneer organisms on bare rock.

Pioneer organisms modify their environment. Seasonal dieback and erosion, for example, would create pocket of *soil* in the crevices and hollows on the bare rock.

b. Changes
Each community modifies the environment, often making it more unfavorable for itself and, apparently, more favorable for the following community which infiltrates the first community over a period of years.

A typical successional sequence in New York State might be: pioneer, grass, shrub, conifer, and deciduous woodland.

Plant species (flora) dominate in the sense that they are the most abundant food sources. Plant succession is a major limiting factor for animal (fauna) succession.

Communities are composed of populations able to exist under the prevailing conditions and are identified by their dominant plant species -- the one that exerts the most influence over the other species present. Some examples include: pine barrens and sphagnum bog.

c. Climax Community
A climax community is a self-perpetuating community in which populations remain stable and exist in balance with each other and the environment. A climax community persists until a catastrophic change of a major abiotic or biotic nature alters or destroys it, thus producing non-climax conditions.

Thereafter, succession once again occurs leading to a climax community. The original climax community may be reestablished or a new climax may be established if the abiotic environment has been permanently altered. Examples include: forest fires, abandoned farmlands, and areas where topsoil has been removed.

The oak-hickory and the hemlock-beech-maple associations represent two climax communities found in New York State.

2. Competition
Competition occurs when different species or organisms living in the same environment (habitat) utilize the same limited resources, such as food, space, water, light, oxygen, and minerals.

The more similar the requirements of the organisms involved, the more intense the competition.

If two different species compete for the same food or reproductive sites, one species may be eliminated. This usually establishes one species per niche in a community. The niche is the organism's role in the community.

3. Biomes
The term biome refers to the most common climax ecosystem that will form in large climatic areas.

Biomes may be terrestrial or aquatic. The temperate deciduous forest of the northeastern United States is a terrestrial biome. The ocean is an aquatic biome.

a. Terrestrial Biomes
The major plant and animal associations on land are determined by the major climate zones of the world, modified by local land and water conditions.

Climates will vary as to temperature, solar radiation and precipitation. The presence or absence of water is a major limiting factor for terrestrial biomes.

1) Characteristics
Land biomes are characterized and sometimes named by the climax vegetation in the region. The major land biomes, and their characteristics, flora, and fauna are listed below.

Biome	Characteristics	Climax Flora	Climax Fauna
Tundra	Permanently frozen subsoil	Lichens, mosses, grasses	Caribou, snowy owl
Taiga	Long, severe winters; summers with thawing subsoil	Conifers	Moose, black bear
Temperate-Deciduous Forest	Moderate precipitation; cold winters, warm summers	Trees that shed leaves (deciduous trees)	Grey squirrel, fox, deer
Tropical Forest	Heavy rainfall; constant warmth	Many species of broad-leaved plants	Snake, monkey, leopard
Grassland	Considerable variability in rainfall and temperature; strong prevailing winds	Grasses	Pronghorn antelope, prairie dog, bison
Desert	Sparse rainfall; extreme daily temperature fluctuations	Drought-resistant shrubs and succulent plants	Kangaroo rat, lizard

2) Geographic Factors
Climatic conditions change with latitude and altitude.

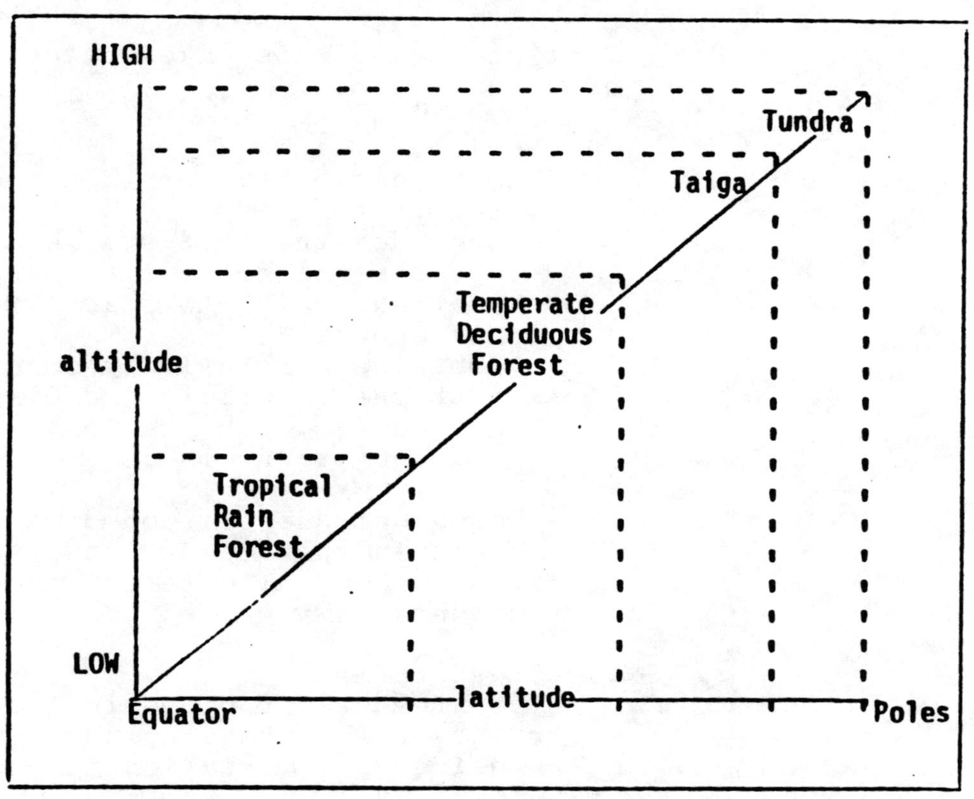

b. Aquatic Biomes
These represent the largest ecosystem on earth. More than 70 percent of the earth's surface is covered by water and most of the life on the planet exists under conditions where water is the principal external medium.

The temperature variation in aquatic biomes is not as great as in the terrestrial biomes, due to the ability of water to absorb and hold heat. In addition, moisture is not a limiting factor. Thus, aquatic biomes are typically more stable than terrestrial biomes.

Such factors as the quantity of available oxygen and carbon dioxide, temperature, light, dissolved minerals and suspended particles are the major factors affecting the kinds and numbers of organisms in an aquatic biome.

Aquatic organisms are well adapted to remove oxygen which is dissolved in water. They must also maintain a proper water balance. This water balance is affected by the concentration of dissolved salts in the water.

Most photosynthesis takes place near the surface of aquatic systems.

1) Marine
The oceans of the world are a continuous body of water that
- provides the most stable aquatic environment
- absorbs and holds large quantities of solar heat and helps to stabilize the earth's atmosphere
- contains a relatively constant supply of nutrient materials and dissolved salts
- serves as a habitat for a large number of diverse organisms

A great amount of food production in the world occurs in the oceans along the edges of the land masses (coastal waters), the deeper regions being too dark.

2) Fresh Water
The fresh water biome includes ponds, lakes, and rivers. The areas which comprise this biome show considerable variation in
- size
- current velocity
- temperature
- concentration of dissolved gases
- suspended particles
- rate of succession

Ponds and small lakes, for example, fill in due to seasonal dieback of aquatic vegetation and erosion of their banks, and eventually enter into terrestrial succession terminating in a terrestrial climax community.

IV. Biosphere and Humans

A. Past and Present
Humans, in exercising a unique and powerful influence on the physical and living world, have modified their environment.

1. Negative Aspects
Natural systems have been upset because humans have not realized that they not only influence other individuals, other species, and the nonliving world, but are, in turn, influenced by them.

Although most ecosystems are capable of recovering from the impact of minor disruptions, human activities have sometimes increased the magnitude of such disruptions so as to bring about a more lasting and less desirable change in the environment upon which all life depends.

Such disruptions will directly affect at least one of the components of an ecosystem and this, in turn, may affect the remaining components.

a. Human Population Growth
The total population of humans has risen at a rapid rate, partly because of the removal of natural checks on the population, such as disease. This continued increase in the human population has far exceeded the food-producing capacities of many ecosystems of the world. The change in the world population of humans is illustrated below:

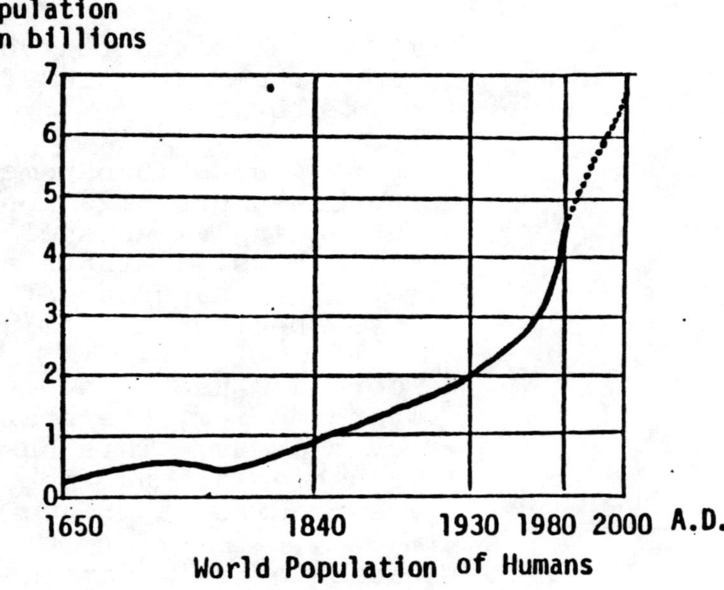

World Population of Humans

b. Human Activities
Some human activities have led to the extinction or endangerment of numerous species of plants and animals as well as producing less favorable living conditions for many species, including humans. Such activities include:

1) Overhunting
Uncontrolled hunting, trapping, and fishing still occur in many parts of the world. The extinction of the dodo bird and the passenger pigeon resulted from such activities. Endangered species include the blue whale.

Updated lists of endangered organisms may be obtained through the Department of Environmental Conservation.

2) Importation of Organisms
Humans have accidently and/or intentionally imported organisms to areas where they have no natural enemies leading to the disruption of existing ecosystems. Examples include: the Japanese beetle, gypsy moth, and disease-causing organisms such as those that cause Dutch Elm disease.

3) Exploitation
The exploitation of wildlife, both flora and fauna, for their products and the pet trade has led to threatened populations and ecosystem disruptions. Examples include: the African elephant and the Pacific walrus - ivory; the Colombian parrot - pet trade; tropical rain forests - plywood.

It is estimated that only one in 50 parrots survives the transition from the wild to private collectors.

4) Poor Land Use Management
Increased urbanization/suburbanization claims increasing amounts of agricultural lands, modifie watersheds, disrupts natural habitats (including wetlands), and threatens the existence of wildlife species.

Poor land use management practices have led to overcropping, overgrazing, and failure to use cover crops. This has resulted in the loss of valuable soil nutrients and topsoil. Many years are required to renew lost topsoil.

5) Technological Oversight
Technological oversights have led to unplanned consequences which have contributed to the pollution of the water, air, and land.

   a) Water Pollution
   Major water pollutants include: heat, sewage and chemicals such as phosphates, heavy metals, and PCBs.

   b) Air Pollution
   Major air pollutants include: carbon monoxid hydrocarbons, and particulates. Nitrogen oxides and sulfur dioxide combine with water vapor creating acid rain problems.

c) Biocide Use
The use of some biocides (such as pesticides and herbicides) without a complete assessment of their environmental impact has contaminated the soil, atmosphere, water supply, and has disrupted food webs. Examples include: DDT effects on the bald eagle and peregrine falcon. Other examples include dioxin (Agent Orange) and the use of Temick on Long Island.

d) Disposal Problems
The affluent lifestyle of humans currently requires increasing supplies of products and energy, the production of which produces considerable wastes: solid, chemical, and nuclear.

2. Positive Aspects
Through increased awareness of ecological interactions, humans have attempted to prevent continued disruption of the environment and to counteract the results of many of our past negative practices.

a. Population Control
Methods of controlling the human reproductive rate have been, and continue to be, developed.

b. Conservation of Resources
Soil cover plantings (reforestation and covercropping) serve as erosion controls. Water and energy conserving measures are currently being implemented. The economic significance of recycling is now being realized.

c. Pollution Controls
Attempts are being made to control air and water pollution by laws and by the development of new techniques of sanitation.

d. Species Preservation
Some efforts to sustain endangered species have included habitat protection (wildlife refuges and national parks) and wildlife management (game laws and fisheries).

Animals which were once endangered but are presently successfully reproducing and increasing their numbers are the bisons and egrets.

Endangered animals which are currently responding to conservation efforts and beginning to make a comeback are the whooping crane, bald eagle, and peregrine falcon.

The future of some species is still in doubt.

e. Biological Control
Biological control of insect pests continues to be encouraged. This method is less likely to: affect those species which are beneficial to humans, disrupt food webs, and contaminate the land. Examples include: the use of sex hormones and natural parasites.

f. Laws
There are laws which regulate and guide the use of natural habitats.

A state law designed to provide the opportunity for citizen review and comment of the environmental impact of any proposed development that has been determined to have significant effect on the environment.

Freshwater Wetlands Act - A state law designed to regulate the use of large or unique freshwater wetlands both publicly and privately owned so as to prevent their destruction and thus maintain valuable wetlands for all life forms.

B. The Future
While human technological advances have led to a higher standard of living for many, the environment has often suffered. Through a greater awareness of ecological principles, wise use of our energy resources, and concern for future generations not only of humans, but also of all species, each individual can help to assure that there will be suitable environments for succeeding generations.

ANSWER SHEET

EST NO. ____________ PART ______ TITLE OF POSITION ______________________________
(AS GIVEN IN EXAMINATION ANNOUNCEMENT - INCLUDE OPTION, IF ANY)

LACE OF EXAMINATION ______________________________ ______________________________ DATE ______________
(CITY OR TOWN) (STATE)

RATING

USE THE SPECIAL PENCIL. MAKE GLOSSY BLACK MARKS.

1 A B C D E	26 A B C D E	51 A B C D E	76 A B C D E	101 A B C D E
2 A B C D E	27 A B C D E	52 A B C D E	77 A B C D E	102 A B C D E
3 A B C D E	28 A B C D E	53 A B C D E	78 A B C D E	103 A B C D E
4 A B C D E	29 A B C D E	54 A B C D E	79 A B C D E	104 A B C D E
5 A B C D E	30 A B C D E	55 A B C D E	80 A B C D E	105 A B C D E
6 A B C D E	31 A B C D E	56 A B C D E	81 A B C D E	106 A B C D E
7 A B C D E	32 A B C D E	57 A B C D E	82 A B C D E	107 A B C D E
8 A B C D E	33 A B C D E	58 A B C D E	83 A B C D E	108 A B C D E
9 A B C D E	34 A B C D E	59 A B C D E	84 A B C D E	109 A B C D E
10 A B C D E	35 A B C D E	60 A B C D E	85 A B C D E	110 A B C D E

Make only ONE mark for each answer. Additional and stray marks may be counted as mistakes. In making corrections, erase errors COMPLETELY.

11 A B C D E	36 A B C D E	61 A B C D E	86 A B C D E	111 A B C D E
12 A B C D E	37 A B C D E	62 A B C D E	87 A B C D E	112 A B C D E
13 A B C D E	38 A B C D E	63 A B C D E	88 A B C D E	113 A B C D E
14 A B C D E	39 A B C D E	64 A B C D E	89 A B C D E	114 A B C D E
15 A B C D E	40 A B C D E	65 A B C D E	90 A B C D E	115 A B C D E
16 A B C D E	41 A B C D E	66 A B C D E	91 A B C D E	116 A B C D E
17 A B C D E	42 A B C D E	67 A B C D E	92 A B C D E	117 A B C D E
18 A B C D E	43 A B C D E	68 A B C D E	93 A B C D E	118 A B C D E
19 A B C D E	44 A B C D E	69 A B C D E	94 A B C D E	119 A B C D E
20 A B C D E	45 A B C D E	70 A B C D E	95 A B C D E	120 A B C D E
21 A B C D E	46 A B C D E	71 A B C D E	96 A B C D E	121 A B C D E
22 A B C D E	47 A B C D E	72 A B C D E	97 A B C D E	122 A B C D E
23 A B C D E	48 A B C D E	73 A B C D E	98 A B C D E	123 A B C D E
24 A B C D E	49 A B C D E	74 A B C D E	99 A B C D E	124 A B C D E
25 A B C D E	50 A B C D E	75 A B C D E	100 A B C D E	125 A B C D E

ANSWER SHEET

TEST NO. ______________ PART ______ TITLE OF POSITION ______________________________
(AS GIVEN IN EXAMINATION ANNOUNCEMENT - INCLUDE OPTION, IF ANY)

PLACE OF EXAMINATION ______________________ (CITY OR TOWN) ______________________ (STATE) DATE ______________

RATING

USE THE SPECIAL PENCIL. MAKE GLOSSY BLACK MARKS.

1 A B C D E	26 A B C D E	51 A B C D E	76 A B C D E	101 A B C D E
2 A B C D E	27 A B C D E	52 A B C D E	77 A B C D E	102 A B C D E
3 A B C D E	28 A B C D E	53 A B C D E	78 A B C D E	103 A B C D E
4 A B C D E	29 A B C D E	54 A B C D E	79 A B C D E	104 A B C D E
5 A B C D E	30 A B C D E	55 A B C D E	80 A B C D E	105 A B C D E
6 A B C D E	31 A B C D E	56 A B C D E	81 A B C D E	106 A B C D E
7 A B C D E	32 A B C D E	57 A B C D E	82 A B C D E	107 A B C D E
8 A B C D E	33 A B C D E	58 A B C D E	83 A B C D E	108 A B C D E
9 A B C D E	34 A B C D E	59 A B C D E	84 A B C D E	109 A B C D E
10 A B C D E	35 A B C D E	60 A B C D E	85 A B C D E	110 A B C D E

Make only ONE mark for each answer. Additional and stray marks may be counted as mistakes. In making corrections, erase errors COMPLETELY.

11 A B C D E	36 A B C D E	61 A B C D E	86 A B C D E	111 A B C D E
12 A B C D E	37 A B C D E	62 A B C D E	87 A B C D E	112 A B C D E
13 A B C D E	38 A B C D E	63 A B C D E	88 A B C D E	113 A B C D E
14 A B C D E	39 A B C D E	64 A B C D E	89 A B C D E	114 A B C D E
15 A B C D E	40 A B C D E	65 A B C D E	90 A B C D E	115 A B C D E
16 A B C D E	41 A B C D E	66 A B C D E	91 A B C D E	116 A B C D E
17 A B C D E	42 A B C D E	67 A B C D E	92 A B C D E	117 A B C D E
18 A B C D E	43 A B C D E	68 A B C D E	93 A B C D E	118 A B C D E
19 A B C D E	44 A B C D E	69 A B C D E	94 A B C D E	119 A B C D E
20 A B C D E	45 A B C D E	70 A B C D E	95 A B C D E	120 A B C D E
21 A B C D E	46 A B C D E	71 A B C D E	96 A B C D E	121 A B C D E
22 A B C D E	47 A B C D E	72 A B C D E	97 A B C D E	122 A B C D E
23 A B C D E	48 A B C D E	73 A B C D E	98 A B C D E	123 A B C D E
24 A B C D E	49 A B C D E	74 A B C D E	99 A B C D E	124 A B C D E
25 A B C D E	50 A B C D E	75 A B C D E	100 A B C D E	125 A B C D E